Lecture Notes in Computer Science   7308

Commenced Publication in 1973
Founding and Former Series Editors:
Gerhard Goos, Juris Hartmanis, and Jan van Leeuwen

Editorial Board

David Hutchison
  Lancaster University, UK
Takeo Kanade
  Carnegie Mellon University, Pittsburgh, PA, USA
Josef Kittler
  University of Surrey, Guildford, UK
Jon M. Kleinberg
  Cornell University, Ithaca, NY, USA
Alfred Kobsa
  University of California, Irvine, CA, USA
Friedemann Mattern
  ETH Zurich, Switzerland
John C. Mitchell
  Stanford University, CA, USA
Moni Naor
  Weizmann Institute of Science, Rehovot, Israel
Oscar Nierstrasz
  University of Bern, Switzerland
C. Pandu Rangan
  Indian Institute of Technology, Madras, India
Bernhard Steffen
  TU Dortmund University, Germany
Madhu Sudan
  Microsoft Research, Cambridge, MA, USA
Demetri Terzopoulos
  University of California, Los Angeles, CA, USA
Doug Tygar
  University of California, Berkeley, CA, USA
Gerhard Weikum
  Max Planck Institute for Informatics, Saarbruecken, Germany

Mats Brorsson   Luís Miguel Pinho (Eds.)

Reliable Software Technologies – Ada-Europe 2012

17th Ada-Europe International Conference
on Reliable Software Technologies
Stockholm, Sweden, June 11-15, 2012
Proceedings

 Springer

Volume Editors

Mats Brorsson
KTH Royal Institute of Technology
Department of Software and Computer Systems
Forum 120, 164 40 Kista, Sweden
E-mail: matsbror@kth.se

Luís Miguel Pinho
Polytechnic Institute of Porto
CISTER Research Unit
Rua Dr. António Bernardino de Almeida, 431, 4200-072 Porto, Portugal
E-mail: lmp@isep.ipp.pt

ISSN 0302-9743   e-ISSN 1611-3349
ISBN 978-3-642-30597-9   e-ISBN 978-3-642-30598-6
DOI 10.1007/978-3-642-30598-6
Springer Heidelberg Dordrecht London New York

Library of Congress Control Number: 2012938027

CR Subject Classification (1998): D.3, D.2, F.3, C.2, H.4, C.3

LNCS Sublibrary: SL 2 – Programming and Software Engineering

Typesetting: Camera-ready by author, data conversion by Scientific Publishing Services, Chennai, India

Printed on acid-free paper

Springer is part of Springer Science+Business Media (www.springer.com)

Organization

The 17th International Conference on Reliable Software Technologies – Ada-Europe 2012—was organized by Ada-Europe and Ada-Sweden, in cooperation with ACM (SIGAda, SIGBED and SIGPLAN).

Organizing Committee

Conference Chair

Ahlan Marriott · White Elephant GmbH, Switzerland

Program Co-chairs

Mats Brorsson · KTH Royal Institute of Technology, Sweden
Luís Miguel Pinho · CISTER Research Centre/ISEP, Portugal

Tutorial Chair

Albert Llemosí · Universitat de les Illes Balears, Spain

Industrial Chair

Jørgen Bundgaard · Rovsing A/S, Denmark

Publicity Chair

Dirk Craeynest · Aubay Belgium & K.U.Leuven, Belgium

Local Chair

Rei Stråhle · Ada-Sweden

Program Committee

Ted Baker
Johann Blieberger
Mats Brorsson
Jørgen Bundgaard
Bernd Burgstaller
Alan Burns
Dirk Craeynest
Alfons Crespo

Michael González Harbour
José Javier Gutiérrez
Peter Hermann
Jérôme Hugues
Jan Jonsson
Albert Llemosí
Kristina Lundqvist

Franco Mazzanti
Julio Medina
Jürgen Mottok
John McCormick
Stephen Michell
Laurent Pautet
Luís Miguel Pinho
Erhard Plödereder

Juan A. de la Puente   Ed Schonberg   Tullio Vardanega
Jorge Real   Theodor Tempelmeier   Juan Zamorano
José Ruiz   Elena Troubitsyna
Sergio Sáez   Santiago Urueña

Industrial Committee

Jamie Ayre   Hubert Keller   Jean-Pierre Rosen
Ian Broster   Ismael Lafoz   Alok Srivastava
Jørgen Bundgaard   Ahlan Marriott   Jean-Loup Terraillon
Rod Chapman   Paolo Panaroni   Erik Wedin
Dirk Craeynest   Paul Parkinson   Rod White

External Reviewers

Gøran Bertheau   Linas Laibinis   Robert Pathan
Néstor Cataño   Risat Pathan   Kristian Wiklund
Etienne Borde

Supporting Organizations

The organizers of the conference are grateful to the exhibitors and supporters of
the conference.

Exhibitors, at the time of writing:
     AdaCore
     Altran Praxis
     Ellidiss Software
     Rapita Systems Ltd
     Vector Software Inc
     Objektum Solutions

Supporters, at the time of writing:
     Siemens Switzerland
     KonAd GmbH

Table of Contents

Real-Time Systems

Ada Ravenscar Code Archetypes
for Component-Based Development

Marco Panunzio and Tullio Vardanega

University of Padova
Department of Mathematics
via Trieste 63, 35121 Padova, Italy
{panunzio,tullio.vardanega}@math.unipd.it

Abstract. We promote a model-driven software development that centres on component-orientation. In keeping with Dijkstra's principle of separation of concerns, we want the user design space to be limited to the internals of components – for which strictly sequential functional code is to be used – and the interfaces provided to and required from other components, where extra-functional requirements are declaratively specified by means of annotations. We want the user model to be directly amenable to response time analysis. To this end we prescribe that the component model must statically bind to a computational model that matches the analysis theory in use. We want to ensure semantic preservation across the entire transformation chain, from the user model, to the analysis model, to the implementation model (i.e., the code) and, eventually to the execution environment. The Ada Ravenscar Profile is an excellent candidate implementation language for use in our endeavour. In this paper we present a set of code archetypes written against the constraints of the Ravenscar Profile, which we developed in conformance with our notion of separation of concerns, to drive the model to code transformation step of our development infrastructure.

1 Introduction

Approaches based on Component-Based Software Engineering (CBSE) [15] and Model-Driven Engineering (MDE) [14] are gaining industrial acceptance in the domain of embedded real-time systems. This is no surprise since those two development paradigms promise important advantages: better and more disciplined software design and increased reuse potential for the former; greater abstraction level and powerful automation capabilities for the latter.

In anticipation of that trend, we have recently prototyped a novel component-based method for the development of high-integrity real-time software and put it to trial in two parallel and complementary efforts: one under the auspices of the European Space Agency (ESA), for the development of on-board software; the other in the context of the CHESS project[1], which targets space, telecom and railway applications.

---

[1] "Composition with Guarantees for High-integrity Embedded Software Components Assembly", ARTEMIS JU grant nr. 216682, 2009-2012 http://chess-project.ning.com

M. Brorsson and L.M. Pinho (Eds.): Ada-Europe 2012, LNCS 7308, pp. 1–17, 2012.

Our development method rests on the cornerstone of a long-known yet often neglected practice, first advocated by Dijkstra in [6]: *separation of concerns*. This principle aims to cleanly separate distinct aspects of software design and implementation, as well as to enable separate reasoning and focused specification. In accord with that principle, in our approach:

a) components comprise functional (sequential) code only: all extra-functional properties (in the regard of tasking, synchronization, timing) are dealt with outside of the component by the component infrastructure;

b) the extra-functional properties that the user requires to be held by components are declaratively specified by decoration of component interfaces with an ad-hoc annotation language.

c) the realization of extra-functional properties is performed by a code generator, which uses a set of predefined and separately compilable code patterns to generate the complete infrastructural code (the component infrastructure for components and their assemblies, and the entities to realize extra-functional properties). Therefore, the user has solely to implement the functional code of components.

Our approach is described in detail in [11] and [10].

One asset of our method is the support for model-based schedulability analysis in a manner that facilitates early consolidation of the software system design [1]. This particular ability results from the cohesive union of the following four constituents:

1. a component model, which is the essential tool for the user to develop reusable software units;

2. a computational model, which relates components and their extra-functional attributes to a set of schedulability analysis equations;

3. a programming model, which conveys in the implementation the assumptions of the analysis and the attributes used as input to it;

4. a conforming execution platform, which preserves at run time the properties asserted in the specification and confirmed by the analysis.

We consider the Ada Ravenscar profile (RP) [3] to be particularly fit to help us realize our vision. The RP expunges all language constructs that are exposed to unbounded execution time or non-determinism. The reduced tasking model that the RP defines was designed in perfect match with the assumptions and communication model of real-time theory in general, and the response-time analysis [8] in particular.

To complement the RP in the definition of our reference programming model, we adopt a set of code archetypes that help us realize elements 3 and 4 of the above list.

Our allegiance to Dijkstra's separation of concerns earns us a number of interesting advantages. The separation of the functional part from extra-functional concerns facilitates the reuse of the sequential code of the functional part independently of the realization of the extra-functional concerns that applied when the component was first created; this may considerably increase the reuse potential of the software (i.e., the opportunity of its possible reuse under different functional and extra-functional requirements).

Moreover, the infrastructural code dealing with concurrency, real-time, communication and component interfacing can be generated automatically in accord with a set of fixed, well-defined and fully deterministic rules; hence the automation capabilities of our approach deliver the designer from the burden of error-prone delicate programming so as to focus on the algorithmic code (e.g., control laws), which is the value added of the software system.

The ASSERT project[2] was the first, large, international initiative that pursued this vision. The results were very encouraging: the strategic importance and the industrial applicability of our vision were sanctioned by the industrial partners at the end of the project [5].

The code archetypes adopted to complete the formulation of the programming model of our interest shall support this vision, while also striving to fit the needs of systems with the limitation and resource constraints typical of embedded platforms. The RP is very apt also in this case, as a Ravenscar-compliant system can use a dedicated Ada run-time, which is more compact in footprint and amenable to qualification/certification according to the applicable standards of the target domains.

One of the results of ASSERT was the development of a set of RP-compliant code archetypes adhering to our vision on separation of concerns and amenable to automated code generation [12]. Those archetypes were developed as an evolution of previous work on code generation from HRT-HOOD to Ada (cf. e.g., [13] and [2]).

In [9] we described how we extended the archetypes to provide property preservation and discussed how to include mechanisms to identify and react to timing faults.

In the CHESS follow-up project, we are revising those code archetypes along two axes: (i) to increase their expressive power, by adding features and lifting some of their current limitations; (ii) to revamp their structure to better express them with the applicable elements of the latest evolution of Ada.

The remainder of the paper is organized as follows: in section 2 we provide a short overview on our design approach; in section 3 we describe how we map to code our design entities; in section 4 how we enforce extra-functional properties in our infrastructural code; in section 5 we highlight the advantages of our evolution of the code archetypes; in section 6 we compare our code archetypes to others' work; and finally we draw some conclusions.

2   Overview of the Design Approach

Before discussing the new code archetypes, we first need to survey our design approach and briefly present the abstractions we offer to the user (see fig. 1).

2.1   User Model Entities in the Platform Independent Model Space

Data types: The designer can create a set of project-specific data types. The categories of interest for data types are: Scalar types (Integer, Rational, and Rational Fixed

---

[2] "Automated proof-based System and Software Engineering for Real-Time systems", FP6 IST-004033 2004-8.

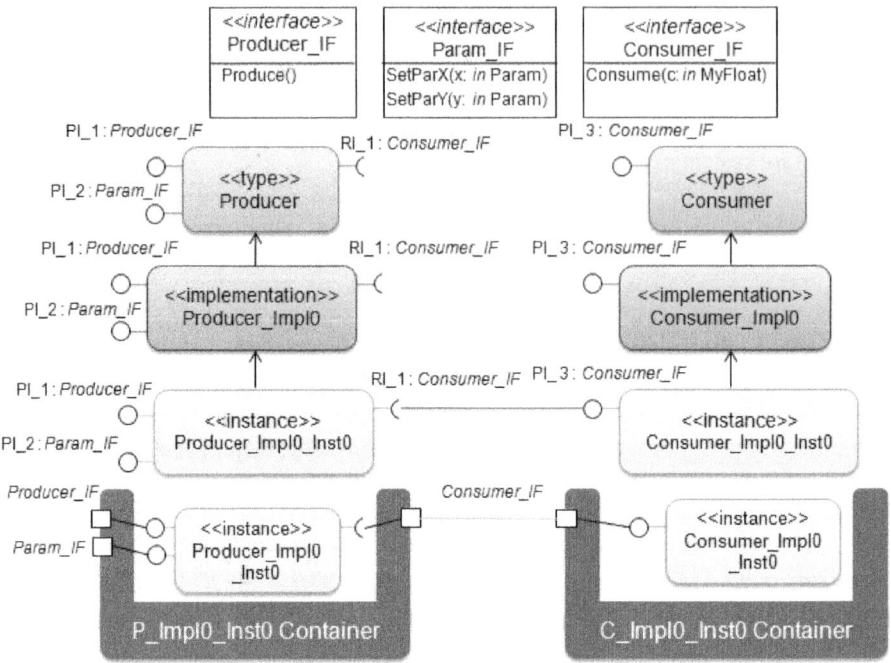

Fig. 1. Example of design entities

Point) with optional range constraints or required precision and enumerations, Boolean types, Arrays, composite data types (similarly to a C struct or an Ada record).

Interfaces: A software interface that enlists a set of operations. Each operation has a signature that includes the name, and a set of ordered parameters. Parameters have a mode (in, out, inout) and are typed with an already defined data type.

Component type: Component types are defined in isolation and are used to declare relationships with other components and the system in general. They encompass a set of Provided Interfaces (PI) – the services the component offers to other components – and a set of Required Interfaces (RI) – the services required by the component to provide its own services. Each PI or RI references an already defined interface.

Component implementation: A component entity that represents a concrete realization of a component type. It is functionally identical to a component type. Source code is added to the component implementation. A component implementation provides an implementation for every operation exposed in its PI.

Component instance: An instantiation of a component implementation. The designer binds the RI of a component instance to a PI of another component instance to fulfill the functional needs of the requiring component. Component instances are deployed on a processing unit. Finally, their PI operations are decorated with extra-functional attributes related to concurrency and real-time concerns.

2.2 Implementation Entities in the Platform Specific Model Space

Container: The software entity responsible for the realization of the extra-functional attributes declared for component instances. Tasks and protected objects are automatically generated inside the container in accord with the extra-functional properties to fulfill.

Connector: The software entity responsible for the realization of interaction concerns. It might be realized for example as a simple subprogram call (function or procedure), a message transmission delegation chain, or an I/O request.

3 Mapping of Design Entities

Let us now illustrate how we map our design entities to the infrastructural code we generate with our model-to-code transformations (see in fig. 2 the mapping for the example of fig. 1).

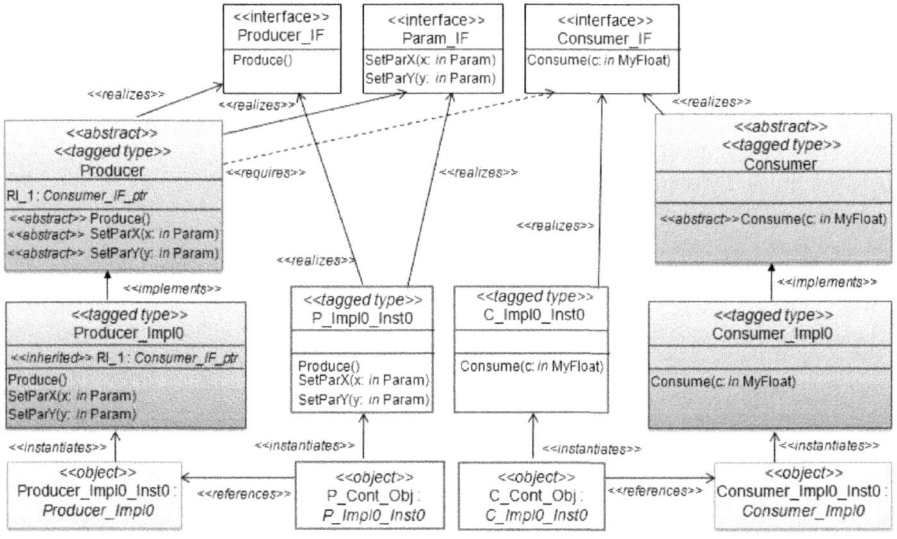

Fig. 2. Mapping of the design entities

3.1 Interface

An interface is mapped as an Ada package, containing the declaration of the interface. For each operation of the interface, an abstract procedure subprogram is added. The first parameter is the variable on which the subprogram is called (a subtype of the interface). Then all other possible parameters of the operation are added. An access type to the whole hierarchy of classes defined as subtypes of the interface is also declared.

Listing 1.1. Mapping of interfaces

```
1   package <Interface_Name> is
2     type <Interface_Name> is interface;
3     --[for each operation of the interface]
4     procedure <Operation_Name> (Self : in out <Interface_Name> ;
5           --[for each parameter]
6                                  <Parameter_Name> : <direction> <ParameterType>)
7       is abstract;
8     -- Declare a named class-wide access type to the interface
9     type <Interface_Name>_ptr is access all <Interface_Name>'Class;
10  end <Interface_Name>;
```

3.2 Component Type

A component type needs to fully specify the means for instances of it to connect with other components. This design entity maps to an Ada package, which contains the declaration of the component type as an abstract tagged type. The tagged type implements all the interfaces declared as PI of the component type. In the private part of the package, the tagged type declaration is completed by adding members to store a pointer for each RI. Finally, a setter for each RI is declared in the public part of the package. The setter subprograms are used at system start up to correctly set the bindings between RI and PI. This setting is part of the system deployment phase.

Listing 1.2. Mapping of component types

```
1   --[for each PI or RI]
2   with <Interface_Name>;
3
4   package <ComponentType_Name>s is
5     type <ComponentType_Name> is abstract new <PI1_Name> and ..
6                                  <PIn_Name> with private;
7     --[for each RI]
8     procedure Set_<RI_Name> (Self: in out <ComponentType_Name>;
9                         ptr: in <RI_Interface_Package>.<Interface_ptr>);
10
11  private
12    type <ComponentType_Name> is abstract new <PI1_Name> and .. <PIn_Name>
13                         with record;
14    --[for each RI]
15      <RI_Name> : <RI_Interface_Package>.<Interface_ptr>;
16    end record;
17
18  end <ComponentType_Name>s;
19
20  package body <ComponentTypeName>s is
21    --[for each RI]
22    procedure Set_<RI_Name> (Self: in out <ComponentTypeName>;
23                         ptr: in < RI_Interface_Package>.<Interface_ptr>) is
24    begin
25       Self.<RI_Name> := ptr;
26    end Set_<RI_Name>;
27
28  end <ComponentTypeName>s;
```

3.3 Component Implementation

A component implementation is declared in a child package of the package containing the definition of the component type. This allows the child package to have visibility

over the declarations in the private part of the parent package (similarly to the Java protected visibility). The component implementation itself is a concrete tagged type that extends its single component type. The package body shall then contain the implementation of all the operations of the PI of the component type.

Listing 1.3. Mapping of component implementations

```
1  package <ComponentType_Name>s.<ComponentImpl_Name>s is
2    type <ComponentImpl_Name> is new <ComponentType_Name> with private;
3
4  --[for each PI operation]
5    overriding procedure <OperationName> (Self: in out <ComponentImpl_Name>;
6  --[for each parameter]
7                      <Parameter_Name> : <direction> <ParameterType>);
8  private
9    type <ComponentImpl_Name> is new <ComponentType_Name> with null record;
10  end <ComponentType_Name>s.<ComponentImpl_Name>s;
```

The implementation of an operation can call a required operation by directing the call to the RI pointers stored in its component type. In the example of figure 2, operation *Produce* of component implementation *Producer_Impl0* can call operation *Consume(MyFloat)* of interface *Consumer_IF* as shown in Listing 1.4:

Listing 1.4. Example of call of an operation on an RI

```
1  package body Producers.Producer_Impl0s is
2    [...]
3    overriding procedure Produce (Self : in out Producer_Impl0) is
4    begin
5       -- other implementation code
6
7       Self.RI_1.Consume(27.0); -- call with implicit pointer dereference
8
9    end Produce;
10    [...]
11  end Producers.Producer_Impl0s;
```

This mechanism is a crucial enabler to warrant the implementation and preservation of the desired extra-functional properties at the callee side (the providing component), as we see in the next section.

3.4 Component Instance and Container

A component instance is an object of the tagged type that represents its component implementation. It is instantiated by the container, which is mapped as a package that contains a new tagged type that implements all the PI interfaces provided by the instance embedded in the container.

Listing 1.5. Mapping of containers

```
1   --[for each PI or RI]
2   with <Interface_Name>;
3   -- the implementation of the embedded instance
4   with <ComponentImplementation_Name>;
5   --[additional with'ed packages to enforce extra-functional properties]
6   package <Container_Name> is
7    --[for each RI]
8   procedure Set_<RI_Name> (<RI_Name> : <RI_Interface_Name>.<RI_Name>_ptr);
9    --[for each PI]
10  function Get_<PI_Name> return <PI_Interface>.<PI_Interface>_ptr;
11
12  private
13   --[Wrapper procedures]
14   -- The component instance
15   <InstanceName>: aliased <ComponentType_Pkg>.<ComponentImpl_Pkg>.
16                                        <ComponentImpl_Name>;
17   --[Entities to enforce extra-functional properties]
18   type <Container_Type> is new <PI1_Name> and ... <PIn_Name> with null record;
19   --[for each PI operation]
20   overriding procedure <OperationName> (Self: in out <Container_Type>;
21   --[for each parameter]
22                              <Parameter_Name> : <direction> <ParameterType>);
23   -- An instance of the container
24   <Container_Instance>: <Container_Type>;
25  end <Container_Name>;
```

The package also provides the getters and setters needed by the deployment utilities to correctly set the RI of component instances, so that they call required operations.

The getters return a reference to the container and that reference is stored in the pointer to a RI (specified in a component type, as described in the previous section). In this way, every time an operation of a RI is called in the source code of a component implementation, the actual call is issued on the container embedding the target component instance; the container can then enforce the necessary concurrency and real-time properties before executing the sequential code of the operation. Section 4 below shows how we achieve this.

4   Realization of Concurrency and Real-Time Properties

In our development method, concurrency and real-time properties are specified by annotations on operations of provided interfaces of component instances. The realization of the desired property is realized with a specific delegation chain rooted on the equivalent operation on the PI of the container.

The containers comprise three main constituents: (i) an *OBCS* (Object Control Structure), which is the protection agent in charge of recording inbound PI invocations as well as of handling the synchronization behaviour attached to the PI; (ii) a *Thread*, which is in charge of calling the functional operation attached to the PI in guaranteed compliance with the extra-functional properties attached to it; (iii) an *OPCS* (Operation Control Structure), which contains the functional code to be executed, and –in schedulability analysis terms– corresponds to all the jobs that can be issued by the task. In our approach the OPCS corresponds to a *component instance*.

The reader may have recognized that those terms are inherited from HRT-HOOD [4], although our equivalent entities have slightly different goals.

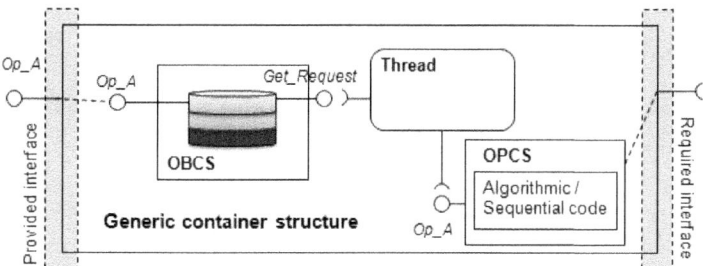

Fig. 3. Generic container structure

4.1 Delegation Chains

Unprotected Operation. An operation declared as unprotected: 1) is executed in the context of the calling thread; 2) does not require any protection from concurrent access. The delegation chain includes just an indirection from the container object to the component instance, where the operation implementation is called.

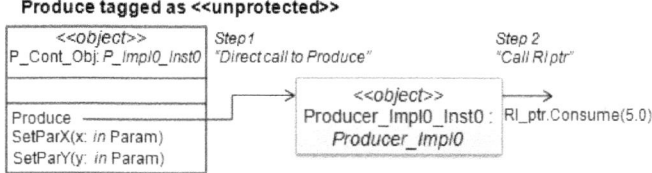

Fig. 4. Delegation chain for a unprotected operation

Figure 4 depicts the delegation chain that would be created if operation Produce exposed through a PI of instance *Producer_Impl0_Inst0* were marked as unprotected. For every concurrent pattern, the possible call to an operation of the RI is performed in the code of the implementation, by using the pointer defined in the corresponding component type.

Protected Operation. An operation declared as protected: 1) is executed in the context of the calling thread; 2) requires protection so that concurrent access is performed in mutual exclusion. The delegation chain includes an indirection from the container object to the OBCS, which is an Ada protected object equipped with a synchronization protocol (the Immediate Ceiling Priority Protocol). The OBCS then enforces mutual execution of the protected operation, which then simply calls its corresponding operation on the component instance.

Figure 5 depicts the delegation chain that would be created if operation Produce exposed through a PI of instance *Producer_Impl0_Inst0* were marked as protected.

Produce tagged as <<protected>>

Fig. 5. Delegation chain for a protected operation

Cyclic Operation. An operation declared as cyclic: 1) is executed in the context of a dedicated thread executor; 2) is triggered periodically by the execution platform, typically as part of the system clock interrupt handler. Hence there is no software client for the operation. From the description above, the execution of a cyclic operation will require the creation (at program elaboration time) of a thread. A thread is initialized with the operation to be executed (*Produce* in this case), which it executes at the specified rate. At the beginning of each task activation, the thread enqueues in the entry of a protected object from where it returns immediately. The guard of the entry can be closed to prevent further execution of the thread if that is required due to a change in the operational mode or for fault containment reasons. In this case, there is no real delegation from the operation on the container to another entity, as the container operation is never called. The creation of the container object is still necessary if any other operation declared on one of the implemented PI had been marked with a non-cyclic concurrent kind.

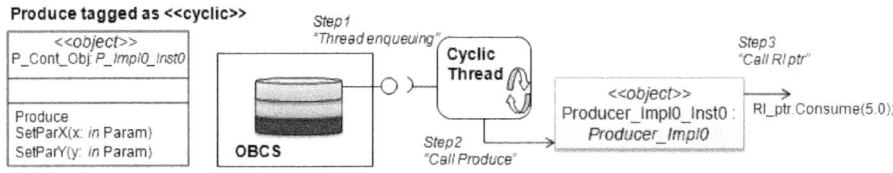

Fig. 6. Delegation chain for a cyclic operation

Figure 6 depicts the delegation chain that would be created if operation Produce exposed through a PI of instance *Producer_Impl0_Inst0* were marked as cyclic.

Sporadic Operation. An operation declared as sporadic: 1) is executed in the context of a dedicated thread executor; 2) is triggered when a new request of execution is posted by a client into a protected buffer; 3) two subsequent releases of the sporadic operation shall be separated by a minimum timespan called minimum inter-arrival time (or MIAT), which is enforced by the code pattern. A call to a sporadic operation (on the container) is redirected to an OBCS, where the request is encoded in a request descriptor. When the request is deposited, the call returns. On the callee side, a sporadic thread is enqueued on the single entry of the protected object, waiting for the arrival of execution requests. When the buffer of requests is not empty, the thread fetches the first request and executes the corresponding operation. Parameter passing between the caller and callee is explained in detail in a later section. At the end of the execution of the sporadic operation, the sporadic thread will self-suspend to enforce its MIAT, and then will enqueue again to the OBCS. If the request buffer is empty, the sporadic thread simply blocks on the call until a new request is posted to the OBCS.

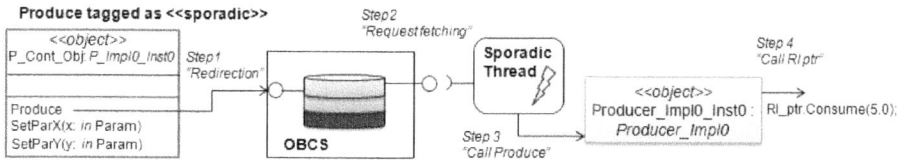

Fig. 7. Delegation chain for a sporadic operation

Figure 7 depicts the delegation chain that would be created if operation Produce exposed through a PI of instance *Producer_Impl0_Inst0* were marked as unprotected.

4.2 Archetypes for Threads

Cyclic Thread. The code archetype for threads shown in listing 1.6 is quite simple. In fact, we only need to create a task type (Thread_T) that periodically executes a given operation with a fixed rate.

Listing 1.6. Cyclic task structure (spec)

```
1  with System; with Ada.Real_Time;
2  package Cyclic_Task is
3     task type Thread_T (Thread_Priority : System.Any_Priority;
4                         Static_Offset : Natural; Period : Natural;
5                         Enqueue_for_Release :
6                         access procedure (Release : out Ada.Real_Time.Time);
7                         Operation : access procedure) is
8        pragma Priority (Thread_Priority);
9     end Thread_T;
10  end Cyclic_Task;
```

The operation is specified by passing an access procedure during the instantiation of the task specification of the task defines the task type for the cyclic thread. The thread is instantiated with a statically assigned priority, a period which stays fixed throughout the entire lifetime of the thread, and an optional static offset to phase the release of the task. Finally, an operation where to enqueue the task at the beginning of each activation is passed with the same language mechanism (an anonymous access procedure).

Listing 1.7. Cyclic task structure (body)

```ada
1  with System_Time;
2  package body Cyclic_Task is
3     use Ada.Real_Time;
4     task body Thread_T is
5        Task_Static_Offset : constant Time_Span := Milliseconds(Static_Offset);
6        Task_Period : constant Time_Span := Milliseconds(Period);
7        Next_Time : Time := System_Time.System_Start_Time +
8                            System_Time.Task_Activation_Delay + Task_Static_Offset;
9        Release_Time : Time;
10    begin
11       loop
12          delay until Next_Time;
13          -- First action : enqueue for release
14          Enqueue_for_Release.all (Release_Time);
15          -- Execute the sequential operation
16          Operation.all;
17          -- Calculate new release time
18          Next_Time:= Next_Time + Task_Period;
19          end loop;
20    end Thread_T;
21 end Cyclic_Task;
```

The body of the task is composed by an endless loop. Just after elaboration, the task enters the loop and is immediately suspended until a system-wide start time (System_Start_Time + Task_Activation_Delay). This initial suspension is used to synchronize all the tasks that are to execute in phase and let them have the first release at the same absolute time. If the task needs to have a certain phase with respect to the synchronous release, this is taken into account by adding the static offset. When resuming from the suspension (which notionally coincides with the release of the task), the task contends for the processor and enqueues in the entry accessed through operation *Enqueue_for_Release*. After returning from the entry, the task executes its cyclic operation specified through the operation access procedure. Then it calculates the next time it has to be released (Next_Time) and as first instruction of the subsequent loop, it issues a request for absolute suspension until the next period.

Use of the construct delay until is required by the Ravenscar profile so as to prevent the drift of the period that might occur with a relative delay.

4.3 Sporadic Thread

This section describes the code pattern for the sporadic task.

Listing 1.8. Sporadic Thread structure (code)

```ada
1  with System;
2  with Data_Structure;
3  with Ada.Real_Time;
4  package Sporadic_Task is
5     task type Thread_T (Thread_Priority : System.Any_Priority; MIAT : Natural;
6                 Get_Request : access procedure (Req : out Data_Structure.
7                                                 Request_Descriptor_T;
8                 Release : out Ada.Real_Time.Time)) is
9           pragma Priority (Thread_Priority);
10    end Thread_T;
11 end Sporadic_Task;
```

A sporadic task is a task such that any two subsequent activations of it are always separated by no less but possibly more than a minimum guaranteed time span, known as the MIAT for minimum inter-arrival time. Our sporadic task comprises: (i) an OBCS, which external clients use to post their requests for execution; (ii) a thread of control that waits for incoming requests, fetches the first of them from the protected object in the OBCS (according to a given queuing policy, which defaults to FIFO) and executes with sporadic guarantees the requested operation as provided by the OPCS. In this section we focus on the structure of the Thread. The sporadic thread requires being instantiated by passing the access procedure to the enqueuing entry of the OBCS. Similarly to the cyclic task, it is instantiated with a fixed priority.

Listing 1.9. Sporadic Thread structure (body)

```
1   with System_Time;
2   with Ada.Real_Time; use Ada.Real_Time;
3   package body Sporadic_Task is
4     task body Thread_T is
5       Req_Desc : Data_Structure.Request_Descriptor_T;
6       Release : Time;
7       Task_MIAT : constant Time_Span := Milliseconds(MIAT);
8       Next_Time : Time := System_Time.System_Start_Time +
9                           System_Time.Task_Activation_Delay;
10    begin
11     loop
12       delay until Next_Time;
13       -- Enqueue in the release entry of the OBCS
14       Get_Request(Req_Desc, Release);
15       -- Execute the sequential operation
16       Data_Structure.My_OPCS(Req_Desc.Params.all);
17       -- Calculate the new earliest release time
18       Next_Time := Release + Task_MIAT;
19     end loop Task_Loop;
20    end Thread_T;
21  end Sporadic_Task;
```

Similarly to the cyclic thread, the body of the task is composed by an endless loop. The thread enters its infinite loop and suspends itself until the system-wide start time. After that: (i) it calls *Get Request(Request_Descriptor_T, Time)*, which is an indirection to the single entry of the OBCS; (ii) after the execution of the entry (off which, it obtains a timestamp of when release actually occurred and a request descriptor), the task executes the sporadic operation requested by the client task, i.e. *My_OPCS(Req_Desc.Params.all)*; (iii) it calculates the next earliest time of release (*Next_Time*) so as to respect the minimum separation between subsequent activations. At the subsequent iteration of the loop therefore the task issues a request for absolute suspension until that time and thus it will not probe the OBCS for execution requests until the required minimum separation will have elapsed.

The use of the dispatching operation *My_OPCS(...)* is the key to supporting sporadic operations with parameters, and will be detailed in section 4.4 below.

4.4 Parameter Passing for Sporadic Operations

Our code archetypes support sporadic operations with parameters. The code of the sporadic thread stays invariant with respect to the signature of the operation to call and the parameters to use. Instead of presenting the complete code that describes the mechanism to pass the parameters of a sporadic call, we explain it in more abstract terms.

A reification procedure encodes and stores the parameters of the call to a sporadic operation into a request descriptor. The sporadic thread fetching the descriptor will then dispatch to the desired call with the corresponding parameters.

First of all, we define an abstract tagged record that is the root of all parameter types, an associated operation *My_OPCS* and a class-wide access type.

Listing 1.10. Definition of an abstract parameter

```
1  type Param_Type is abstract tagged record
2    In_Use : Boolean := False;
3  end record;
4
5  procedure My_OPCS (Self : in out Param_Type);
6  type Param_Type_Ref is access all Param_Type'Class;
```

Then we create a request descriptor, to store a set of parameters.

Listing 1.11. Definition of a request descriptor

```
1  type Request_Descriptor_T is
2  record
3    Params : Param_Type_Ref;
4  end record;
```

Suppose then that we want to call a sporadic operation with the following signature:

```
1  procedure Op1 (a: in T1; b: in T2);
```

A request descriptor for this procedure and its overridden procedure *My_OPCS* would be declared as follows:

Listing 1.12. Example of request descriptor

```
1  type Op1_Param_T is new Param_Type with record
2    OPCS_Instance : <Interface_Package>.<Interface_ptr>;
3    a: T1;
4    b: T2;
5  end record ;
6
7  procedure My_OPCS (Self : in out Op1_Param_T) is
8  begin
9    Self.OPCS_Instance.Op1(Self.a, Self.b) ;
10 end My_OPCS;
```

Members *a* and *b* are used to store the parameters of the call. *OPCS_Instance* is a pointer to the interface type that provides this operation. The pointer will be set so as to reference the component instance that has to be called when executing the sporadic operation. Executing *My_OPCS* hence simply redirects to the corresponding operation on the component instance. A configurable number of these request descriptors are statically allocated in the OBCS of the sporadic task. When *Op1* is called on a container through an RI, the container redirects the call to the OBCS, where it is executed under mutual exclusion. The OBCS code simply encodes a request descriptor for the call.

5   Discussion

The code archetypes presented in this paper are based on previous work, in particular regarding the Thread and the mechanisms for reification of sporadic calls to the OBCS. The reader is referred to [2] and [12] for the details of those constituents.

Nevertheless, our work shows considerable improvements on a number of aspects. First, it takes full benefit of the *interface* construct of Ada 2005, which enables the user of our modeling framework to develop components independently, each in isolation. The binding between components is therefore declared on component instances at a stage of development that is distinct and successive to that of component specification. Consequently, the code that implements component binding is mapped with a call from the functional code of a component implementation to a container, which is where we perform the enforcement of the extra-functional properties as specified by the user on component interfaces. Our use of interfaces is interesting also for its flexibility; in fact we are experimenting with adding domain-specific layers in front of the container, so as to support domain-specific needs (e.g. the PUS services [7] that regulate the communication between ground stations and onboard services in space systems) and more complex connectors that intercept outgoing calls from the component implementation code so as to support desired connection properties or domain-specific communication protocols. In this way: (i) the code of component implementations remains domain-neutral; (ii) the core part of the archetypes is domain-neutral and offers extension points to address domain-specific needs.

Secondary to the focus of this paper, but of paramount importance in our development process, the code archetypes constitutes a very elegant mapping of our reference component model [10,11] to Ada code.

Finally, our evolution completely replaces Ada *generics* with *interfaces* and *tagged types*. We consider this a good news because – as we reported in [12] – generics can hinder *timing analysis* and make it harder to achieve tight bounds on the worst-case execution time (WCET) of operations. As an additional bonus, since our development process is based on MDE, the information on the bindings between component instances is known at design time and stored in the model. This makes it possible to automatically generate annotations for timing analysis, in particular to precisely characterize the dispatching calls of our framework. We are currently working on this aspect. The information of the model also enables us to account for the timing overhead of the framework while performing model-based schedulability analysis, as we did in [1].

6 Related Work

Initial proposals for Ravenscar code patterns for the realization of real-time systems in Ada were included in [3].

The most known Ada framework for the development of real-time software is by Wellings and Burns [16]. Their framework is based on a hierarchy of "task states" (realized as tagged types) which are used to specify the information relative to the release pattern of a task (periodic, sporadic and aperiodic). The "task state" is then coupled with a concrete release mechanism and possibly with mechanisms for the detection and reaction to WCET overruns and deadline misses. The different release mechanisms are specified in a hierarchy of synchronized interfaces, and then realized with support of protected objects with entries, timing events and execution-time timers. The framework also offers support for the execution of aperiodic tasks under a server.

The main differences between that framework and ours are the following:

- The framework of Wellings and Burns is not –and does not intend to be– Ravenscar-compliant (which instead was a goal in ours since its outset), as it uses language constructs that are forbidden by the profile (not considering execution-time timers and group budgets, it nevertheless leverages on protected objects with multiple entries, requeues and "select then abort") and supports task termination;
- Their framework supports parameterless sporadic tasks only;
- Their framework is expression of a task-centric notion typical in real-time systems development, and the sequential code to be executed by the task is embedded in the task structure itself: the user must implement the desired task operation to fully realize the task's tagged type provided by the framework. Our archetypes instead are designed after methodologies (e.g. component-oriented approaches) where the functional (i.e. sequential) code to execute is separately specified (typically in a "component" and possibly by a software supplier) and tasking is a later concern under the responsibility of the software integrator: tasks are just executors of code allocated on them (at software deployment time) and not the basic design entities. This difference is typified in our separation between the Thread and the OPCS.

7 Conclusions

There arguably is a lot to be gained, industrially, from the adoption of model-driven component-based development. Further value is added by strengthening the user model with characteristics that make it amenable to response time analysis in a direct and seamless model-to-model transformation chain, by construction.

The Ada Ravenscar Profile was defined with schedulability analysis in mind in the first place, hence it fully matches our needs in that respect. In this paper we have shown that some advanced features of the sequential part of Ada 2005 and its Ravenscar Profile are a best-fit choice for the implementation language for use in the model-to-code leg of our transformation engine.

In contrast with other well-known Ada programming frameworks for use in the development of real-time systems, our Ravenscar code archetypes were designed in a manner that corresponds specific code artefacts to each and every element of our component model and also preserves clear-cut separation between the user's functional code and the provisions of our infrastructure in the way of tasking, time and synchronization.

Acknowledgments. This work was supported by the Networking/Partnering Initiative of ESA/ESTEC and by the CHESS project (ARTEMIS JU grant nr. 216682, 2009-2012). The views presented in this paper are however those of the authors' only and do not necessarily engage those of the other partners of the CHESS consortium.

References

1. Bordin, M., Panunzio, M., Vardanega, T.: Fitting Schedulability Analysis Theory into Model-Driven Engineering. In: Proc. of the 20th Euromicro Conference on Real-Time Systems, pp. 135–144. IEEE Computer Society (2008)
2. Bordin, M., Vardanega, T.: A New Strategy for the HRT-HOOD to Ada Mapping. In: Vardanega, T., Wellings, A.J. (eds.) Ada-Europe 2005. LNCS, vol. 3555, pp. 51–66. Springer, Heidelberg (2005)
3. Burns, A., Dobbing, B., Romanski, G.: The Ravenscar Tasking Profile for High Integrity Real-Time Programs. In: Asplund, L. (ed.) Ada-Europe 1998. LNCS, vol. 1411, pp. 263–275. Springer, Heidelberg (1998)
4. Burns, A., Wellings, A.J.: HRT-HOOD: A Structured Design Method for Hard Real-Time Ada Systems. Elsevier (1995)
5. Cancila, D., Passerone, R., Vardanega, T., Panunzio, M.: Toward Correctness in the Specification and Handling of Nonfunctional Attributes of High-Integrity Real-Time Embedded Systems. IEEE Transactions on Industrial Informatics 6(2), 181–194 (2010)
6. Dijkstra, E.W.: The humble programmer. Communications of the ACM 15(10), 859–866 (1972) ISSN 0001-0782
7. European Cooperation for Space Standardization: Space Engineering – Ground systems and operations – Telemetry and telecommand packet utilization, ECSS-E-70-41A (2003)
8. Joseph, M., Pandya, P.K.: Finding Response Times in a Real-Time System. The Computer Journal 29(5), 390–395 (1986)
9. Mezzetti, E., Panunzio, M., Vardanega, T.: Preservation of Timing Properties with the Ada Ravenscar Profile. In: Real, J., Vardanega, T. (eds.) Ada-Europe 2010. LNCS, vol. 6106, pp. 153–166. Springer, Heidelberg (2010)
10. Panunzio, M.: Definition, realization and evaluation of a software reference architecture for use in space application. Ph.D. thesis, University of Bologna, Italy (July 2011), http://www.informatica.unibo.it/ricerca/ublcs/2011/UBLCS-2011-07
11. Panunzio, M., Vardanega, T.: A Component Model for On-board Software Applications. In: Proc. of the 36th Euromicro Conference on Software Engineering and Advanced Applications, pp. 57–64. IEEE (2010)
12. Panunzio, M., Vardanega, T.: Charting the evolution of the Ada Ravenscar code archetypes. In: Proc. of the 15th Int. Real-Time Ada Workshop, ACM SIGAda Ada Letters (2011)
13. de la Puente, J.A., Alonso, A., Alvarez, A.: Mapping HRT-HOOD Designs to Ada 95 Hierarchical Libraries. In: Strohmeier, A. (ed.) Ada-Europe 1996. LNCS, vol. 1088, pp. 78–88. Springer, Heidelberg (1996)
14. Schmidt, D.C.: Model-Driven Engineering. IEEE Computer 39(2), 25–31 (2006)
15. Szyperski, C.: Component Software: Beyond Object-Oriented Programming, 2nd edn. Addison-Wesley Professional, Boston (2002)
16. Wellings, A.J., Burns, A.: Real-Time Utilities for Ada 2005. In: Abdennahder, N., Kordon, F. (eds.) Ada-Europe 2007. LNCS, vol. 4498, pp. 1–14. Springer, Heidelberg (2007)

An Integrated Framework for Multiprocessor, Multimoded Real-Time Applications*

Sergio Sáez, Jorge Real, and Alfons Crespo

Instituto de Automática e Informática Industrial,
Universitat Politècnica de València,
Camino de vera, s/n, 46022 Valencia, Spain
{ssaez,jorge,alfons}@disca.upv.es

Abstract. In this paper we propose an approach for building real-time systems under a combination of requirements: specification and handling of operating modes and mode changes; implementation on top of a multi-processor platform; integration of both aspects within a common framework; and connection with schedulability analysis procedures.

The proposed approach uses finite state machines to describe operating modes and transitions, and a framework of real-time utilities that implements the required behaviour in Ada 2012. Automatic code generation plays an important role: the system is derived from the functional and timing specification, and implemented according to the abstractions provided by the framework. Response time analysis enables assessing the schedulability of the different operating modes and the transitions between modes.

Keywords: Real-Time Framework, Mode Changes, Multiprocessor Scheduling, Ada 2012.

1 Introduction

This paper continues a series of developments around a framework for real-time utilities in Ada. The aim of such effort is to provide a set of high-level abstractions to ease the development of real-time systems, by using the very convenient but low-level facilities provided by Ada. The first version of that framework was introduced in [1]; a second version was proposed for extending the original framework to multimoded systems [2], and then the framework was substantially redesigned to accommodate execution on multiprocessor platforms [3], with an incipient support for modes and mode changes. As a continuation of that work, the framework version used in this paper integrates and extends the support for both multiprocessor and multimoded real-time systems, making use of Ada 2012.

* This work was partially supported by the Vicerrectorado de Investigación of the UPV (PAID-06-10-2397), Ministerio de Ciencia e Innovación (TIN2011-28567-C03-03) and European Union (FP7-ICT-287702).

M. Brorsson and L.M. Pinho (Eds.): Ada-Europe 2012, LNCS 7308, pp. 18–34, 2012.

We consider task-partitioned scheduling across processors, where tasks are statically pre-allocated to processors – the method for deciding this allocation is however out of the scope of this paper. We enrich this model by considering also job-partitioning for selected tasks and task migration between modes.

Another contribution of this paper is the integration with a tool for specifying the behavioral aspects of the system, in terms of operating modes and transitions among them. From this description, additional code generation tools produce code for handling the conditions that lead to mode changes at run time, and implement the adequate handlers at the task level (local mode-change handlers). Within these handlers, tasks' attributes such as period, priorities, deadline and CPU affinity are adequately changed, and also ceiling priorities of shared protected objects are readjusted by their responsible task in each mode.

The paper illustrates the design process and implementation details by using an example system from the very beginning. Section 2 presents the example system and underlying hardware platform. Section 3 sketches the development process workflow. Section 4 briefly discusses the results of the schedulability analysis of the system, both in the steady state (each of the modes) and during mode transitions. Section 5 shows the specification process and support. Section 6 discusses the implementation within the framework. Finally, Section 7 concludes the paper.

2   Example System

This section describes an example system to illustrate the rest of the paper. We have chosen to use a real example system, but we have omitted a number of details that would only make it harder to follow. Although all tasks in the example are periodic, the concepts herein are also applicable to sporadic tasks with a bounded pattern for the arrival of the activation event, i.e., tasks with a bounded minimum inter-arrival time.

2.1   Functional Description

The example system is in charge of classifying different mechanical pieces into two categories: cylinders and cubes. Figure 1 shows the example plant. Pieces are supplied to the system by means of a conveyor belt. A video camera is located on top of the conveyor belt and takes images of the first section of the belt. These images therefore reflect the input load to the system. According to that input, up to two manipulator robots will pick the pieces from the belt and place them separately depending on their type (cylinder or cube). In figure 1, this is represented by other two conveyor belts that we will not consider as a part of the system. There is also a console screen that shows information about the process.

After considering the physical elements of the system, figure 2 shows the software elements and their interconnections. A two-stage process (*segmentation* and *recognition*) analyzes the images captured by the camera. The segmentation part simply detects the number of pieces and their position in each image frame.

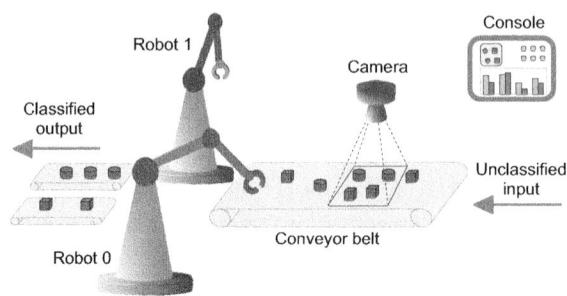

Fig. 1. View of the example plant

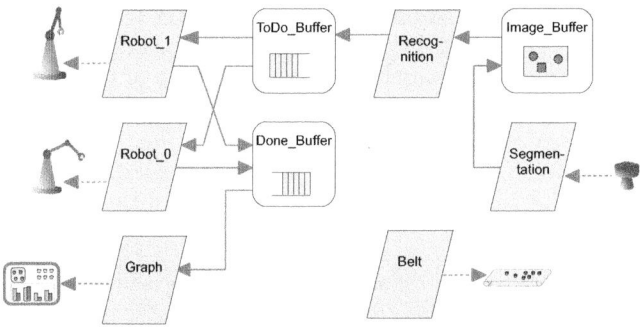

Fig. 2. Software elements of the example system

The output from the segmentation stage is inserted in the *Image_Buffer*. After segmentation, the recognition stage completes the analysis of the images by determining the type of each piece and their exact orientation, so that the robots can properly catch them from the belt. The output from the recognition stage is placed in the *ToDo_Buffer*, from where they are then collected by one or two robots, controlled by tasks *Robot_0* and *Robot_1*. Each time a robot removes one piece from the belt, its corresponding robot task adds the related information to the *Done_Buffer*.

The *Graph* task extracts elements from the *Done_Buffer* and displays status information on the console screen (eg. number and type of pieces processed). Finally, the *Belt* task controls the belt speed. This task is independent from the other tasks, since it does not need to exchange information with them.

2.2   Operating Modes

The flow of pieces is variable, and so is the number of pieces that are to be removed from the belt. In order to adapt to this input variability, and to save energy and resources, three operating modes are defined for the system. The current operating mode depends on the amount of pieces that need to be removed from the belt at a particular time interval:

Normal Mode. During this mode, the number of pieces on each captured frame is within the range {1..Threshold}. In this situation, the system is able to process all the pieces on the belt by using one single robot. The second robot is kept in a standby state in order to save energy. The belt advances at *normal* speed.

Overload Mode. When the number of pieces in a frame is greater than the threshold, the system operates in overload mode. In this mode, both robots collaborate to remove pieces from the belt. When the amount of pieces in scope is again within the threshold, the system will switch back to normal mode. By incorporating the second robot in the overload mode, we can keep the belt running at normal speed.

Fetch Mode. When there are no pieces to be processed on the belt (the input flow has temporarily ceased), both robots standby and the belt moves at *fast* speed in order to fetch pieces at the beginning of the belt as fast as possible. There is no need for the recognition process to run in this mode, since there are no pieces to recognize. But we still need to run the segmentation process in order to detect the arrival of new pieces. The fetch mode is abandoned when a non-empty image frame is detected in the segmentation stage. The details about how this mode change is processed are given in Section 5.

2.3   Hardware Platform and Software Workload Model

We shall assume that the hardware platform is a two-core processor, with the two cores identified as CPU0 and CPU1. A low number of cores keeps the example simple, while it allows us to demonstrate the ability of the proposed framework to take advantage of multi-core processors.

CPU1 is idle during the normal and fetch modes. In normal mode, CPU0 runs the tasks *Segmentation, Recognition, Robot_0, Belt* and *Graph*. In fetch mode, CPU0 runs only *Segmentation, Belt* and *Graph*. These task names correspond with the activities described in Section 2.1. Figure 3 gives the details of the workload in overload mode, which deserves further explanation. Note that both CPUs perform the same sequence of processing steps, with the difference that CPU0 executes the graph task while CPU1 controls the belt. Both CPUs execute the segmentation step at the same rate. By using an appropriate offset (as shown later in this section), we will alternate the execution of the pair segmentation-recognition in both cores, so that each CPU processes a different image frame. The segmentation task is unique, but it is scheduled to execute consecutive instances (jobs) in alternate CPUs: it is *job-partitioned*.

The image buffer is split in two local shared objects, *Image_Buffer_0* and *Image_Buffer_1*. Each instance of the segmentation task uses the buffer corresponding to its current CPU.

Figure 4 compares the execution of the segmentation-recognition process in modes normal and overload. In normal mode, there is time enough for segmentation and recognition to complete within their period, before a new frame is

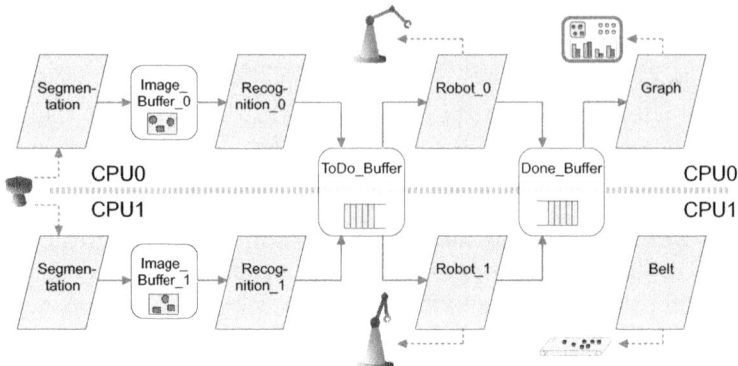

Fig. 3. Workload details in overload mode

taken. But in overload mode, the recognition process takes longer to execute, because there are more pieces to identify. In particular, it can take longer than the frame capture period, and hence one recognition stage could overlap with the next one. Therefore we cannot just job-partition the recognition task. Instead, we will use two different tasks, identified in figure 3 as *Recognition_0* and *Recognition_1*. The overlap of the end of recognition with the processing of the next image frame is therefore solved by using the two cores in parallel.

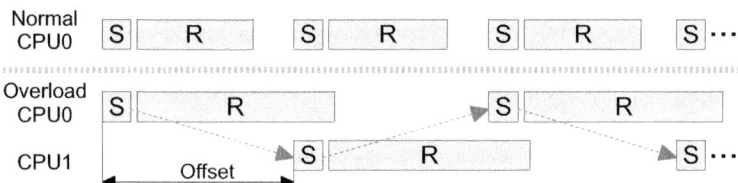

Fig. 4. Segmentation and recognition in modes normal and overload. In overload mode, segmentation (S) is job-partitioned and recognition (R) has a larger WCET.

By using an initial offset for the pair segmentation-recognition when we enter overload in CPU1, we are shifting this pair of tasks with respect to their analogous tasks on CPU0. By doing so, each CPU is processing a different image frame and we keep the system capacity to cope with the overload without reducing the belt speed.

Recognition tasks suffer from input jitter: they perform the recognition stage on the latest image taken by their corresponding segmentation task. We will ensure this relationship by setting a deadline for segmentation equivalent to the maximum input jitter for recognition, and we will use the results of the schedulability analysis to verify that recognition always uses fresh data.

Both recognition tasks share the *ToDo_Buffer*, which is a global resource since it is used from tasks running on both processors.

Robot_0 and *Robot_1* execute on CPU0 and CPU1, respectively. They control the corresponding robots. Both tasks share the common, global resource *Done_Buffer*, where they insert information about pieces already processed. They also share the *ToDo_Buffer* among them and with the recognition tasks.

The task *Graph* collects information from the *Done_Buffer* to display statistics on the screen. The task *Belt*, in charge of keeping the belt speed adequate to the current mode, runs on CPU1 in overload. In modes normal and fetch, *Belt* runs on CPU0. This task serves us to illustrate *task migration* between modes.

3 Real-Time System Development Workflow

Figure 5 shows the development workflow and the resulting real-time application. During the design phase, two specification documents are used to perform the schedulability analysis of steady states and mode changes. These documents are the *Real-Time Workload Specification* and the *Operating Modes Model*. These two models and the *Real-Time Analyses Report* generated by the *Schedulability Analyses Tool* are then used by two code generation tools to generate (i) the *Real-Time Scheduling Support*, that implements the mode-change handlers and real-time behaviour of the application tasks; and (ii) the *Operating Modes Support*, that implements the system *Mode Manager*. Both packages are built on top of the *Real-Time Application Framework* [3] that has been extended to fully support multi-mode applications over multiprocessor platforms using the new Ada 2012 capabilities. Finally, the functional behaviour of the *User-Defined Real-Time Tasks* is implemented by using/extending the automatically generated code.

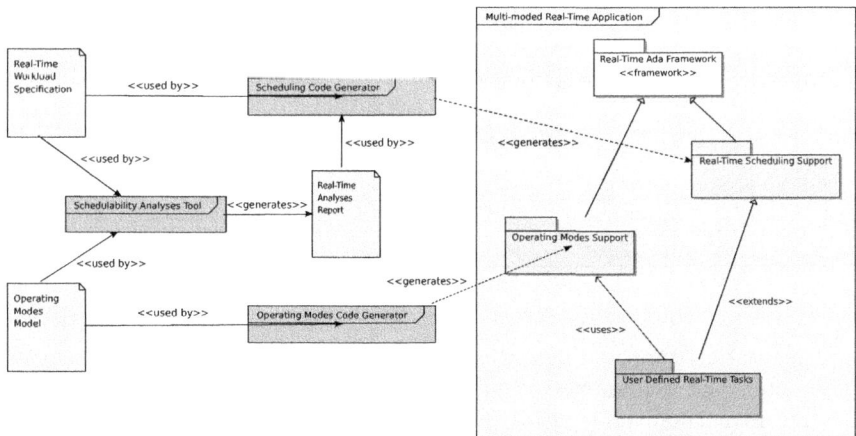

Fig. 5. Multimode Real-Time Application development workflow

4   Schedulability Analysis

4.1   Steady-State Analysis

Table 1 shows the tasks' timing parameters and the worst-case response time analysis of the different operating modes, considered in isolation. We refer to this as the *steady-state* analysis, because it does not consider transitions between modes. All tasks are periodic and the time units used here are abstract. For each mode and CPU, the table shows the tasks' worst-case execution time (C), period (T), deadline (D), and input jitter (J), as well as the calculated worst-case response time (R). This response time has been obtained using the classical response time analysis equations [4,5], with higher priorities assigned to shorter deadlines, and assuming blocking times of 2 time units for all shared resources. Note that all tasks are schedulable in the steady state, that is, in the absence of mode changes: all worst-case response times are below their respective deadlines. Table 1 also shows the utilization ratios for each CPU and mode. Note that the overload mode would not be schedulable in a single CPU, since the total utilization is above 100 %.

Table 1. Parameters and steady-state analysis of tasks on both CPUs, and in all modes. See text above for the meaning of columns.

CPU	Task name	Normal					Overload					Fetch				
		C	T	D	J	R	C	T	D	J	R	C	T	D	J	R
CPU0	Segmentation	3	50	10		8	3	100	10		8	3	25	25		5
	Recognition	20	50	50	10	39										
	Recognition_0						40	100	100	10	66					
	Robot_0	3	10	10		5	3	10	10		5					
	Belt	2	50	50		10						2	25	25		2
	Graph	50	500	500		250	50	500	500		257	50	500	500		65
	CPU0 Utilization	90 %					83 %					30 %				
CPU1	Segmentation						3	100	10		8					
	Recognition_1						40	100	100	10	68					
	Robot_1						3	10	10		5					
	Belt						2	50	50		10					
	CPU1 Utilization	0 %					77 %					0 %				
	Total utilization	90 %					160 %					30 %				

Segmentation runs at different periods. A short period of 25 units in fetch mode, since the belt moves at *fast* speed during fetch. A medium period of 50 units in normal mode, that accommodates the *normal* speed of the belt in this mode. And a larger period of 100 units in overload. In overload mode however, the segmentation task runs on both processors. Hence the effective rate of segmentation is the same in modes normal and overload. In mode overload, an initial offset of 50 time units for segmentation in CPU1 will ensure that segmentation runs once every 50 time units in one or the other CPU – see the mode-change analyses in Section 4.2.

Recognition requires more processing time in overload than in normal mode (40 vs. 20 units), since there are more pieces to process during an overload. The recognition task is modeled with two different task descriptions: we use `Recognition` to describe the task in mode normal, with $C = 20$, and `Recognition_0` and `Recognition_1` for the overload mode, with $C = 40$. Note that this is just an analysis artifact: our model for mode-change analysis allows changes in all tasks' parameters, except in C. There are several reasons that justify this approach [6].

The input jitter of 10 units for recognition tasks models the required behaviour that recognition always uses the freshest image pre-processed by segmentation. This input jitter is set equal to the deadline for segmentation tasks. In practical terms, the *Image_Buffer*s behave like a one-item stack, written with push and read with a blocking pop. So recognition is blocked until there is a new item in the *Image_Buffer*.

4.2 Transition Analyses

There are 5 possible transitions in the example system. They comprise changes in both directions between normal and fetch (four mode changes), and one more from fetch to overload. The only transition excluded is overload to fetch. This will be explained in more detail in Section 5. The mode-change analysis must be applied to both CPUs, hence there is a total of 5 transitions × 2 CPUs = 10 analyses to consider. Some of them are however trivial. For example, all mode switches in CPU1 are schedulable because there is only one active mode in that CPU: there are no old-mode tasks when switching from normal or fetch to overload; there are no new-mode tasks in a switch from overload to normal; and there are no tasks at all involved in switches between normal and fetch in CPU1. Hence all transitions in CPU1 are guaranteed by the steady-state analysis shown in Table 1.

We analyze the schedulability of transitions using the mode-change response time analysis proposed in [6]. Our tool analyzes the transition and, if it is not schedulable, it then finds appropriate offsets for new-mode tasks so that no deadlines are missed in the mode switch. For tasks with a changing period, this offset is relative to the time when the mode change request occurs. For tasks that keep their activation pace across modes, the calculated offset is relative to the first activation of the task in the new mode. We have slightly adapted the tool to enable setting an initial offset in the new mode, since we needed that for the segmentation and recognition tasks in CPU1 in mode overload.

There is no space available here for showing the results of all the mode-change analyses in detail. We will just note that all transitions proved schedulable after applying appropriate offsets when needed.

5   Operating Modes Specification

Section 2.2 has described the possible operating modes of the system and the conditions to move from one mode to another. Two main components will be involved in these mode changes: the *mode manager*, that detects the mode-change conditions and triggers the mode-change process; and the *mode changer*, that performs the mode-change process updating the attributes of the tasks involved in a given change. There are two different approaches to design these components:

Distributed. The logic to detect the mode-change conditions or to update the task attributes is distributed across the system tasks, i.e., the mode-change conditions are detected in the tasks' code, from where the mode-change request is triggered. Each task is also responsible for changing its own attributes for the new mode under the request of a *mode changer*.

Centralized. The logic to detect the mode-change conditions is centralized in a *mode manager* component that receives the relevant system events and decides when to trigger the mode-change process. A centralized *mode changer* processes the mode-change request by updating the attributes of the involved tasks directly.

The design proposed in this work is based on a centralized mode manager that detects all mode-change conditions and sends a mode-change request to a minimalist mode changer when appropriated. The mode changer informs the involved tasks about the mode change request to perform the task attributes updates in a distributed manner. This section deals with the specification and design of the mode manager, while the mode-change process and the mode changer details are explained in section 6.

5.1   Mode Manager Specification

A centralized mode manager has to maintain a global state of system variables that are related with the current operating mode, and to trigger a mode-change request when certain conditions hold. The updating of this state is performed when certain system events occurs, e.g., a piece has been removed from the belt. This behavioral pattern adequately matches the formalism defined by Finite State Machines (FSM) [7,8]. In the proposed framework, the mode manager is specified by means of a detailed behavioral FSM, and the implementation code is derived from this model using a modified version of the framework presented in [9].

5.2   UML Finite State Machine Elements

UML Finite State Machines offer a broad set of elements to model the behavior of any system component. However, when this formalism is used to specify the behavior of a mode manager, only a small subset of these elements are really useful and some of them can have a slightly different semantics. This section describes some of the main FSM facilities that can be used to model complex mode managers.

First of all, although it seems obvious that system operating modes will correspond to states of the mode manager, not every state of the mode manager will represent a different operating mode. Therefore, states of the mode manager that do represent system operating modes have to be annotated somehow. The *non-mode* states can be used to facilitate the modeling of mode-change conditions. An example of this situation can be found in Figure 6. It shows the FSM that describes the operating modes of the example system and the transitions between them. *Fetch, Normal* and *Overload* states represent the system operating modes, while the rest of the states are used to model the internal behavior of the *Overload* state or to group common event responses as can be seen in the OR-state *Working*.

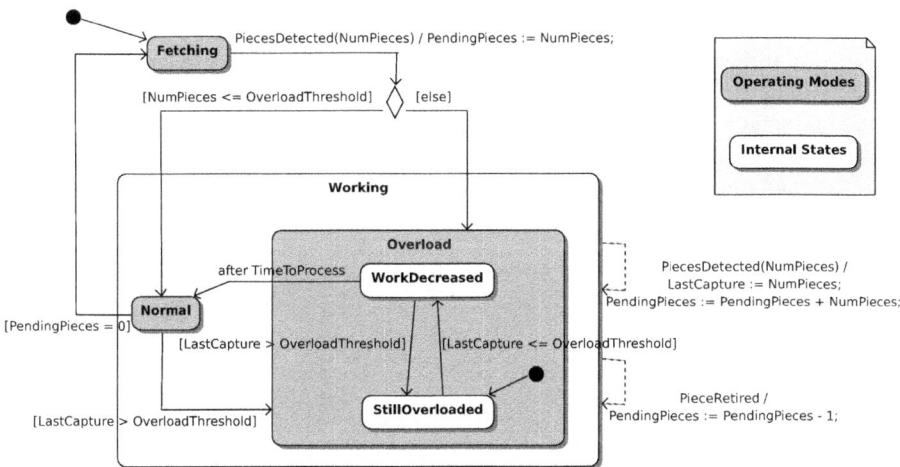

Fig. 6. System mode behavioral state machine

Since the current state of the FSM is always a simple state[1], when OR-states are used to group event management of several simple states, the only requirement is that each simple state was either an operating mode or it had an operating mode among its ancestors or superstates. This ensures that the mode manager is always in a valid operating mode while being in a stable state. The FSM that describes the example mode manager shown in Figure 6 clearly fulfills this condition.

Although the rest of FSM elements can be used to specify the mode manager behavior, such as *timed* events, *entry* and *exit* actions, other constructs, such as *deferred* events or *do* activities, have a limited usefulness. In the case of deferred

---

[1] A state without any nested state.

events, the fact that a given system event management will be postponed until the mode manager is in a different mode does not seem clearly useful. In the same way, *do* activities require that the mode manager is continuously executing a set of actions while staying in a given state. This behavior does not match the role of a system mode manager.

Finally, AND-states allow the FSM to be in more than one state simultaneously. The next subsection explains how this can be applied to the definition of a mode manager.

5.3   Specification of Partial Mode Changes

AND-states can be used to simplify the number of states in a FSM, since they allow different aspects of the component behavior to evolve independently. However, if concurrent states correspond to different system operating modes, the semantics of *being in multiple operating modes* needs to be clarified.

This work proposes to use AND-States to partition the application tasks among several concurrent regions or subsystems, allowing the system designer to specify different operating modes for each subsystem. In such a way, a mode change in a concurrent region or subsystem will not alter the attributes of the tasks associated with the other concurrent regions. In the example shown in Figure 7, a mode change from mode C to E will not change the attributes of the tasks associated with modes A or B.

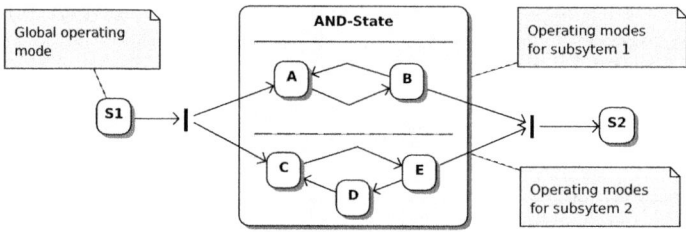

Fig. 7. Concurrent operating modes

However, from the analysis point of view, if the task partitions or subsystems share software or hardware resources, e.g. they are executed in the same set of CPUs, the mode change analysis will require to consider the system as a whole. Although the task attributes of the other partitions do not change, the response times can be affected due to the lack of execution isolation. On the other hand, if the tasks associated with each concurrent subsystem are executed in a different platform, set of CPUs or *Dispatching Domain* [10] and there are no resources shared among the partitions, execution isolation ensures that mode change analysis can be performed independently for each concurrent subsystem, thus reducing the number of transitions to be analyzed.

6   Implementation within the Real-Time Framework

This section deals with the implementation of the example application on top of the Real-Time Framework presented in [3], that has been extended in this work to support multimoded real-time applications. Next sections detail the design and the implementation of the main components.

6.1   Mode Manager

As mentioned above, the mode manager has been specified by means of a behavioral FSM. Although the resulting mode manager component could be an Active Object and the corresponding task be incorporated in the system analysis, a Passive Object is preferred to implement the proposed approach. Accordingly, an Ada protected object implements the centralized mode manager. The Ada specification of the mode manager is shown in Listing 1. This code is automatically generated from the FSM specification in SCXML [11] using an extended version of the tools presented in [9].

Listing 1. Mode manager protected type

```
protected type Example_System_Mode_Manager(Num_Tasks: Positive) is
   new Example_System_Mode_Manager_Interface with
   −− Registers a task in the mode manager
   procedure Add_Task (NM: Any_Notification_Mechanism;
                       TS: Any_Task_Sched_Interface);
   −− Init event to  initialize  the FSM
   procedure Init_Event;
   −− Send event: PiecesDetected
   procedure Pieces_Detected_Event (Num_Pieces: Natural);
   −− Send event: PieceRemoved
   procedure Piece_Removed_Event;
private
   −− Internal events: Timeout and Completion
   procedure Process_Timeout_Event (TE: in out Timing_Event);
   procedure Process_Completion_Event;
   −− FSM context
   Overload_Threshold : Natural := 8;
   Time_To_Process : TimeSpan := Seconds(5);
   Pending_Pieces : Natural := 0;
   Last_Capture : Natural := 0;
   −− FSM attributes
   The_Mode_Changer : Mode_Changer(Num_Tasks);
   ...
end Example_System_Mode_Manager;
```

With respect to the FSM context, that defines the scope of the variables and methods used in the FSM conditions and actions, there are two possible scenarios. If the FSM context is defined only by the state variables, as in the example system shown in Figure 6, these variables can be automatically placed in the mode manager protected type by the code generator and no extra context objects are required, i.e. no user code is required to implement the mode manager. However, if the FSM context also requires some user-defined procedures or functions then a FSM context object has to be passed to the mode manager to complete the implementation of its behavior. In this case, only the FSM context interface and the specification part of the tagged type that implements the FSM context can be automatically generated.

FSM events are directly mapped into protected procedures. Listing 2 shows how the PiecesDetected event is processed, how the decision pseudo-state is implemented and different mode change requests from Fetch to Normal or Overload, depending on the event information. The Process_Completion_Event procedure also shows how the activation and cancellation of a *timed event* is implemented in the *WorkDecreased* state by means of an Ada timing event.

Listing 2. Mode manager PiecesDetected and Completion events handling

```
procedure Pieces_Detected_Event (Num_Pieces: Natural) is
begin
   case Current_State is
   when Fetch_State =>
      −− Event action
      Last_Capture := Num_Pieces; Pending_Pieces := Num_Pieces;
      −− Decision pseudo−state
      if Last_Capture <= Overload_Threshold then
         Current_State := Normal_State; −− Target state
         Current_Mode := Normal_Mode; −− Target mode
         The_Mode_Changer.Change_To(Mode_Name'Pos(Normal_Mode));
      else
         Current_State := Still_Overloaded_State; −− Target state
         Current_Mode := Overload_Mode; −− Target mode
         The_Mode_Changer.Change_To(Mode_Name'Pos(Overload_Mode));
      end if;
   when Normal_State | Still_Overloaded_State | Work_Decreased_State =>
      −− Event action
      Last_Capture := Num_Pieces; Pending_Pieces := Pending_Pieces + Num_Pieces;
   when others =>
      null; −− No transition
   end case;
   −− Check completion conditions
   Process_Completion_Event;
end Pieces_Detected_Event_Event;

procedure Process_Completion_Event is
begin
```

```
case Current_State is
when Normal_State =>
   if Last_Capture > Overload_Threshold then
      Current_State := Still_Overloaded_State;  -- Target state
      Current_Mode := Overload_Mode;  -- Target mode
      The_Mode_Changer.Change_To(Mode_Name'Pos(Overload_Mode));
   elsif  Pending_Pieces = 0 then
      Current_State := Fetch_State;  -- Target state
      Current_Mode := Fetch_Mode;  -- Target mode
      The_Mode_Changer.Change_To(Mode_Name'Pos(Fetch_Mode));
   end if;
when Still_Overloaded_State =>
   if Last_Capture <= Overload_Threshold then
      -- Program timed event
      Timeout.Set_Handler (Time_To_Process, Process_Timeout_Event'Access);
      Current_State := Work_Decreased_State;  -- Target state
   end if;
when Work_Decreased_State =>
   if Last_Capture > Overload_Threshold then
      -- Cancel timed event
      Timeout.Cancel_Handler (Timeout_Cancelled);
      Current_State := Still_Overloaded_State;  -- Target state
   end if;
when others =>
   null;  -- No transition
end case;
end Process_Completion_Event;
```

6.2   Mode Changer

Although the code of the mode changer is also generated from the system specification and the analysis results, the implementation is completely different. The mode changer is based on a minimalist Mode_Changer component that has been added to the Real-Time Framework and a set of automatically generated Mode_Change_Handlers distributed across the system tasks. When a mode change request is triggered, each task in the system receives a Mode_Change_Event, and it is the handler of this event who performs the mode change for that task in two phases. A first step, executed at the task priority, establishes the new task attributes, activates the scheduling mechanisms required for the new mode and updates the ceilings of shared resources. The second step effectively changes the task attributes within a task-specific protected procedure.

Listing 3 shows a fragment of the Mode_Change_Handler that implements the change from *Normal* to *Overload* for the segmentation task. The first part activates the *Job-Partitioning* mechanism in the *Overload* mode, and the second part establishes the specific transition offsets and updates ceilings. Finally, the activation of the second step to be executed within the Release_Mechanism is shown.

Listing 3. Mode-change handler for the *Segmentation* task

```
procedure Mode_Change_Handler (Sched: in out Segmentation_Sched_Type;
                              MCR: in Time;
                              Old_Mode, New_Mode: in Natural) is
  Current_Mode: Mode_Name := Mode_Name'Val(Old_Mode);
  Target_Mode: Mode_Name := Mode_Name'Val(New_Mode);
  Must_Change: Boolean;
begin
  case Target_Mode is
    ...
  when Overload =>
    Sched.Job_Partition_CE.Set_Num_Sched_Sets(2);
    Sched.Job_Partition_CE.Set_Sched_Set(1,
                        Segmentation_Sched_Attrib_Overload_Mode(1));
    Sched.Job_Partition_CE.Set_Sched_Set(2,
                        Segmentation_Sched_Attrib_Overload_Mode(2));
    Sched.RM.Set_Control(Job_Partition_Id, Sched.Job_Partition_CO);
    Sched.SA_Base.all := Segmentation_Sched_Attrib_Overload_Mode(1);
    -- Transition dependent code
    case Current_Mode is
    when Fetch | Normal =>
      Sched.SA_Base.Set_Offset(Milliseconds(4));
      -- Ceiling updates for mode Overload
      Example_System.Resources.Image_Buffer_0.Update_Ceiling(
                        Image_Buffer_0_Ceil_On_Overload_Mode);
    when others => null;
    end case;
  when others =>
    Sched.SA_Base.Set_Activity_Flag(False);
  end case;
  -- Activate second step
  Sched.Mode_Change_CO.Activate_Trigger;
end Mode_Change_Handler;
```

6.3   Shared Objects

As shown in Listing 3, in order to support automatic updates of the ceilings during the mode-change process, the system shared resources have to implement the new Shared_Resource_Interface interface provided by the Real-Time Framework, to ensure that the Update_Ceiling procedure will be available. Also the exact package and object name have to be provided by the system designer to allow the code generation tool to produce the necessary mode-change code.

Listing 4. Global shared resources support

```
-- Ceil updates for mode Normal
To_Do_Buffer_Helper.Must_Change_Ceiling(To_Do_Buffer_Num_Tasks_On_Overload_Mode,
                                To_Do_Buffer_Ceil_On_Normal_Mode,
                                Must_Change);
if Must_Change then
   Example_System.Resources.ToDo_Buffer.Update_Ceiling(
                                To_Do_Buffer_Ceil_On_Normal_Mode);
end if;
```

In the case of global shared resources, the mode change analysis tool cannot easily determine which task is the proper one to update the shared resource ceiling, as the execution order in multiple CPUs cannot be reliably established. In this case, the Shared_Resource_Interface is not enough and a simple helper object is provided for each global resource to determine the last task to process the mode-change event at run-time. Listing 4 shows how this helper object can be used to update global resource ceilings during a mode change.

7   Conclusions

This paper has discussed the current state of a framework of real-time utilities in Ada 2012 for multiprocessor platforms, and its integration with a specification model and a code generation tool for multimoded real-time systems. The main contributions are the update of the framework to support modes on multiprocessors and the specification and code generation tools, connected with the results of the schedulability analysis. The process here described favors separation of concerns between the implementation of tasks and the logic of handling mode changes.

References

1. Wellings, A.J., Burns, A.: A Framework for Real-Time Utilities for Ada 2005. Ada Letters XXVII(2) (August 2007)
2. Real, J., Crespo, A.: Incorporating Operating Modes to an Ada Real-Time Framework. Ada Letters 30(1) (April 2010)
3. Sáez, S., Terrasa, S., Crespo, A.: A Real-Time Framework for Multiprocessor Platforms Using Ada 2012. In: Romanovsky, A., Vardanega, T. (eds.) Ada-Europe 2011. LNCS, vol. 6652, pp. 46–60. Springer, Heidelberg (2011)
4. Joseph, M., Pandya, P.: Finding response times in a real-time system. British Computer Society Computer Journal 29(5), 390–395 (1986)
5. Audsley, N., Burns, A., Richardson, M., Tindell, K., Wellings, A.J.: Applying new scheduling theory to static priority pre-emptive scheduling. Software Engineering Journal 8(5), 284–292 (1993)
6. Real, J., Crespo, A.: Mode Change Protocols for Real-Time Systems: A Survey and a new Proposal. Real-Time Systems 26(2), 161–197 (2004)

7. Harel, D.: Statecharts: A visual formalism for complex systems. The Science of Computer Programming 8(3), 231–274 (1987)
8. Object Management Group: Unified Modeling Language (OMG UML) V2.4 (August 2011), http://www.omg.org/spec/UML/2.4.1
9. Sáez, S., Terrasa, S., Lorente, V., Crespo, A.: Implementing Reactive Systems with UML State Machines and Ada 2005. In: Kordon, F., Kermarrec, Y. (eds.) Ada-Europe 2009. LNCS, vol. 5570, pp. 149–163. Springer, Heidelberg (2009)
10. Burns, A., Wellings, A.J.: Dispatching Domains for Multiprocessor Platforms and their Representation in Ada. In: Real, J., Vardanega, T. (eds.) Ada-Europe 2010. LNCS, vol. 6106, pp. 41–53. Springer, Heidelberg (2010)
11. Barnett, J.: State Chart XML (SCXML): State Machine Notation for Control Abstraction (May 2008), http://www.w3.org/TR/scxml/

Integrating Middleware for Timely Reconfiguration of Distributed Soft Real-Time Systems with Ada DSA*

Marisol García-Valls and Felipe Ibáñez-Vázquez

Distributed Real-Time Systems Laboratory
Department of Telematics Engineering
Universidad Carlos III de Madrid
Av. de la universidad 30, 28911 Leganés (Madrid), Spain
`mvalls@it.uc3m.es, fibanez@pa.uc3m.es`

Abstract. Soft real-time distributed systems are dynamic in nature which poses a number of challenges to their time-deterministic behavior. The communication links between their remote parts are also a source of temporal uncertainty that requires thorough architecting to minimize these undesired effects. Currently, enhanced middleware have appeared for soft real-time domains to support time-bounded reconfiguration capabilities; timely reconfiguration is, however, a futuristic approach for open systems, but it is at the moment possible in a restricted distributed system model. In this paper, we present the adaptation of one of these futuristic middleware implementations, iLAND, to Ada DSA; a vertical real-time platform is presented that allows interoperability between a distributed soft real-time iLAND network and distributed Ada programs. This idea has been implemented and validated in a PolyORB/QNX environment.

Keywords: Distributed systems, real-time, iLAND, middleware, Ada, DSA, QNX, PolyORB, reconfiguration, service oriented applications.

1 Introduction

Distributed soft real-time systems may include a number of heterogeneous nodes across a network domain. Their behavior can be highly dynamic in nature introducing contradictory requirements with respect to their real-time ones. Also, the communication media may add uncertain transmission and latency effects, data loss, etc., posing a number of challenges to their time-deterministic behavior. To reduce their temporal uncertainty a thorough architecting of solutions that can contribute to minimize these undesired effects is required.

* This work has been partly supported by the iLAND project (ARTEMIS-JU 100026) funded by the ARTEMIS JTU Call 1 and the Spanish Ministry of Industry, Commerce, and Tourism (www.iland-artemis.org), ARTISTDesign NoE (IST-2007-214373) of the EU 7th Framework Programme, and by the Spanish national project REM4VSS (TIN 2011-28339).

M. Brorsson and L.M. Pinho (Eds.): Ada-Europe 2012, LNCS 7308, pp. 35–48, 2012.

In modern environments, one of the most powerful characteristics and trends of middleware is the support of timely reconfiguration. By reconfiguration it is meant the ability to undertake a transition from the current structure of the system to a new one. Such a change can be, for instance, the replacement of one task or a task set (or the functionality they execute) by a different one. A middleware that offers this functionality will need to provide not only real-time communication capacities, but also, it will have to embed the necessary logic to store different possible states or modes of the system and the protocols to coordinate the transition from one state to another, i.e., to reconfigure, in a time-bounded way. Still, it is out of the picture to support timely reconfiguration in a completely open system with no restrictions. Some bounds have to be set to the structure of the distributed system (e.g., [1]) in order to achieve real-time reconfiguration.

In this paper, we present the integration of an extended middleware that supports real-time reconfiguration, iLAND [1], and Ada DSA (Ada *Distributed Systems Annex*) in order to have a vertical implementation of iLAND with a core real-time communication backbone technology with the goal of improving its temporal predictability. iLAND [2] provides a vertical real-time architecture (from the applications that are service-based to the operating system and network) considering all the software layers involved in providing real-time. As real-time operating system (RTOS) we have used QNX. This idea has been implemented and validated in a PolyORB [3] over a QNX environment.

The paper is structured as follows. Section 2 describes the background and related work. Section 3 presents an overview of the architecture of the iLAND middleware, describing its platform independence characteristics by means of defining a *common bridge component*, and describing how it overcomes the typical limitations of middleware to support real-time. In section 4, we present the Ada DSA specifics that influence the integration with iLAND; section 5 presents this integration (iLAND/Ada DSA) presenting also its validation over a PolyORB/QNX platform. Section 6 draws the conclusions of the work.

2   Background and Related Work

Already in the 80's, distribution based on the Ada language was subject of different contributions. Later in the 90's, one of the significant open distribution efforts where the Ada language was used focused on the creation of a communications library using Ada 83 (and later Ada 95) named Drago [4][5]. One of the relevant characteristics of Ada 95 was the inclusion of distribution facilities that were not contemplated in the previous version of the language, Ada 83. Still the support for distributed systems included in Ada 95 were very limited with respect to the needs of modern distributed systems programmers. As an example, explained in [6], the standardization of the communication protocols were not contemplated, threatening the interoperability of the implementations generated by different compiler vendors. Moreover, underspecified behavior like partition failures do not appear suitable for the kind of target systems aimed at by Ada. Some research efforts gave birth to the partial implementation of the Ada DSA named GLADE [7] and later PolyORB [3] for improved interoperability to other middleware technologies as CORBA [8].

The needs of today's distributed systems have gone even further, and appealing technologies have appeared that are major competitors in some domains. For instance, ICE [9] is a popular middleware for domains where real-time is not a primary issue but rather just an added value; also, DDS [10] is an attractive alternative in soft real-time domains, although the implementations of this standard are already being refined to improve its efficiency and its support for systems with higher level of real-time requirements. DDS has overcome most of the previous popular technologies that were a promise for real-time distributed systems as RT-CORBA[11], and even Java based solutions where its progress is very slow as real-time RMI (Remote Method Invocation for Java) due to the doubts it poses as far as the suitability of its software stack for real-time.

Anyhow, the communication paradigms of these technologies are not comparable in many ways to that of Ada DSA. Ada's distribution paradigm is based on a much simpler model where the capacity to control the execution of the different parts of the system (or partitions) and their timeliness is the main issue. Even if some of the Ada DSA characteristics are not directly linked to the real-time annex [12], the simplicity of its model is the key enabler to developing real-time implementations.

The fast evolution of distributed systems (and of real-time distributed systems) is a fact; consequently, enhanced middleware solutions have appeared over the recent years that include extra logic to support the dynamics of the next generation systems. Among this extra logic we may find functionality for dynamically upgrading code versions [13] although silent about real-time issues, on-line reconfiguration with bounded-time [14], or dynamic service discovery facilities [15].

In the recent years, Ada DSA has not been a major player in the domain of soft real-time systems, and contributions to adapt it or use it in these domains have not been in the front line. In this paper, we present an integration of the iLAND middleware [2] with distributed real-time technology based on Ada DSA and on top of a real-time operating system. The main motivation is the need for our middleware to evolve and interoperate with real-time nodes based on Ada, so that in the near future a version of iLAND with increased predictability will be available.

3   iLAND Middleware

In a previous work, we described a middleware for supporting dynamic reconfiguration in soft real-time systems [2][14] and we presented also one of its main components for making it portable to different underlying communication middleware technologies that follow different paradigms. Following, we present an overview of the iLAND middleware that supports timely reconfiguration and we recall and briefly describe the structure of its *common bridge* [16] component that enables the porting of the middleware to be interoperable with an Ada environment.

3.1   Architecture Overview

The iLAND architecture has been recently designed, implemented, and experimented in small scale industrial prototypes as well as in industrial demonstrators. iLAND middleware architecture follows the classical principles of a layered middleware [17] adding a number of extensions for specifically providing:

- Support of service oriented applications (precisely, light-weight services in the real-time version of the architecture and web-based services in the soft or QoS version).
- Integration of time-deterministic reconfiguration techniques and service-composition algorithms.
- Real-time communications by defining the complete network protocol stack (i.e., time-triggered level 2 media access control networks for allowing full schedulability analysis, as [18]).
- Possibility of using (and easy porting to) different communication off-the-shelf middleware backbones such as DDS, ICE, or RT-CORBA. It is achieved by the definition of a common communication bridge for synchronous and asynchronous middleware models.

The above mentioned characteristics are reflected in figure 1; it presents an overview of the middleware architecture.

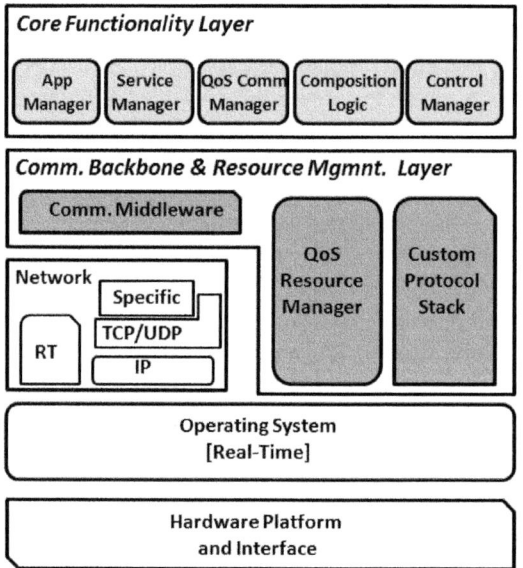

Fig. 1. iLAND middleware architecture

The *Core Functionality Layer (CFL)* contains most of the key added-value functionality (management of services, and time-deterministic composition and reconfiguration):

- *Service Manager (SM)* component contains the primitives for declaration/deletion and modification of the properties (including their resource requirements) of individual services and their particular implementations (service versions or *service implementations* in iLAND terms).

- *Application Manager* (AM) component includes the primitives to define the structure of an application (service graph), i.e., its services and their connections. Application-level QoS parameters (i.e. end-to-end properties for the whole service graph) are specified using this component.
- *Composition Logic* (CL) component contains the algorithms for service-based composition. This logic finds a set of services that allow to construct a specified application that complies with the specified QoS. Examples of criteria can be: minimizing the memory consumption of all services or minimizing/meeting the end-to-end deadline. Since each service can have different versions that realize it, the complete graph to search for a valid solution can be of high complexity. Non-efficient composition algorithms can be too costly (time-consuming) and, therefore, unaffordable to be executed on-line. Examples of time-deterministic composition algorithms used in iLAND with restricted bounds can be found in [19]. Improved ones are being tested in the current demonstrators.
- *Control* Manager (CM) component contains the logic for reconfiguration of applications; it performs high-level monitoring of the application and it controls the reconfiguration times and sequence to be time-deterministic. Reconfiguration time slots are scheduled as part of the overall timing analysis of the system [20] and efficient dynamic resource management algorithms based on dynamic priorities are embedded in this middleware component [21].
- *QoS Communication Manager* (QS) component configures the global QoS parameters for the communication.

The *Communication Backbone and Resource Management Layer (CBL)* has the following components:

- Backbone *Communication Middleware* or core communication models, that allows to port the architecture over different middleware paradigms and technologies.
- The *QoS Resource Manager* component aimed at QoS-based resource management. Scheduling for multi-resource management lies inside this component. This component follows the HOLA-QoS [22] architecture using the required scheduling mechanisms for real-time execution based on contracted resource budgets [20][21][23].
- The *Custom Protocol Stack* provides real-time support (scheduling, network protocols) for either (1) backward compatibility with legacy systems or for (2) supporting applications with hard real-time requirements.

The *Network Layer (NL)* contains the basic functionality for real-time transmission on general networks that offer TCP/UDP over IP. An application-specific communication protocol can be used in the *specific* module, such as streaming communication with specialized protocols as RTP enhanced with RTCP-based communication at transport level. Also, low level synchronization techniques inside the kernel can be used for the time deterministic operation of the network driver [24].

3.2   Platform Independence

Platform independence is achieved through the *common bridge* component contained in the CBL, precisely in the *communication middleware* part. This component presents a simple interface for sending and receiving messages, and it can adjust to different communication paradigms:

- P/S (*publish/subcribe*),
- MOM (*message oriented middleware*),
- DOM (*distributed object middleware*), or
- RPC (*remote procedure call*).

The reference implementation of iLAND follows a *publish/subscribe* model mapped to DDS. The architecture of this common bridge contains three layers:

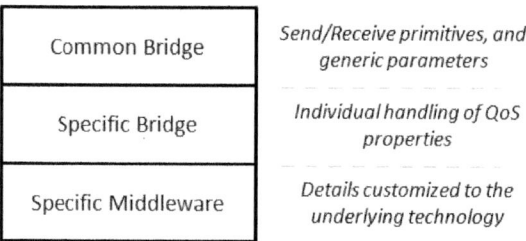

Fig. 2. Common *Bridge* architecture

The upper layer (which coincides in name with the component) offers `send_async` and `send_sync` primitives for implementing any type of communication. Also, it offers *listeners* and *servers* for implementing both asynchronous and synchronous structures, respectively.

3.3   Limitations for Real-Time

iLAND has a vertical architecture, from real-time operating system to the service management components. The level of guarantees over the real-time properties that can be offered depends on the different mechanisms and technologies used at the different layers:

- Operating systems and run-time; this layer must offer real-time guarantees, therefore solutions as real-time operating systems or Ada run-time will provide time-bounded thread/task manipulation primitives and management of time.
- Networking protocols; at this level, different solutions can be found but with limited or non-existing real-time properties. iLAND can be used directly over a real-time protocol (e.g. time triggered) that provides the basic send/receive primitives; in this case, they will be naturally synchronous. For direct usage of real-time network protocols, the middleware offers the *custom protocol stack.*

- Communication middleware; they provide abstraction over the specific networking protocols used at the cost of introducing a number of common intermediate operations that increase uncertainty (marshalling and unmarshalling, machine-independent data conversion, priority translation mechanisms for the invocations, addressing and location of remote objects/entities/partitions, dynamic binding, buffer management for memory efficiency, thread management, etc.). How the different communication middleware solutions implement these specific issues is very different and usually obscure, posing many challenges to the end-to-end schedulability analysis of the system.

To cope with this later uncertainty, in iLAND we have designed alternatives for achieving different levels of real-time guarantees:

- Usage of the custom protocol stack, that can schedule the network traffic and provide real-time guarantees over time triggered protocols (i.e., TTP/C or TT-Ethernet).
- Usage of a real-time middleware, that offers *quality of service* (QoS) in the sense that guarantees are probabilistic and dependant on the efficiency of the communication technology used (e.g., DDS, Ada DSA, ICE, etc.).

It is important to note that, as can be seen in figure 1, this is combined with the presence of a *quality of service resource manager* (QoSRM following the principles of HOLA-QoS) that arbitrates the allocation of resources (mainly processor cycles and network bandwidth) and applies admission control strategies to determine whether a given set of services (or an application) is eligible to run; this depends on the result of the schedulability analysis of the system task set (or service set in iLAND).

4   Adjusting to Ada Distribution Specifics

The communication paradigm used by both middleware implementations, iLAND and DSA, is essentially different. iLAND supports both synchronous (RPC based) and asynchronous (data-centric publish subscribe) communication paradigms. It can be ported to different underlying middleware technologies (following different communication paradigms) and to different real-time operating systems that are POSIX compliant.

On the side of Ada, interoperability with other middleware was initially achieved by PolyORB using an *interface definition language* (IDL) and a CORBA engine. However, Ada DSA is an extension of the language and required a pure Ada language implementation to avoid performance drawbacks. DSA incorporates distribution within the language, preserving the language's abstraction and strong typing features. It is based on the concept of program partitions and remote procedure calls (RPC). Partitions are entities that run independently in the system except when they communicate; if some partition contains procedures that are marked as remote, other partitions can communicate with it and invoke its remote code. The `pragma Remote_Call_Interface` marks the remote nature of the procedures and functions of a given partition. The default communication is synchronous, although asynchronous interaction is also offered through the `pragma Aynchronous [(name)]`.

Once the partitions have been defined, they are later configured which means that they are mapped to the nodes of the distributed system. Figure 3 shows an overview of a distributed Ada program.

DSA contemplates two types of partitions: *passive* and *active*. Passive partitions contain data that is accessible from all active partitions; they do not have threads of control of their own; and all their library units are pre-elaborated. Active partitions contain threads that can be a main program or some task.

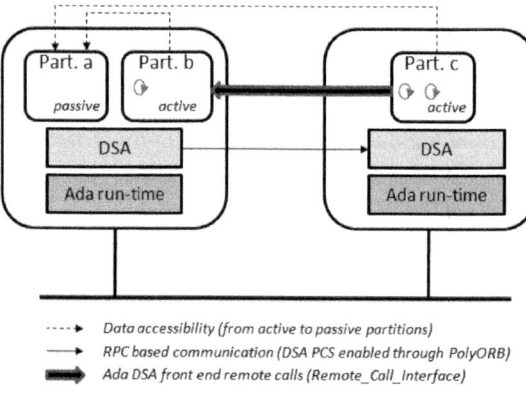

```
- - - ▶   Data accessibility (from active to passive partitions)
  ───▶   RPC based communication (DSA PCS enabled through PolyORB)
  ━━▶   Ada DSA front end remote calls (Remote_Call_Interface)
```

Fig. 3. Distributed programs as partitions in Ada

Whereas DSA supports a pre-defined environment where the program is written in the same language but split into partitions that are placed remotely, iLAND manages applications based on services that have higher dynamics than those targeted by DSA. In an iLAND environment, the structure of the system can change (reconfigure) at run-time connecting and disconnecting parts of the system (*services*, i.e, self contained code entities with well defined interfaces in a more dynamic environment) and this will be done in a time-bounded fashion. To bound the reconfiguration process time, it is required to have a time predictable underlying infrastructure and an a-priori study of the applications and their structure based on services. Even though time guarantees are not hard but probabilistic and based on QoS, integrating an environment as DSA enables the progressive evolution to a more predictable reconfigurable environment.

5   Integrating iLAND with Ada DSA. An Interoperable Solution

In this section, we describe the adaptation of the iLAND middleware to be able to execute over an underlying real-time middleware technology platform based on Ada. Using Ada technology as the core communication backbone allows to increase temporal determinism while preserving the flexibility provided by the communication model of the middleware and its interoperability to an environment that offers real-time reconfiguration.

The concurrency model of iLAND is based on POSIX. Therefore, we have required the presence of a real-time operating system that provides this thread interface for preserving interoperability while introducing the possibility of having nodes that can execute iLAND services and DSA partitions simultaneously. We have selected QNX as the RTOS to be used. Also, we have selected PolyORB as the middleware implementing the Ada DSA. A cross compilation tool chain was, therefore, required and for this purpose we have collaborated with the work of adapting an Ada compiler to PolyORB and QNX [25][26].

5.1   Adaptation to the Common Bridge

The integration requires to first describe the mapping between the *common bridge* of iLAND and the implementation of Ada DSA, PolyORB. Precisely, the implementation of DSA used for the integration is PolyORB. One of the features of PolyORB is that it can support distribution between different middleware technologies and over different operating systems. Although PolyORB initially borrowed some architectural parts and code from CORBA, currently there is a version with the pure implementation in Ada of the DSA that overcomes this initial problem, improving its predictability and light-weight. The concurrency and the real-time mechanisms are supported by the language itself with tasks, protected types, and the services specified in annex D. Like RT-CORBA, Ada DSA does not consider the possibility of passing scheduling parameters to the communications networks; only remote invocations are enabled.

Figure 4 shows how DSA should fit in the iLAND's common bridge, keeping the independence with the upper layers.

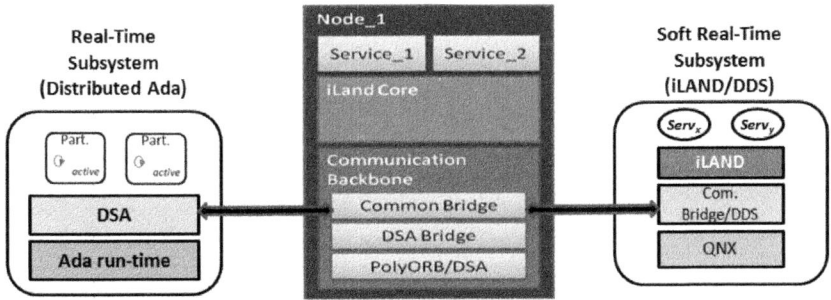

Fig. 4. DSA specific communication backbone as a gateway

In the *common bridge* component, we define a simple API with a transparent interface for the user. It acts as the interoperability enabler since Ada programs will be able to interact with iLAND services by means of invoking send and receive primitives; also, iLAND services will request remote procedures from Ada partitions that are tagged with the `Remote_Call_Interface` pragmas. There are different solutions for this interoperability. The one that is presented here is based on the design of a gateway architecture that contains both DSA/Ada run-time with iLAND middleware; in this case, an extended POSIX compliant RTOS is needed for compatibility with iLAND. Integrating iLAND and DSA in the same machine presents two clear benefits:

- A gateway hides the details of interoperability to other parts of an Ada distributed program, and
- iLAND services and Ada code partitions can easily communicate in the same machine by means of the same interface and, by extension, between remote machines.

```ada
package CommonBridge is
    pragma Remote_Call_Interface;

    procedure create_listener (ptr : String; id : Character)
    procedure close_listener (id : Character)
    procedure send_async (dst_id : Character;
                          message : String;
                          length: Natural)
    pragma Asynchronous (create_listener);
    pragma Asynchronous (close_listener);
    pragma Asynchronous (send_async);

    procedure create_sync_server (ptr : String;
                                  id : Character)
                                  return Integer;
    procedure close_sync_server (id : Character)
                                 return Integer;
    procedure send_sync (src_id : Character;
                         dst_id : Character;
                         message : String;
                         length: Natural);

end CommonBridge;
```

Fig. 5. Ada implementation of the *common bridge*

The integration of both middleware implementations in an interoperable gateway architecture is shown in figure 6.

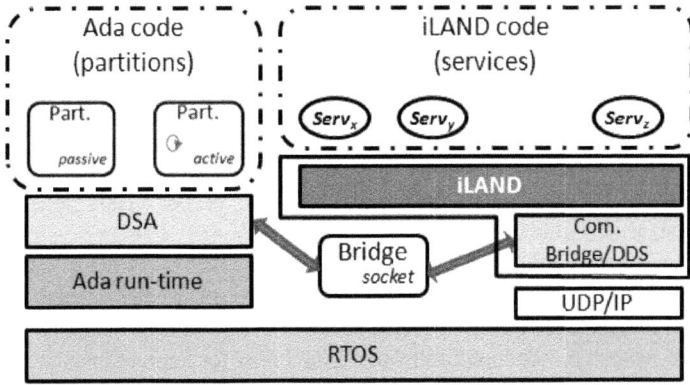

Fig. 6. Interoperable architecture for Ada DSA and iLAND

Here, we present the detailed design of the common bridge gateway from figure 4. It must be noted that in the specific bridge layer, we connect the iLAND implementation based on C language with the Ada part. Sockets are needed to pass the data between the Common Bridge Layer in C and the specific middleware layer in Ada, as shown previously in figure 4.

5.2   Validation

We have validated this interoperable architecture implementing a gateway node that contains both PolyORB and iLAND in the same execution environment. Sockets are used to exchange information between both middleware in the same node; it is the most straightforward solution since sockets are implemented on a wide spectrum of operating systems and platforms being well-known, flexible and a de facto industry standard for TCP/IP network programming. There are two ways to implement sockets in Ada; using the standard mapping of POSIX to Ada (IEEE 1003.5b-1996) or using the GNAT.Sockets library.

All of our Ada nodes run the version of Ada DSA implemented in GNAT, so we can choose the second option. The implementation of sockets with standard POSIX binding is more unmanageable and error-prone. GNAT provides a solid binding with GNAT.Sockets and it is portable to other GNAT platforms.

Management of multiple simultaneous requests is done by creating and Ada task per client to conduct each session independently. There is a limitation to the number of connections, as it is the usual approach in all middleware technologies. It requires synchronization between tasks when there are shared structures, but it is easy to design and control in our service-oriented middleware.

The different structures involved in the communication are created in the specific middleware layer thanks to the PCS (Partition Communication Subsystem) defined by Ada DSA and implemented by PolyORB. The PCS provides facilities for supporting communication between the active partitions of a distributed program. The package System.RPC is a language-defined interface to the PCS. An implementation conforming to this annex shall use the RPC interface to implement remote subprogram calls. The communications between different partitions follows the same structure regardless of whether the calling and called partitions reside in the same node or not.

PCS implementation is reentrant, thereby allowing concurrent calls to service concurrent remote subprogram calls into the server partition. This means that at the implementation level the PCS manages a pool of helper tasks. This (apart from performance) is invisible to the user.

The integration of Ada DSA in a RTOS such as QNX is not a trivial step. At the moment of carrying out this work, there is no commercially available version of PolyORB over QNX. Therefore, we have undertaken a joint effort together with [25][26] in order to develop a cross compiler from a Linux host for a target machine running Ada DSA (the PolyORB implementation) on QNX. This setup of such a cross environment instead of using the native environment has some advantages as the following:

- There are no integrated development environments for ADA on QNX,
- Native compilation is slower than cross compilation, and
- QNX does not support most of the modern hardware; so it is more common to use cross compiler for para-virtualization.

Following, table 1 shows a comparative view of the integration of different technologies with iLAND and the level of timely guarantees that can be achieved with each of them.

Table 1. Technology integration

OS	Middleware	Network	Timing Guarantees	Efficiency
Linux/RT	Sockets	UDP/TCP / IP	Best effort	High
Linux/RT	DDS	UDP/IP	Soft (QoS, probabilistic)	Medium
QNX	DDS	UDP/IP	Soft (QoS, probabilistic)	Medium
Linux	ICE	UDP/IP	Best effort (probabilistic)	Medium
Linux/RT	-	TT	Real-time	High
Ada run-time	DSA/PolyORB	TCP/IP	Real-time	High
QNX	DSA/PolyORB	TCP/IP	Real-time	High

The very high level of *efficiency* is not assigned to any technology integration since it would imply an *optimized usage of the communications, a minimum level of buffering and threading overheads*, and global control over temporal predictability. Some selected implementation of TT (time triggered) protocols could be a strong candidate for the highest efficiency, but there are very few efficient open solutions that can be integrated in an open project as iLAND; current TT porting can only be classified as *high* though *not very high*. It can be observed that iLAND middleware in combination with Ada DSA offers a high efficiency and control over the execution not only in a local node but also in remote communications. We have, therefore, validated our interoperable architectural solution for integrating iLAND with Ada DSA using as key enablers the pure Ada language implementation of PolyORB implementation and a real-time operating system as QNX that keeps threading compatibility with the rest of iLAND nodes.

6   Conclusions

One of the most powerful future characteristics of middleware is the support of timely reconfiguration of distributed systems. However, this poses a number of contradicting requirements with real-time environments. Enhanced middleware solutions have appeared over the recent years that include extra logic to support the dynamics of the next generation systems; this is the case of the iLAND middleware that aims at supporting timely reconfiguration in distributed soft real-time systems under certain bounds and limitations to the open nature of such systems.

Using Ada technology as the core communication backbone inside iLAND middleware allows to increase temporal determinism while preserving the flexibility provided by the communication model of the middleware, and also keeping its interoperability with an environment that offers real-time reconfiguration. Their integration requires the mapping between the *common bridge* of iLAND and Ada DSA communication paradigm and language model. We have presented an architecture for this integration of iLAND middleware in combination with Ada DSA in order to offer higher efficiency and control over the execution not only in a local node but also in remote communications. We have implemented this interoperable architecture between Ada DSA (precisely the PolyORB implementation of DSA) and iLAND middleware, and we have discussed benefits of DSA core communication backbone compared to the other middleware technologies.

References

1. García Valls, M., Gómez Molinero, F.: Real-Time Reconfiguration in Complex Embedded Systems: A Vision and its Reality. In: IEEE International Conference on Industrial Informatics (IEEE INDIN 2011). IEEE Computer Society Press, Caparica (2011)
2. García Valls, M., Rodríguez López, I., Fernández Villar, L.: iLAND: An Enhanced Middleware for Real-Time Reconfiguration of Service Oriented Distributed Real-Time Systems. IEEE Transactions on Industrial Informatics (2012) (accepted for publication)
3. PolyORB, http://polyorb.objectweb.org/
4. Guerra, F., Miranda, J., Álvarez, A., Arévalo, S.: An Ada Library to Program Fault-tolerant Distributed Applications. In: Hardy, K., Briggs, J. (eds.) Ada-Europe 1997. LNCS, vol. 1251, pp. 230–243. Springer, Heidelberg (1997)
5. Miranda, J., Álvarez, A., Arévalo, S., Guerra, F.: Drago: An Ada Extension to Program Fault-tolerant Distributed Applications. In: Strohmeier, A. (ed.) Ada-Europe 1996. LNCS, vol. 1088, pp. 235–246. Springer, Heidelberg (1996)
6. Pautet, L., Quinot, T., Tardieu, S.: Building Modern Distributed Systems. In: Strohmeier, A., Craeynest, D. (eds.) Ada-Europe 2001. LNCS, vol. 2043, pp. 123–135. Springer, Heidelberg (2001)
7. Pautet, L., Tardieu, S.: GLADE: a Framework for Building Large Object-Oriented Real-Time Distributed Systems. In: IEEE International Conference on Object-Oriented Real-Time Distributed Computing (ISORC), USA, pp. 244–251 (2000)
8. OMG: Common Object Request Broker Architecture (CORBA) Specification, Version 3.1. Interfaces (2008)
9. ZeroC Inc: The Internet Communications Engine (2003)

10. OMG: A Data Distribution Service for Real-time Systems Version 1.2. Real-Time Systems (2007)
11. OMG: Real-time CORBA Specification (2005)
12. Campos, J.L., Gutiérrez, J.J., González Harbour, M.: The Chance for Ada to Support Distribution and Real-Time in Embedded Systems. In: Llamosí, A., Strohmeier, A. (eds.) Ada-Europe 2004. LNCS, vol. 3063, pp. 91–105. Springer, Heidelberg (2004)
13. Villa, D., Martín, C., Villanueva, F., Moya, F., López, J.C.: A Dynamically Reconfigurable Architecture for Smart Grids. IEEE Transactions on Consumer Electronics 57(2), 411–419 (2011)
14. García-Valls, M., Rodríguez-López, I., Fernández-Villar, L., Estévez-Ayres, I., Basanta-Val, P.: Towards a middleware architecture for deterministic reconfiguration of service based networked applications. In: Proc. of the 15th IEEE Int'l Conference on Emerging Technologies and Factory Automation - ETFA 2010, Bilbao, Spain, September 13-16 (2010)
15. Park, J., Kang, S., Moon, K.: Middleware Architecture for Supporting both Dynamic Reconfiguration and Real-Time Services. IEEE Transactions on Consumer Electronics 46(3), 795–801 (2000)
16. Rodríguez-López, I., García-Valls, M.: Architecting a Common Bridge Abstraction over Different Middleware Paradigms. In: Romanovsky, A., Vardanega, T. (eds.) Ada-Europe 2011. LNCS, vol. 6652, pp. 132–146. Springer, Heidelberg (2011)
17. Schantz, R., Smidth, D.: Middleware for Distributed Systems: Evolving the Common Structure for Network-Centric Applications. In: Encyclopedia of Software Engineering. Wiley and Sons (2002)
18. Kopetz, H., Bauer, G.: The Time-Trigger Architecture. Proceedings of the IEEE 91(1), 112–126 (2003)
19. Estévez Ayres, I., García Valls, M., Basanta-Val, P., Díez-Sánchez, J.: A hybrid approach for selecting service-based real-time composition algorithms in heterogeneous environments. Concurrency and Computation: Practice and Experience 23(15), 1816–1851 (2011)
20. García-Valls, M., Basanta-Val, P., Estévez-Ayres, I.: Real-time Reconfiguration in Multimedia Systems. IEEE Transactions on Consumer Electronics 57(3), 1280–1287 (2011)
21. García-Valls, M., Alonso, A., de la Puente, J.A.: A Dual-Band Priority Assignment Algorithm for QoS Resource Management. Future Generation Computer Systems (2011), http://dx.doi.org/10.1016/j.future.2011.10.005
22. García Valls, M., Alonso Muñoz, A., Ruíz Martínez, F.J., Groba, A.: An Architecture of a QoS Resource Manager for Flexible Multimedia Embedded Systems. In: van der Hoek, A., Coen-Porisini, A. (eds.) SEM 2002. LNCS, vol. 2596, pp. 36–55. Springer, Heidelberg (2003)
23. Alonso, A., García-Valls, M., de la Puente, J.: Assessment of Timing Properties of Family Products. In: van der Linden, F.J. (ed.) Development and Evolution of Software Architectures for Product Families. LNCS, vol. 1429, pp. 161–169. Springer, Heidelberg (1998)
24. Breuer, P., García-Valls, M.: Raiding the Noosphere: the open development of networked RAID support for the Linux Kernel. Software: Practice and Experience 36(4), 365–395 (2005) ISBN: 0038-0644
25. Trojanek, P.: Ada Annex E with PolyORB under QNX. Warsaw University of Technology. Web report (2011)
26. Trojanek, P.: GNAT cross compiler on a Linux host for QNX target. Warsaw University of Technology. Web report (2009)

Source Code as the Key Artifact in Requirement-Based Development: The Case of Ada 2012

José F. Ruiz, Cyrille Comar, and Yannick Moy

AdaCore 46 rue d'Amsterdam, 75009 Paris, France
{ruiz,comar,moy}@adacore.com

Abstract. Developing high-integrity software requires the production of many interrelated collections of artifacts which must be kept up-to-date and in synchrony; traceability in particular must be captured to ensure coherence across the various development and verification phases.

This paper proposes a new approach to the development of high-integrity systems, in which various artifacts (low-level requirements, modules, relationships among modules, test case obligations, etc.) are represented directly in the source code.

Package specs in general, and Ada 2012 aspects in particular, are very well suited for expressing some of these artifacts, facilitating reuse and maintainability, and obtaining traceability automatically. Review activities are made more effective and efficient because the context of the reviewed artifact is in full view, and when something is modified it is easy to know which other artifacts need to be re-verified.

The software architecture derived from the design activity consists in the definition of software components, their interfaces and their relationships. All those elements are well represented by Ada package specs and the "with" clauses between packages. Low-level requirements, which define the detailed functionality, can in part be formally expressed through Ada 2012 contracts. Test cases associated with low-level requirements can then be described using Test_Case aspects. Test procedure skeletons can be automatically generated from the test cases.

1 Introduction

When human lives depend on the correct operation of software, strict processes must be put in place to ensure, as much as possible, the absence of errors. In the avionics safety-critical world a strict guidance/audit of the development process is imposed before authorization to fly is granted.

According to the DO-178 [10,11] avionics standards, developing a certified safety-critical system consists of various interrelated activities that produce collections of artifacts as evidence of successful completion. The software development processes (requirements, design, production/coding, and integration) create the final system (and many intermediate artifacts), and the software verification process (reviews, analyses, tests, etc.) aims at detecting and reporting errors that may have been introduced during the software development processes.

M. Brorsson and L.M. Pinho (Eds.): Ada-Europe 2012, LNCS 7308, pp. 49–59, 2012.
© Springer-Verlag Berlin Heidelberg 2012

Maintaining such complex software in an Agile [8] way is challenging. It involves not only the software (source code) but also the rest of interrelated artifacts. Traditional activity-centric approaches for managing certification artifacts focus on the temporal and causal dependencies among activities. The artifact-centric approach proposed here consists in including directly relevant artifacts in the source code itself in order to simplify traceability and enforce consistency and and coherence.

For instance, some requirements can be expressed either informally as comments associated with the subprograms implementing them or more formally as pre and post conditions of these subprograms. In Ada 2012, the latter can be expressed using the `Pre` and `Post` aspects. Whether formal, partially formal, or completely informal, keeping the requirement close to the code implementing it creates traceability by proximity and decreases the risk of incoherence.

Similarly, a software architecture consisting of an organized set of software components and their relationships can be expressed directly in Ada through packages and their dependencies, or in a graphical representation.

In this way, review activities are more effective and efficient because the context of the reviewed artifact is easily accessible. For example, when a requirement (contract) in the package specification is modified, the implementation that needs to be reviewed (and potentially modified) is in the corresponding package body. Many verification activities (such as those checking traceability between artifacts) are greatly simplified by proximity and some can even be guaranteed by coding standard rules (e.g. a subprogram must have a `Post` aspect) or by simply checking the Ada semantics: the implementation (subprogram body) must comply with its spec (subprogram spec + contract).

The following sections describe the different artifacts produced by the development and verification processes, highlighting when and how the required information can be kept in the Ada code, and the advantages of following this approach. The DO-178 standard is used as the reference to define the artifacts to be produced and the kind of information and verification required, but the general methodology can be applied to other safety or security standards.

2   Requirements

The software requirement process produces high-level requirements (HLRs), representing "what" is to be designed. Then, these high-level requirements are further refined through one or more iterations during the software design process, producing the low-level requirements (LLRs), which represent "how" to implement the design. Low-level requirements are thus software requirements from which source code can be directly implemented without needing further information.

This idea of specifications defining the exact functionality to implement is the cornerstone of Design-by-Contract [9]. A contract is given by a precondition, which the caller must *pay* to be entitled to the service provided by the callee, and a postcondition, which is the service the callee must *provide* to the caller. Ada 2012 defines such subprogram contracts, using the new aspects syntax of `Pre` for preconditions and `Post` for postconditions. These are defined as Boolean expressions over program variables and functions. Additionally, the expression in a postcondition can refer to the value returned by a function F as `F'Result`, and to the value in the pre-state (at the beginning of the call) of any variable or parameter V as V'Old. Expressing properties in contracts is greatly facilitated by the use of several new Ada 2012 features: conditional expressions, case expressions, universal and existential quantified expressions, and expression functions (an expression function is a simple function whose body is defined by a single expression).

As an example, here is the contract for a procedure that doubles the value of its formal parameter. It expects its input to be within some bounds in order to avoid overflow, and it returns the doubled value in its output.

```
procedure Double (X : in out Integer) with
   Pre  => X >= Integer'First / 2
           and then X <= Integer'Last / 2,
   Post => X = 2 * X'Old;
```

If the expressions used in contracts do not have side-effects, then they can also have an interpretation as logic formulas. The precondition is a property of the input state. The postcondition is a relation (two-state property) between the input state and the output state.

Expressing LLRs as contracts helps meet the following DO-178 objectives that apply to reviews and analyses of LLRs:

- Accuracy and consistency: The objective is to ensure that each low-level requirement is accurate and unambiguous, and that the low-level requirements do not conflict with each other.
- Verifiability: The objective is to ensure that each low-level requirement can be verified.

If LLRs are expressed as code, and indeed Ada 2012 contracts are part of the code, then their meaning is accurately defined by the static and dynamic semantics of the programming language. In general, code can be ambiguous due to compiler permissions, for example the different orders of evaluation of expressions. By following suitable restrictions, typically mandated by coding standards for critical software development, we can ensure that the code and thus the contracts are unambiguous.

In the appropriate mode, the compiler will insert assertions in the executable to check at run-time that contracts are respected. Thus, LLRs are naturally verifiable by testing. For a subset of subprograms and contracts, additional tools provide formal verification of LLRs, for example the tools developed in project Hi-Lite [7]. These tools translate contracts into logical formulas that must be proved, using Hoare logic to interpret programs. Each subprogram can be proved in isolation, because calls can be abstracted by the corresponding callee's contract. And some subprograms can be proved while others are tested, thanks to the combination strategy that we have developed [4].

3   Software Architecture

The software architecture defines the software structure chosen to implement the requirements. Usually this structure is represented by software components or subsystems interacting with one another. The interactions are based on the component interfaces and their relationships; typical relationships are client/provider and inheritance.

The key point is that when using a language such as Ada, with support for encapsulation and modularization, a good part of the architectural design can be represented by package specs and dependencies between packages. The package spec itself is an effective textual representation of the interface offered by a software component. The relations between the packages, represented for example by with clauses or child package hierarchies, are critical elements of the software architecture. These two elements – package specs and their relationships – are clearly more in the category of design artifacts than coding artifacts even if they are expressed using programming language syntax. In fact, having compilable design artifacts insures a high level of coherence and facilitates traceability between design and implementation. The implementation is represented principally by the bodies of the package specs for the design and architecture artifacts.

When appropriate, tools like GPS (GNAT Programming Studio) can generate a graphical representation of such an architecture, as shown in figures 1 and 2 for package and class diagrams respectively. This clear visualization of the architecture makes it easier to manually review the compatibility with HLRs.

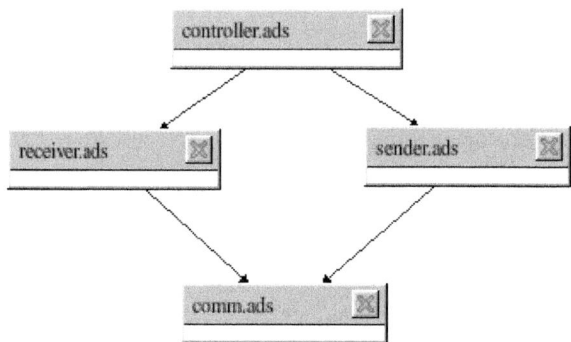

Fig. 1. Software (package) architecture

Thus some of the Ada sources are part of the design, and others are part of the implementation. This should not be confused with an attempt to reverse engineer the Ada source code to obtain the architecture. It is part of a top-down approach where the architecture is defined first, in a manner making it very convenient to insert the code implementing it afterwards.

This concept works well within an Ada partition, and when the application is made up of several partitions (for example, with the Integrated Modular Avionics (IMA) architecture approach [2]), some additional mechanisms are required for representing the partitioning architecture).

One of the certification activities related to the architecture is to check its consistency, ensuring that the data flow and control flow relationships are correct. The graphical representation of package dependencies exposes these relationships explicitly, facilitating its verification. Additionally, Ada visibility rules define the namescopes accessible

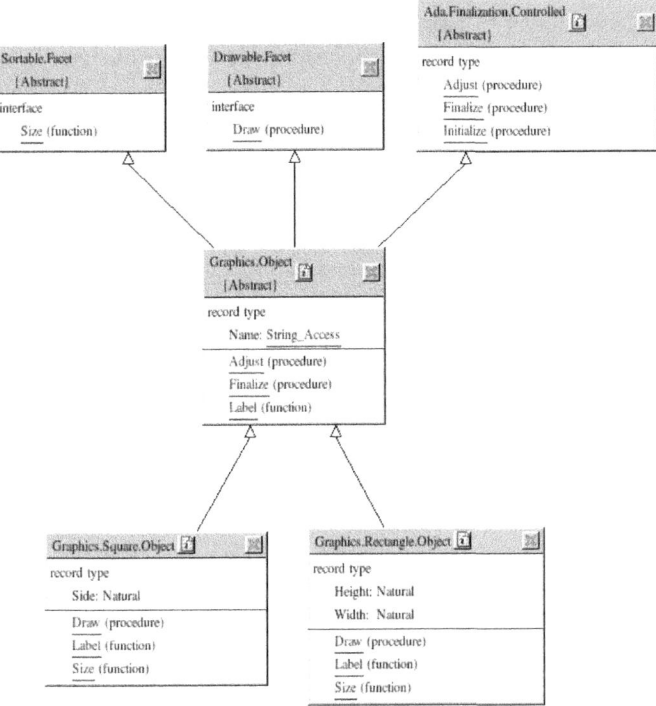

Fig. 2. Class architecture

within the different compilation units, so coding standard rules can easily restrict unde-sired data and control coupling.

An advantage of using Ada as a design notation is that basic data flow information is already present in the subprograms' parameter modes: in, out or in out. When the target programming language is less design-friendly, the design notation must provide similar capabilities and tools need to be used to ensure coherence between the design and the code as described for instance in [5].

The SPARK subset of Ada goes even further, by allowing users to precisely spec-ify both data flow and information flow (e.g., which output depends on which inputs). The SPARK tools check statically that a unit's implementation respects the flows spec-ified in the spec. As an example, here is the SPARK specification of a procedure which computes some outputs from some inputs; both the outputs and the inputs involve pa-rameters and a global (state) variable:

```
procedure Process (Output : out T; Input1, Input2 : in T);
--# global out Global_Output;
--#        in Global_Input;
--# derives Output from Input1, Input2 &
--#         Global_Output from Global_Input, Input2;
```

SPARK's annotation language allows the state to be abstracted, which is crucial for scaling specifications to large applications. For example, `Global_Input` and `Global_Output` above may be either concrete variables or abstract ones, which represent in fact a set of concrete variables.

The modularity provided by Ada packages makes it suitable for directly representing key aspects of the software architecture, and additional encapsulation and visibility rules help address the verification of the architecture. In other words, some of the Ada sources can be considered as artifacts of design process, as opposed to the coding process. This applies particularly to package specs when they express both the LLRs and the architectural relationships.

4   Code

From a DO-178 perspective, the source code is produced by the software coding process based upon the software architecture and the LLRs. If the latter are already provided in the form of Ada package spec source code, the coding process can be summarized as providing the implementation of the LLRs through the corresponding Ada package bodies' source code.

The DO-178 standards, and similar high-integrity standards, require that the source code reviews and analyses fulfill the following objectives:

- Compliance with the low-level requirements
- Compliance with the software architecture
- Verifiability
- Conformance to software coding standards
- Traceability to the low-level requirements
- Accuracy and consistency

The first objective, compliance with LLRs, has two implications. First, the code must be accurate and complete with respect to the requirements: i.e., the code must implement all the required functionality as it has been specified. Second, the code should not implement more than what is expressed in the contract: no unintended functionality. Accuracy and completeness have been mentioned in section 2: a mismatch between the contract and the implementation will be detected either dynamically during the testing or statically by contract proving. Detection of unintended functionality is difficult and usually accomplished through several complementary activities. The first is code reviews, where having the contract and the implementation in the same notation is a help. The second is structural coverage analysis, which detects code that is not exercised by requirement-based testing. However, this testing can exercise nonrequired code by chance. For example, while implementing a required functionality the developer may want to add a logging mechanism to trace its execution. This unintended functionality can be exercised during testing, and hence not detected by structural coverage analysis. When using contract proving, the prover could detect that all the statements related to the logging functionality do not contribute to prove the contract, hence highlighting it as unintended functionality. Tools such as SPARK [3] detect these "ineffective" statements during flow analysis.

Showing that the source code complies with the software architecture means, in the DO-178 sense, ensuring that the code matches the data flow and control flow defined in the architecture. The design process defines the appropriate architecture (see section 3), with the required data and control dependencies, together with their imposed characteristics (protection mechanisms, sequencing of activities, scheduling, etc.) In order to compare what has been implemented against what is in the design architecture, fine-grained flow information (which can be extracted with tools from the implementation) helps. For example, the GNAT compiler can show detailed control flow information (per-subprogram call graph) with the *-fcallgraph-info* flag. GPS can also graphically show this call graph information (see figure 3). The compiler can also check that input and output parameters (defined in the specification) are used as such in the implementation.

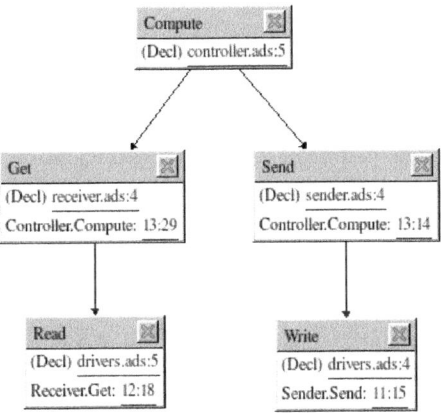

Fig. 3. Control flow information

Verifiability implies avoiding statements and structures that cannot be verified. What can be easily verified by testing is everything defined in the public interface provided by the visible part of Ada specifications. Variables and subprograms defined in the private part of a package can be tested by child units. Items declared in the scope of package bodies (including nested packages in bodies) must be exercised by the tests created for those entities using these "hidden" variables or subprograms (tests use the visible interface, and these subprograms must use those declared in package bodies).

Conformance to software coding standards can be easily verified using an automatic tool, such as GNATcheck [1], which in addition can be qualified to obtain certification credit for its use.

Traceability to the LLRs is straightforward because these LLRs are directly expressed as contracts in the source code for the specs of the subprograms that implement them.

Finally, the objectives of accuracy and consistency relate to the correctness and consistency of the source code. Here tools like CodePeer can be used effectively, mathematically analyzing every line of software, and considering every possible input and every path through the program.

Thus a multifaceted approach – using the source code for the reference architecture, contracts to define the requirements, an appropriate coding standard, and tools to automate static analyses – greatly reduce the manual effort to achieve the source code objectives specified in the DO-178 standards.

5   Testing

Testing is used to demonstrate that the software satisfies its requirements, and to demonstrate with a high degree of confidence that errors that could lead to unacceptable failure conditions, as determined by the system safety assessment process, have been removed.

There are three kinds of requirements-based testing methods addressed in the DO-178 documents: hardware/software integration testing, to verify correct operation in the target computer environment, software integration testing, to verify the correct interrelationship among requirements, design and implementation, and low-level testing, to verify the correct implementation of low-level requirements.

Testing a subprogram might be performed with manually coded oracles that translate the LLRs for the subprogram into code. If LLRs are expressed as contracts, as described in Section 2, then testing the subprogram reduces to calling it on suitable inputs. Indeed, the compiler inserts assertions for contracts in the executable, so that any violation of contracts will be detected at run-time.

Additionally, exercising the subprogram on representative inputs that "cover" the input space is recommended. In other words, there must be enough test cases to functionally cover the LLRs. Furthermore, since testing is non-exhaustive, there may be invocations of the subprogram from unexpected contexts. For such cases a desired outcome should be specified, in order to make the code robust. DO-178 differentiates these two kinds of test cases:

- the *normal range* test cases, that verify the subprogram with respect to its requirement, and
- the *robustness* test cases, that verify the behavior of the subprogram in abnormal circumstances.

In many cases, these test cases can be expressed as additional contracts that a subprogram should respect. Using the permission in Ada 2012 to create compiler-dependent aspects, the GNAT compiler has defined a new Test_Case aspect that allows users to describe test cases in subprogram specifications, along with contracts. A test case is either in nominal mode (to test in an expected calling context) or robustness mode (to test in an unexpected calling context). A nominal test case may refine the subprogram contract by defining a requires-clause (added to precondition) and an ensures-clause (added to postcondition). A robustness test case replaces the subprogram contract with its requires-clause and ensures-clause so that the program can be exercised outside of the range of its contract.

For example, test-cases can be defined for function `Double` as follows:

```
procedure Double (X : in out Integer) with
  Pre  => ...,  -- As above
  Post => ...,  -- As above
  Test_Case => (Name     => "positive",
                Mode     => Nominal,
                Requires => X >= 0
                Ensures  => X >= 0),
  Test_Case => (Name     => "lower-bound",
                Mode     => Nominal,
                Requires => X = Integer'First / 2,
                Ensures  => X = Integer'First),
  Test_Case => (Name     => "off-by-one-positive",
                Mode     => Robustness,
                Requires => X = Integer'Last / 2 + 1,
                Ensures  => X = Integer'Last);
```

The test cases "positive" and "lower bound" exercise the nominal mode of function `Double`, in which its contract should be respected. Here, we want to test additionally that the output value respects some constraints. The test case "off by one positive" should exercise function `Double` outside its nominal mode. Here, we ignore the contract of `Double`, because we are testing under abnormal circumstances which are outside the contract. Instead, we require that `Double` be called in a context where the input value is too large by one, and that the result saturates at the larger integer value.

By expressing test cases in the same formalism as contracts, we are able to perform much more verification automatically. For example, we may want to check automatically that a test procedure implements a test case. This is what the GNATtest unit testing tool does. GNATtest generates a test harness for a project, with a separate test procedure for each test-case, or a single test procedure for a subprogram when no test-case is defined. The user only has to complete each of these procedures with a proper call sequence to the subprogram under test (the person writing the tests should use input data respecting the preconditions and the `Requires` attributes, and assert that the correct output is achieved), then simply compile and run the test harness, to get a report detailing which test-cases and contracts are adequately tested. Thus, the definition of formal test cases allows automating the verification of functional coverage of the subprogram contract by its test cases. Much more automatic verification is possible: ensuring that robustness test cases exercise the subprogram outside the range where its precondition holds; ensuring that nominal test cases partition the input space defined by the precondition.

DO-178 specifies testing objectives to ensure an adequate coverage of the program behaviors despite the non-exhaustive nature of testing. These testing objectives, such as Modified Condition/Decision Coverage (MC/DC), account for a large part of the high cost of testing. It is therefore of practical value to turn to alternate verification techniques which do not incur this cost. Formal methods have the potential for exhaustively analyzing all behaviors of a program, without the need for additional coverage objectives. Contract-based formal program verification, which consists in verifying statically that a subprogram respects its contract, has already been pioneered in avionics industry on C and SPARK programs [12,6]. The new DO-178C Formal Methods Supplement recognizes such usage and explicitly gives permission to replace some of the prescribed testing activities by formal methods. The tool GNATprove allows partial replacement of low-level testing by contract-based formal verification [4]. We do not aim at completely replacing low-level testing with formal verification, because the latter may be much too difficult (hence, costly) for some parts of the program. Instead, we aim at fully automated formal verification on most of the program, completed with low-level testing on the parts that are not formally verified. The GNATprove tool sensibly combines formal verification and testing, based on executable contracts.

6   Traceability

Traceability information is used to show the bi-directional associations between artifacts. This association links together the inputs and outputs of the various development and verification activities. The goal of traceability is to make sure that when there is a modification in an artifact (for example one of the requirements) the artifacts that depend on that one (related requirements, architecture, code, tests, etc.) are verified and modified if needed. According to the DO-178 standards, the following traceability associations need to be captured:

- System requirements to software and HLRs
- HLRs and LLRs
- LLRs and source code
- Software Requirements and test cases
- Test cases and test procedures
- Test procedures and test results

Linking LLRs (which are expressed in the source code as contracts) to HLRs and system requirements is typically handled by tools external to the software. They are not usually produced by software engineer; it is usually the task of system engineers with a view of the whole system and not only the software part.

One of the major advantages of the approach proposed in this paper, which keeps the source code as the reference artifact, is that traceability is automatically achieved. The source code contains the reference to LLRs (in the form of contracts), to the software architecture (the Ada package to which it belongs) and the associated test cases (using the Test_Case aspects).

In the approach that we are proposing (see section 5), test procedures are automatically created from the test case specifications by GNATtest. This is an ASIS-based utility that creates unit-test stubs as well as the test driver infrastructure (harness). Hence, traceability between test cases and test procedures is automatically achieved by design. Note that the Test_Case aspect includes the Requires and Ensures attributes, achieving the required traceability between test procedures and test results.

The source code contains all the required traceability information related to the artifacts generated by the software design, coding, and testing processes (LLRs, architecture, code, tests cases, test procedures, and test results).

7   Conclusion

This paper proposes some techniques to help requirements-based software development. Instead of maintaining the different artifacts used for software development and verification (requirements, architecture, code, test cases, test procedures, and test results) in different physical locations (files or documents), we propose a source code-centric approach, where the code contains most of the relevant artifacts. It is therefore much easier to ensure coherence among them, and traceability information is obtained at lower cost.

Ada packages and their dependencies are used as a very practical and simple way to represent the design (software architecture), and the encapsulation and visibility control helps in verifying the architecture.

Contracts (Ada 2012 pre- and post-conditions) can accurately define the required functionality (low-level requirements), and they are naturally verifiable by either formal proofs or testing.

Software testing information (test cases, test procedures and test results) can be easily linked to the code they test using a new Ada 2012 aspect, facilitating their traceability and review, and helping to keep tests up-to-date when the code changes.

Using the source code as the reference architecture, contracts to define the requirements, and test aspects for software testing information, many of the verification activities can be either automated or facilitated. Maintainability and evolution of the resulting system is made easier because we have direct access to interrelated artifacts.

References

1. AdaCore: GNATcheck Reference Manual, http://www.adacore.com/wp-content/files/auto_update/asis-docs/gnatcheck_rm.html
2. ARINC: ARINC Specification 653, Avionics Application Software Standard Interface. Aeronautical Radio, Inc. (2005)
3. Barnes, J.: High Integrity Software. In: The SPARK Approach to Safety and Security. Addison Wesley (2003)
4. Comar, C., Kanig, J., Moy, Y.: Integrating formal program verification with testing. In: Proceedings of the Embedded Real Time Software and Systems Conference, ERTS^2 2012 (February 2012)
5. Delmas, D., Cuoq, P., Lamiel, V.M., Duprat, S.: Fan C, a Frama-C plug-in for data flow verification. In: Proceedings of the Embedded Real Time Software and Systems Conference, ERTS^2 2012 (February 2012)
6. Hall, A., Chapman, R.: Correctness by construction: Developing a commercial secure system. IEEE Software 19(1), 18–25 (2002)
7. Project Hi-Lite, http://www.open-do.org/projects/hi-lite/
8. Martin, R.C.: Agile Software Development: Principles, Patterns, and Practices. Prentice Hall (2003)
9. Meyer, B.: Object-Oriented Software Construction, 1st edn. Prentice-Hall, Inc., Upper Saddle River (1988)
10. RTCA SC-167/EUROCAE WG-12: DO-178B – Software Considerations in Airborne Systems and Equipment Certification (December 1992)
11. RTCA SC-205/EUROCAE WG-71: DO-178C – Software Considerations in Airborne Systems and Equipment Certification, Draft IP 50 (2011)
12. Souyris, J., Wiels, V., Delmas, D., Delseny, H.: Formal Verification of Avionics Software Products. In: Cavalcanti, A., Dams, D.R. (eds.) FM 2009. LNCS, vol. 5850, pp. 532–546. Springer, Heidelberg (2009), http://dx.doi.org/10.1007/978-3-642-05089-3_34

Teaching 'Concepts of Programming Languages' with Ada

Theodor Tempelmeier

University of Applied Sciences, Rosenheim, Germany
tempelmeier@fh-rosenheim.de

Abstract. In many universities programming is taught using the current main-stream languages C, C++, C#, or Java. For Universities of Applied Sciences (Fachhochschulen) in Germany this is almost mandatory, as the contents of their curricula are always scrutinized with respect to (immediate) practical applicability. This contribution presents the concepts behind an elective course on 'Concepts of programming Languages' in the master's degree program of the computer science department of the Fachhochschule Rosenheim. The course has been taught over the years, using the programming language Ada as a central subject throughout the course. In spite of the contrast to mainstream languages the use of Ada in this course has received positive feedback from the students and the colleagues and may well be designated as successful.

Keywords: Teaching, programming, concepts of programming languages, Ada, University of Applied Sciences.

1   Introduction

Universities of Applied Sciences (Fachhochschulen) in Germany have a very strong focus on practical applicability of the contents of their curricula. As a consequence, all teaching related to programming is usually centered on mainstream programming languages, which means, currently, on C, C++, C#, and Java. The computer science department of the University of Applied Sciences in Rosenheim does not (and cannot) deviate from this in the general course of studies.

Computer science education at the Rosenheim University is done in a seven semester bachelor program, including one practical semester in industry, and a three semester master program. Students have the choice between specializing on business applications, on applications in technology, or else studying computer science in general. In all branches the curriculum includes courses on basics of computer science, operating systems, computer architecture, programming, software engineering[1], etc.

---

[1] For historical reasons the general computer science branch is termed software engineering. But of course, software engineering is necessary and included in form of mandatory courses in all branches to a significant extent. Thus, using this term for general computer science is unfortunately a complete misnomer.

M. Brorsson and L.M. Pinho (Eds.): Ada-Europe 2012, LNCS 7308, pp. 60–74, 2012.

Elective courses may be included in the curriculum of a German University of Applied Sciences to a greater or lesser extent. In Rosenheim, the students are given great freedom by having the percentage of elective modules in the curriculum at around 15% in the Bachelor's degree curriculum, and above 30% in the Master's degree curriculum[2].

Specialization as described above is achieved by making appropriate elective modules mandatory and by recommending elective modules. As an example, students selecting the specialization in technology will typically take the courses assembler, microcontrollers, image processing, safety-critical systems, VHDL, and, in the master program, real-time systems and advanced computer architecture[3]. Similar schemes exist for the other branches.

A course on programming languages has been held for about twenty years within this curriculum under varying names and experimenting with varying content. The course now has remained in a relatively stable state for more than five years, and has recently been moved to the master program by the faculty council. It is now termed "Concepts of Programming Languages" and is in a pool of three courses, where all master students of all branches of study have to select two of these courses[4].

Scanning the internet and the book stores for courses on Concepts of Programming Languages brings up a variety of ideas (e.g. [2-10] and [11, 12]). Some of these courses treat all aspects of programming languages with examples from various languages, others focus on one language and try to treat all aspects of programming languages along the lines of the chosen language. In the latter case, often a functional language is used.

The concept presented here is different from these concepts in some aspects, and the main contributions of this presentation may be summed up as follows:

- The programming language Ada, a language following the imperative paradigm, is used as a central theme throughout the course. Given the emphasis on mainstream languages as described above, which is unavoidable at a German University of Applied Sciences, using Ada is at least unusual.
- A focus is set on programming language concepts which are important for embedded and safety-critical systems, rather than overemphasizing high-level abstract concepts as courses based on functional languages do. The course is aimed at helping the everyday programmer by providing a deep understanding of the consequences of using various concepts of programming languages.
- A segment "Questions and Discussions" is the most important part of the course, as it forces the students to think about (and discuss) many important topics *for themselves.*
- Positive feedback from the students as well as from the colleagues shows that the concept may well be appropriate.

---

[2] Master students have to agree their selection of courses with their supervising professor.

[3] More details on the concepts behind this branch of studies may be found in [1]. An up-to-date version accounting for recent additions and changes is planned for the near future.

[4] The other courses in this pool currently are Advanced Computer Architecture and Advanced Data Communication, with the course Functional Programming Languages probably to be included in the future.

This contribution is only a personal experience report on teaching "Concepts of Programming Languages" at a German Fachhochschule, using Ada. There is no claim that the presented ideas are better (in what sense?) than other ways of teaching such a course. The only claim is that, even with the overwhelming focus on practical applicability, the presented concept and using Ada are well received.

In the following chapter 2 the design of the course is described. Chapter 3 deals with the most important segment in the course termed "Questions and Discussions". In chapter 4 a few cross-references to other courses are mentioned. Chapter 5 gives some information on the results of the evaluation of the course.

Finally, a note on terminology seems to be appropriate in order to clarify different usage of some educational terms in different countries. The terms "course", "unit", and "module" are used synonymously in this contribution for a unit of teaching, Such units of teaching at a German Fachhochschule typically last one semester (15 weeks) and typically comprise four semester credit hours (60 contact hours during one semester). Taking account of the students' work for preparation and repetition at home this results in five credit points in the European Credit Transfer System ECTS. Of course, there are also other courses, spanning two semesters, having a different number of semester credit hours or contact hours, etc.

2   Design of the Course "Concepts of Programming Languages"

2.1   Organization

The course reported here is a one-semester course having four semester credit hours or, equivalently, 5 credit points. The course is divided into a lecture (two hours per week) and a practical (2 hours per week). There are 15 to 20 participants on average, allowing for seminar-like tuition[5] instead of pure lecturing, occasionally.

Lecture notes are provided to the students with some omissions to be supplemented during the lecture. These lecture notes serve as main source of information. In addition, the students are given references to textbooks [11, 12] and to other resources as background reading material.

Due to the highly interactive nature of the course (see chapter 3 Course Segment "Questions and Discussions" and consider the seminar-like tuition as described above) there is no fixed correspondence between lecture hours and course chapters. Instead, the course is basically a consecutive sequence of teaching Ada with many asides and lots of references and comparisons to other languages, progressing as the interaction with the students permits.

2.2   Introductory Chapters

The course "concepts of programming languages" starts with an introductory overview of the history of programming languages and short characterizations of some more influential languages. Two lessons of 45 minutes each are spent on COBOL and

---

[5] "Seminaristischer Unterricht" in German.

FORTRAN 77, because it is felt that some (very) basic knowledge of these languages should be mandatory for every computer scientist.

2.3   Basic Decisions in Designing the Course

Several basic decisions had to be made in designing the course. These decisions are presented in the following. Of course, one might arrive at decisions different from the ones reported here, leading to a different course.

The decisions are mostly based on the personal experience in teaching and in industrial embedded and safety-critical projects over the past 30 years of the author.

Only One Language in the Practical

The course consists of lectures and a practical, one half each. Based on former negative experience, only one programming language should be used in the practical by the students. This does not preclude discussions about any programming language during the lectures, but refers to active programming by the students on their own. Switching to different programming languages during the practical has proven unsuitable during earlier courses.

It is obvious that the language selected for the practical should also be used as a recurrent theme in the lectures.

Choosing Ada as the Central Theme

There is a number of programming languages that come to mind when thinking about the central subject of such a course, e.g. Ada, Eiffel, Occam, Lisp, Smalltalk, ML, Erlang, Haskell, Python, Ruby, Esterel, but also C, C++, C#, Java, and others.

To serve as a central theme, a programming language should encompass as many concepts and paradigms as possible. Further, it seems reasonable to bring a new, different world to the students[6]. This rules out C, C++, Java, and C# in the setting at the University of Applied Sciences Rosenheim. And the language should at least syntactically bear some resemblance to other languages in use.

Ada fulfills these requirements with an extensive set of features in the fields of imperative and object-oriented programming, as well as in the field of real-time programming. There are also syntactical and conceptual similarities (more or less) to VHDL, FORTRAN, Structured Text in PLC programming, conditional and looping constructs in some Unix shells, etc.

Ada is not a language for functional programming. Unlike many other courses on concepts of programming languages, no functional language was chosen for the following reasons.

- First, there is an elective module in the computer science department in Rosenheim, where functional languages are studied in depth.
- Second, the focus of "concepts of programming languages" is admittedly biased towards applications in technical systems, most notably in embedded and safety-

---

[6] E.g. to show them that there is a world without curly brackets.

critical systems. This is done on one hand in view of the German automotive industry – still using mostly C –, and on the other hand in view of the German aerospace industry – using at least some Ada. Functional programming without side effects seems strange to the author for embedded systems, where side effects are used continuously when reading sensors and setting actors. Similarly, garbage collection, lazy evaluation, etc. may be in contrast to safety-critical systems. However, an outlook on functional programming is given in Ada 2005 (see chapter 4, Cross-References to other Courses).

Some more practical reasons for choosing Ada were the availability of a free excellent compiler (GNAT) and the availability of a free ISO standard.

Emphasis on Type Systems, Packages, and Generics
After the introductory chapter the course continues with a crash course in Ada in order to enable the students to start doing exercises in the practical. A rough explanation of subtypes and unconstrained arrays is given very early, and some simple exercises make the students familiar with Ada.

Thinking about what is really important for a deeper understanding of programming languages, the following subjects are given special emphasis:

- type systems (including subtypes, derived types, decimal and binary fixed point types, modular types, string types, dynamic type systems, type equivalence, polymorphism, type extension, safe pointers) ,
- packages including child packages and issues in visibility and the concept of abstract data types, and
- generic units with type and subprogram parameters.

The emphasis on these subjects is based on experience from industrial projects in the embedded domain.

Confusion of different (numeric) types in the interfaces of modules has shown to be one of the most common and nastiest errors in practice to the author[7], so a clear understanding of types and of (often erroneous) automatic type conversions is necessary. Another aspect are widely used graphical block diagramming tools such as MATLAB/Simulink or ASCET [14], where some reports exist on problems of correctly generating binary fixed point arithmetic [15] (sometimes even without precise semantics [16][8]). In view of this, a thorough understanding of binary fixed point types is even more important.

As for the second item, a clean and strong partitioning of large projects into modules without side effects across module boundaries has proven as most valuable.

And finally, having fought code bloat due to templates in a large industrial C++ project for years, a deep understanding of generic units seems equally important.

---

[7] In a direct comparison of student projects done in C and in Ada, a similar conclusion was drawn, when "the accurate modeling of scalar quantities" was seen as the most significant contribution to project success. [13].

[8] "Semantics are defined by the code generator. And the code generator is proven by use" [16].

Continuous Comparison of the Concepts of Ada to other Programming Languages

A mere course in Ada would not make up a course on concepts of programming languages, of course. So the concepts taught throughout the course in Ada are always compared to the concepts in other languages, mostly to the concepts in the languages the students are familiar with. The comparison may result in finding similarities or dissimilarities among the concepts. To give some examples, generics and memory management are well suited for such comparisons.

The method of teaching these differences between programming languages is a direct inclusion of the comparisons in the lectures on one hand, and on the other hand to a large percentage done with self-directed learning by the students as reported in the following chapter 3.

Additional Subject Matter: Multitasking and "Trivia"

Though not the main focus of the course, some insight in multitasking and real-time systems is given to the students, also with exercises in the practical. A more in-depth treatment of these topics is available to the students with the elective course on real-time systems.

In addition, a number of (presumed) trivia are treated, such as the number of bits in an integer, machine addresses, short-circuit operations, variant records, volatile and atomic objects, name mangling, array slicing, and random numbers.

3   Course Segment "Questions and Discussions"

3.1   Background

A part of the course termed "questions and discussions" started a number of years ago with only a few items. Over the years the number of questions and discussions has increased to about fifty topics. These may now well be deemed *the most important part of the course*. These questions and discussion are also given to the students as a handout, without solutions, however.

The idea behind these questions and discussions is to guide the students to *think about (and discuss) these topics for themselves*.

The questions are interspersed with the normal lecture, sometimes together with the subject in focus, sometimes one or two weeks after the subject has been treated, as a form of repetition. Some questions are very easy, some are more difficult. The following subchapters give a few examples.

In the text below example-questions will be written using italics, and remarks about the questions will be in normal text.

3.2   Examples: Easy Level

One of the very easy questions is as follows.

A student's error in the first semester practical on programming - what is (probably) wrong?
```
for (i=1;i<max;i++);
    {
    ...
    }
```

The students usually get the error immediately. However, discussion should not stop here. One can continue with discussing MISRA C guidelines, always requiring the use of curly brackets, even when there is only one statement in the loop body, and one can contrast this guideline to the Ada loop construct, rendering such guidelines superfluous.

3.3   Examples: Medium Level

Some medium level examples are given here.

Which style guide is right?
- *"A switch statement must <u>always</u> contain a default branch which handles unexpected cases." [17]*
- *"<u>Never</u> use an others choice in a case statement." [18]*

What is allowed?
```
-------- Ada
N : integer := 5;
My_Array : array (1..n*n) of float; -- ok?

//////// C89, C99 and C++98
int N=5;                 // or maybe  const int N=5; ?
float myArray[N*N];      // ok?
```

What are the "best" strings of the three categories (fixed-length, bounded-length, unbounded-length) discussed? Hint: Where are strings to be stored?

What should a pace maker do when new *raises storage error (or bad_alloc)?*

Given a parameter of type access function (l,r : integer) return boolean, *why is it not possible to use* ">" 'access *as an actual? (The error message is "prefix of access attribute cannot be intrinsic").*

What happens in x:=x+1.23; *(Ada) or in* x=x+1.23; *(C, C++, Java) respectively? (x be of type float)?*

A discussion about universal types and mixed mode expressions has to follow. One can extend this example to the difficult level with the following question.

How should x+i *be computed (x be float, i be integer)? Should the required type as in* variable_of_some_type := x+i; *be considered? How about an overloaded function call in the expression?*

The students usually propose rules similar to Java, allowing widening, but no narrowing. They best learn about the problems by showing them the extremes, e.g. the coercion chart of Algol 68 [19] on one hand, or, on the other hand, simply disallowing mixed mode expressions as in Ada.

3.4   Examples: Difficult Level

In the difficult level, the students normally get the answers only partially right, and thus have to be guided somehow. The questions seem nevertheless to be of value to them. Again some examples

In Ada the short-circuit operations `or else` *and* `and then` *formally are no operators, and they cannot be overloaded – why?*

Giving some help to the students, e.g. referring them to [20], which is available as an electronic book to them interactively during the lecture, usually lets them find the right answer.

What does the following code do?
How can it be that <u>no code at all</u> is generated with optimizations turned on?
```
inline unsigned64 Swap_64(unsigned64 x) {
  unsigned64 tmp;
  (*(unsigned32*)&tmp)= Swap_32(*(((unsigned32*)&x)+1));
  (*(((unsigned32*)&tmp)+1)) = Swap_32(*(unsigned32*)&x);
  return tmp;
}
```

The students usually get the answer to the first question right. For the second question, help must be given with referring them to the C++ standard, 3.10-15[9]. The most important part is the footnote: "The intent of this list is to specify those circumstances in which an object may or may not be aliased." So, even though the students were not aware of the fact, they learn about the alias problem. And discussion may turn back to Ada, focusing on the keyword `aliased`.

Why has Ada two dots in a range (1..10), VHDL on the other side uses the reserved words `to` *and* `downto`, *e.g.* `(1 to 10)` `(10 downto 1)?`

This question opens the possibility to talk about null ranges in Ada.

Why does Ada use `in  out`, *while VHDL uses* `inout` *(without blank)?*

3.5   Programs for Trying out and Discussing

Recently, some simple short programs have been provided to the students, just to try out some aspect of the language. The reason behind these programs is that many things which come naturally to an Ada programmer are surprising to students having been exposed to the C family of languages. And, providing complete programs lets the students get to the point of the intended discussion very fast.

The first and simplest example is about loops. It may start a discussion on reasoning about programs. Can you tell how often a loop is executed from inspecting the loop parameter specification?

---

[9] 1998 version of the standard.

```
N := 4;
for I in 1..N loop
    put(I);
    N := 10*N;
end loop;
```

There are also more complicated programs in this segment, e.g. a program showing how unsafe assignments to global access variables are prevented in Ada (a simplified version of the example in [21, 22]).

```
procedure Evil_Pointers is
    type P_Object_T is access all Integer;
    Evil_Obj_P : P_Object_T;
    procedure P (Objptr : access Integer) is
    begin
        Evil_Obj_P := Objptr;
    end P;
begin
    Put_Line ("Let's start!");
    declare     ---------------------- nested block
        An_Obj : aliased Integer;    -- |
    begin                            -- |
        P (An_Obj'access);           -- |
    end;        ---------------------- end of nested block
    Evil_Obj_P.All := 123;
end Evil_Pointers;
-- How to compile without errors?
-- Maybe "p_objec_t" instead of "access integer"  ??
-- Maybe a type conversion ... := p_object_t(objptr)  ??
```

It is a new experience to the students that pointers are safe and that they cannot beat the Ada system. The same example is also given in C, where the nested block is replaced with a local function (this is possible in GNU C beyond the standard).

```
typedef int* object_p_t;
object_p_t   evil_obj_p ;
void p(int* objptr){
    evil_obj_p = objptr;
}
int main (){
    void x (){          // local function instead of
        int an_obj;     // the nested block
        p(&an_obj);     // (possible in GNU C)
    }
    printf("Let's start!\n");
    x();
    *evil_obj_p = 123;
    printf("Result: %i\n",*evil_obj_p);
    return 0;
}
```

This version runs "perfectly", of course. Fortunately however, the students usually discover the trick immediately, easing the mind of the lecturer.

4   Cross-References to Other Courses

In the view of the author it is very important to include cross-references to other courses in a lecture. This helps the students to build up an overall picture of their studies.

As a first example, building a generic package for vector arithmetic with components of *arbitrary* type in the practical, the students learn that they need a generic formal object parameter `Null_Element`. One may refer the students to their first year course in mathematics, showing them that teaching contents such as group theory, requiring a neutral element, were not "useless" at all.

Or, considering again the question *Given a parameter of type* `access function (l,r : integer) return boolean`, *why is it not possible to use* `">"'access` *as an actual? (Error message is "prefix of access attribute cannot be intrinsic")* from chapter 3.3. Giving the students a hint to think about their course in assembler programming, they usually get the right answer.

As the author had come into contact with level A software [23] during his career [24], there are also numerous cross-references to the course on safety-critical software systems. As an example, the question about the fictitious pace maker running out of heap storage (see chapter 3.3), may be contrasted to a situation where using heap memory was simply disallowed in a level A project.

Finally, a discussion about functional programming is appropriate. The first example of a Scala tutorial, "Quicksort ... in functional style" [25], is given in Ada in an identical style to build a bridge to the course in functional programming.

```
-- Quicksort in functional style in Scala [25]

-- def sort(xs: Array[Int]): Array[Int] = {
-- if (xs.length <= 1) xs
-- else {
-- val pivot = xs(xs.length / 2)
-- Array.concat(
-- sort(xs filter (x => pivot > x)),
--       xs filter (x => pivot == x),
-- sort(xs filter (x => pivot < x)))
-- }
-- }

with predicates; use predicates; -- not shown
with filters; use filters;        -- not shown
-- ArrayInt is defined with index type natural

function sort (xs : ArrayInt) return ArrayInt is
begin
   if xs'length <= 1 then  return xs;
   else
      declare
         pivot : constant integer := xs(xs'length/2);
      begin
         return sort(filter(xs,  pivot,  greater)) &
                     filter(xs,  pivot,  equal)    &
                sort(filter(xs,  pivot,  less));
      end;
   end if;
end sort;
```

So, is Ada a functional programming language? How is the performance of this version of quicksort as compared to doing the operations in place? (This gives another cross-reference to the course on algorithms and data structures).

It should be clear from these questions that this style of programming is not recommended to the students when using an imperative language. The example is only used as an outlook on the course in functional programming and on the necessary or possible optimizations with functional programming languages.

5   Evaluation of the Course

5.1   How to Evaluate a University Course?

In general, it is difficult to evaluate the quality of a university course, let alone to compare the quality of different courses or different course concepts in an objective way. In some cases it may be fairly easy, though. For instance, letting similar groups of students implement similar projects with different programming languages as in [13] allows for a conclusion on the influence of the programming language. However, in a course on concepts of programming languages the learning objectives are more abstract as compared to implementing a project. Further, as it is the case with this contribution, focusing on the aspects of embedded and safety-critical systems makes the course incomparable to courses focusing on e.g. monads, continuations, lazy evaluation and the like.

As a consequence, evaluation of the quality of a course is basically restricted to subjective judgment in the form of

- feedback from peers,
- feedback from industry,
- feedback from the students, and
- self-reflection of the lecturer.

Feedback from industry is usually only concerned with the overall picture and gives no clue on the quality of a particular course. Feedback from the peers in the faculty was positive, but this need not mean necessarily that the course achieves, what its learning objectives demand. So, feedback from the students seems to be the most important source for discussing the quality of a course.

5.2   Evaluation by the Students

According to the Bavarian University Law all courses have to be evaluated by the students on a regular basis. It is the responsibility of the dean of studies of each faculty to supervise these evaluations. Evaluation in the Faculty of Computer Science at the University of Applied Sciences Rosenheim is done on the following basis.

- Every teacher evaluates his own course and discusses the results with his students.
- Every teacher may use *an individual questionnaire* (usually with a five-level scale for answering the questions) *or even only a form with two open-ended questions* "What was good?" and "What should be improved?"
- The dean of studies supervises the evaluation process.

Table 1. Some Evaluation Results of the Presented Course – Questionnaire

Winter Semester 2005/06	++	+	o	-	- -
... data concerning the presenter personally have been deleted ...					
Exercises, Examples	‖‖ ‖‖ I	‖‖ III			
Course is interesting	‖‖ ‖‖ ‖‖	IIII			
Course is understandable	‖‖ ‖‖ ‖‖	IIII			
Course is challenging	‖‖ ‖‖	‖‖ I	III		
Course is important	‖‖ IIII	‖‖ III	II		
Course is instructive	‖‖ ‖‖ III	‖‖ I			
Overall assessment	‖‖ ‖‖ II	IIII			

As a consequence of using individual questionnaires, evaluation results cannot simply be compared on a uniform scale all over the university. Evaluation is done in this way deliberately and as accepted by the Bavarian Ministry of Education [26]. The reason behind this is that, for instance, a first semester course in mathematics should not (and cannot) be compared to a course on game programming simply by one single average mark of a standardized questionnaire. The evaluation results of the course on concepts of programming languages must be seen with this evaluation method in mind.

Table 2. Some Evaluation Results of the Presented Course – Clustering of answers to a form with only two open-ended questions

Winter Semester 2011/12	
"What was good?"	
Questions and Discussions	‖‖ III
Examples from the real world, references to practice, cross-references to safety-critical software systems	‖‖
...	
"What should be improved?"	
Not enough prior knowledge of C++ to follow all parts of the lecture	II
÷	
General remarks	
"Keep up the good work!"	I

5.3   Advantages and Drawbacks of the Course as Seen by the Lecturer

Of course, every lecturer should also evaluate his/her course in an act of self-reflection retrospectively. Personal experience from industrial projects and insights gained from supervising student projects in industry on one hand should match with the contents of the particular course and the curriculum as a whole on the other hand. Thus the advantages and drawbacks of a particular course set-up should show up.

- The main advantage of the presented concept is that the content of the course is specifically tailored to programmers of technical, embedded, and safety-critical systems, giving them very practical help in everyday programming. Moreover, the course even builds a bridge to electrical engineering and FPGA programming by including parts of the hardware description language VHDL.
- A drawback of the presented course concept is that functional and logic programming languages are not treated. Consequently, but unfortunately, the ramifications concerning the implementation of these languages are not treated either. As for the functional languages the drawback is mitigated by a separate course on this subject mentioned above, which the students may take additionally or alternatively to the presented course.
- A more serious drawback of the presented course is the omission of the synchronous programming paradigm [27, 28], because this is indeed of high relevance in technical, embedded, and safety-critical systems.[10] The cause behind this omission is just lack of time in the given time frame of the presented course. Solving this problem, i.e. including synchronous programming languages, will be a task for the next revision of the whole curriculum.

Another omission concerning graphical block diagramming tools such as MATLAB/Simulink or ASCET mentioned in chapter 2.3 is not considered a serious drawback. Such modeling tools, though often used in a style more akin to programming than to modeling, are normally beyond the scope of a course as described here.

6   Conclusion

Using Ada as the central theme in a course on concepts of programming languages can be seen as successful, as shown by positive feedback from the students and colleagues. This holds even for a situation where the students are educated almost exclusively in mainstream programming languages due to the focus on practical applicability of Universities of Applied Sciences.

The presented course has a certain bias towards technical, embedded, real-time, safety-critical systems and is more aimed at concepts of programming languages with respect to everyday practical usage in such systems than at theoretical concepts. It is a good idea to complement such a course with a more theoretical course on functional programming languages as described above.

---

[10] Synchronous programming languages are not included in the textbooks [11,12] either.

Acknowledgement. The author would like to thank the reviewers for their valuable comments and their arduous work in convincing the author to make many additions and amendments to the original and to intermediate versions of the paper. Any shortcomings of the paper or of the presented course are of course nevertheless in the sole responsibility of the author.

References

1. Tempelmeier, T.: Embedding Practical Real-Time Education in a Computer Science Curriculum. In: Nawrocki, J., Schwarz, J.-J., Zalewski, J. (eds.) Real-Time Systems Education III. Proceedings of the IEEE Workshop, November 21, 1998. Scientific Centre of the Polish Academy of Sciences, IEEE Computer Society, Poznan, Los Alamitos (1999)
2. Fiore, M.: Concepts in Programming Languages. University of Cambridge (2010), http://www.cl.cam.ac.uk/teaching/1011/ConceptsPL/ (accessed February 15, 2012)
3. Göers, J.: Programmiersprachenkonzepte. Universität Osnabrück (2010), http://www-lehre.inf.uos.de/psk/1011/ (accessed February 15, 2012)
4. Klaeren, H.: Konzepte höherer Programmiersprachen. Universität Tübingen (January 24, 2012), http://pu.inf.uni-tuebingen.de/users/klaeren/ko.pdf (accessed February 15, 2012)
5. Mezini, M.: Concepts of Programming Languages. TU Darmstadt (2011), http://www.stg.tu-darmstadt.de/teaching/courses/ss2011/concepts_of_programming_languages_ss2011/cpl_schedule_2/index.en.jsp (accessed February 15, 2012)
6. Mitchell, J.: Programming Languages. Stanford University (2008), https://courseware.stanford.edu/pg/courses/214531/cs242-fall-2011 (accessed February 15, 2012)
7. Zhang, T.: Principles of Programming Languages. Iowa State University (2010), http://www.cs.iastate.edu/~tingz/classes/cs342/Fall2010/ (accessed February 15, 2012)
8. Ploedereder, E.: Konzepte der Programmiersprachen. Universität Stuttgart, http://www.iste.uni-stuttgart.de/ps/lehre/ueberblick/konzepte-der-programmiersprachen.html (accessed February 15, 2012)
9. Sieber, K.: Konzepte höherer Programmiersprachen. Universität Siegen (2006), http://www.informatik.uni-siegen.de/sieber/public/2006_SS_KP/Main.html (accessed February 15, 2012)
10. Zimmermann, W., Picht, R.: Konzepte höherer Programmiersprachen. Universität Halle-Wittenberg, http://swt.informatik.uni-halle.de/lehre/lehrveranstaltungen_im_ws_2010/konzepte_hoeherer_programmierspra/#anchor2361387 (accessed February 15, 2012); To appear: Oldenbourg-Verlag, München (September 2012)
11. Sebesta, R.W.: Concepts of Programming Languages, 9th edn. Addison-Wesley (2009)
12. Watt, D.A.: Programming Language Design Concepts. John Wiley & Sons (2004)
13. McCormick, J.W.: Ada and Software Engineering Education: One Professor's Experience. In: Session "Ada and Software Engineering Education" at the 13th International Conference on Reliable Software Technologies, Ada-Europe 2008, Venice, Italy, June 16-20 (2008); Ada User Journal 29(3), 203–207 (September 2008)

14. ETAS Group: ASCET Software Products,
    `http://www.etas.com/en/products/ascet_software_products.php?langS=true&` (accessed March 2, 2012)
15. Eisemann, U.: Guidelines for a Model-based Development Process with Automatic Code Generation. In: Niggemann, O., Giese, H (Hrsg.) Proceedings of the 3rd Workshop on Object-oriented Modeling of Embedded Real-Time Systems (OMER 3). HNI-Verlagsschriftenreihe, Paderborn, Band 191, Heinz Nixdorf Institut, Universität Paderborn (2005)
16. Blache, G.: Model based development & automatic code generation for safety critical systems with ASCET. In: Ada Deutschland, Workshop Entwicklung Zuverlässiger Software-Systeme, Hochschule Regensburg (Juni 18, 2009),
    `http://www.ada-deutschland.de/sites/default/files/tagungen/ws2009/presentations/006_Blache_GI_Ada2009.pdf` (accessed March 2, 2012)
17. Henricson, M., Nyquist, E.: Programming in C++, Rules and Recommendations. Original translation from Swedish by Joseph Supanich. Ellemtel Telecommunication Systems Laboratories, Sweden, `http://www.doc.ic.ac.uk/lab/cplus/c++.rules/` (accessed November 25, 2011)
18. Ada 95 Quality and Style: Guidelines for Professional Programmers. SPC-94093-CMC. Version 01.00.10. Software Productivity Consortium, Herndon, Virginia (October 1995) `http://www.adaic.org/resources/add_content/docs/95style/95style.pdf` (accessed November 25, 2011)
19. Lindsey, C.H., Van Der Meulen, S.G.: Informal Introduction to Algol 68. North-Holland Publishing Company (1973)
20. Meyers, S.: More Effective C++: 35 New Ways to Improve Your Programs and Designs. Addison-Wesley (2011); second e-book release
21. Barnes, J.: Rationale for Ada 2005. John Barnes Informatics, Reading, England (2006), `http://www.adaic.org/standards/05rat/Rationale05.pdf` (accessed November 25, 2011)
22. Barnes, J.: Programming in Ada 2005. Addison-Wesley, Harlow (2006)
23. DO-178B Software Considerations in Airborne Systems and Equipment Certification. RTCA, SC-167, EUROCAE, WG-12, December 1 (1992)
24. Roßkopf, A., Tempelmeier, T.: Aspects of Flight Control Software - A Software Engineering Point of View. In: 24th IFAC/IFIP Workshop on Real-Time Programming, Schloss Dagstuhl, Saarland, Germany, May 31-June 2. Pergamon, Elsevier Science, Oxford (1999); Also in: Control Engineering Practice 8(6), 675–680 (2000)
25. Odersky, M.: Scala By Example. Draft. Programming Methods Laboratory, EPFL, Switzerland (May 24, 2011), `http://www.scala-lang.org/docu/files/ScalaByExample.pdf` (accessed November 25, 2011)
26. Michl, W. (Hrsg.): Evaluation und Lehrbericht - Empfehlungen für Studiendekane. DiZ - Zentrum für Hochschuldidaktik der bayerischen Fachhochschulen, Workshop of the Bavarian Deans of Studies, November 11-12. ZIEL Verlag, Augsburg (1999) (in German); under presence and approval of a representative of the Bavarian Ministry of Education
27. Halbwachs, N.: Synchronous programming of reactive systems. Kluwer Academic Pub. (1993)
28. Halbwachs, N.: A synchronous language at work: the story of Lustre. In: Third ACM and IEEE International Conference on Formal Methods and Models for Co-Design, MEMOCODE 2005, Verona, Italy (2005), `http://hal.archives-ouvertes.fr/hal-00190883/fr/`

Designing the API for a Cryptographic Library
A Misuse-Resistant Application Programming Interface

Christian Forler, Stefan Lucks, and Jakob Wenzel

Bauhaus-University Weimar, Germany
{Christian.Forler,Stefan.Lucks,Jakob.Wenzel}@uni-weimar.de

Abstract. Most of the time, cryptography fails due to "implementation and management errors". So the task at hand is to design a cryptographic library to ease its safe use and to hinder implementation errors. This is of special interest when the implementation language is celebrated for its qualification to write reliable safe and secure systems, such as Ada.

This paper concentrates on the handling of nonces ("number used once") and on authenticated encryption, i.e., on establishing a safe communication channel between two parties which share a common secret key. Cryptographers consider it as a "nonce misuse", if a nonce value is ever reused. Avoiding nonce-misuse is easy in theory, but difficult in practice. One problem with authenticated encryption is that a naive combination of a secure authentication and a secure encryption scheme may turn out to be insecure. Another problem is that decryption temporarily provides an incomplete plaintext, that may eventually found to be unauthentic.

We discuss how to ease the proper usage of cryptosystems, how to hinder unintentional misuse, and how one may possibly limit the damage in the case of a misuse.

Keywords: cryptography, library, specification, misuse-resistance.

1 Introduction

In the area of cryptography there exist a lot of different kinds of cryptosystems. At first, there are symmetric cryptosystems handling secret-key encryption and authentication of confidential data. Another type is described by asymmetric cryptosystems which are used in terms of public-key encryption and digital signatures. Furthermore, the cryptography provides systems for the management of keys and certificates. Next, we have sophisticated protocols which suite for special applications, such as anonymous digital money, and anonymous and verifiable digital elections. Beside the listed ones there are a lot more cryptosystems which are not mentioned here. To maintain a clear focus in the current paper, we will only consider symmetric cryptosystems below. The issues we discuss are representative for cryptography in general, though.

Abstractly, a cryptographic library can support three different levels of cryptosystems:

M. Brorsson and L.M. Pinho (Eds.): Ada-Europe 2012, LNCS 7308, pp. 75–88, 2012.

1. cryptographic primitives, such as the AES block cipher, or the RSA public-key scheme,
2. modes of operation for these primitives, *e.g.*, the CBC mode for encryption based on a block cipher, or the OAEP mode to use RSA for public-key encryption and key transmission, and
3. standardized protocols combining different of these modes, such as SSL/TLS.

Without proper modes of operation, the primitives are essentially useless – and easy to misuse by application programmers without proper expertise in cryptography. A recent example is the communication between the German law-enforcement "spyware" – commonly referred to as the "Staatstrojaner" – and the command and control server [8]. Beyond a flawed (or rather missing) key management, this setting had three major flaws: The data flow from

1. ... server to contagious system was neither encrypted nor authenticated.
2. ... contagious system to server was not authenticated.
3. ... contagious system to server was encrypted, using the well-established AES block cipher, but in an insecure mode of operation[1] .

The lack of authentication could allow malicious adversaries to generate any kind of false evidence against honest people. The weak encryption is an example of the misuse of a secure cryptographic primitive – which is why a good cryptographic library needs to support modes of operation, not just primitives. In fact, a proper solution would have provided authenticated encryption both from the server to the contagious system and vice versa.

Authenticated Encryption (AE). A common requirement for cryptographic applications is to establish a secure channel between two parties (the sender "Alice" and the receiver "Bob") who share a secret key[2]. Sometimes, the secure channel requires privacy. That means an eavesdropper will not find out anything about the data sent from Alice to Bob, except their length. The cryptographic technique to ensure this is "encryption". Sometimes, authenticity and integrity are required, i.e., an adversary cannot forge messages, or tamper with them undetected. This is cryptographically ensured by "authentication". But most of the time, users need both encryption and authentication: *"authenticated encryption"*.

In the past decade, cryptographers published a lot of block cipher based authenticated encryption schemes. These share the following two properties: 1) they are generic, in the sense that one can use different block ciphers, and 2) they are provably secure. I.e., under certain assumptions, one can formally prove that they provide both authenticity and privacy. The assumptions for provable security include obviously the security of the underlying block cipher, but also the proper use, *e.g.*, most schemes need a nonce or even an unpredictable random value for security (below we elaborate on nonces).

---

[1] It used the "Electronic CodeBook" (ECB) mode [9].

[2] Note that these roles can be assumed by the same entity, *e.g.*, the same person can first write sensitive data to an insecure storage, and later read these data.

Most schemes – even when claimed "chosen ciphertext secure" – also assume that if a ciphertext has been forged, the adversary learns nothing about the corresponding would-be plaintext. Otherwise, this is a case of "plaintext leaking". **If any of these assumptions fail, the proof of security is questionable. Furthermore, most authenticated encryption schemes actually fail badly if any of these assumptions fail [14].** Fougue *et al.* present a generic construction called Decrypt-Then-Mask in [16] that defends against plaintext leaking by "masking" (actually re-encrypting) the decrypted ciphertext. Only when the authenticity of the ciphertext has been confirmed, the key to unmask (re-decrypt) the plaintext is given out. Our library follows that approach.

There exist several cryptographic libraries which do not provide authenticated encryption [37, 17, 33, 1]. In this case the application developers have to combine an encryption scheme and a message authentication code on their own. As we will elaborate below, this is rather error-prone, certainly not misuse-resistant, and can cause critical security issues.

Nonces. A "number used once" usually provides an initial value for an encryption process. Often, one can use unique values from other protocol levels, or, *e.g.*, a counter incremented each time when a new nonce is drawn. The nonce concept is simple in theory, but challenging in practice. It is hard to ensure that a nonce is only used once, and flawed implementations are ubiquitous [6, 20, 24, 32, 35]. On the one hand implementation failures – *e.g.*, constant nonces – are responsible for security issues. On the other hand there are several reasons why software developers cannot always prevent nonce reuse in practice. A persistently stored counter, which is increased and written back each time a new nonce is needed, may be reset by a backup – usually after some previous data loss. Similarly, the internal and persistent state of an application may be duplicated when a virtual machine is cloned. Another case of nonce reuse occurs when using a counter-based setting producing an overflow.

Many common authenticated encryption schemes [26, 10, 3, 21] are based on the counter mode, producing a keystream, which is XORed with the plaintext. The keystream – generated by the encryption of a counter – only depends on the user provided initial value N – the nonce – and the key. The keystream does not depend on the message. For a fixed key the ciphertext C is computed by $C = P \oplus K_N$, where P denotes the plaintext and K_N denotes the keystream, generated by the counter mode, under the nonce N. Assume the case that the same nonce is used at least twice to encrypt two distinct messages P_1 and P_2 to C_1 and C_2, respectively. An adversary that knows P_1 and C_1 can easily compute the keystream by $K_N = P_1 \oplus C_1$. This adversary can then easily compute the plaintext $P_2 = K_N \oplus C_2$ without knowledge of the key. Even if an adversary does not have any information about P_1 and P_2 she can compute $C_1 \oplus C_2 = P_1 \oplus P_2$. Hence, there exists a key independent relation between both plaintexts and both ciphertexts, which can be exploited. Only very few authenticated encryption schemes provide provable security against nonce misuse [14].

Our Contribution and Outline. We present an API for nonce generators and authenticated encryption schemes based on the `libadacrypt` [15]. The nonce API is designed under the objective of resistance against nonce reuse. This allows an application developer to get access to a reliable implementation of nonce generators, which can be used in a cryptographic secure setting. Furthermore, our API for authenticated encryption schemes solves the problem of plaintext leaking. Thus, a secure channel based on our authenticated encryption scheme implementation is resistant against both nonce reuse and plaintext leaking.

This paper is organized as follows. The next section introduces the basis of our work, the `libadacrypt`, which we expanded including our implemented API. In Section 3 we discuss in detail the problems when handling secure authenticated encryption schemes, and in Section 4 we present our package specification. Section 5 contains a comparison of different cryptographic libraries regarding to our mentioned topics. Finally, Section 6 concludes the paper.

2   Introducing the `libadacrypt`

The `libadacrypt`-0.2.0 is the most advanced and comprehensive cryptographic library written in Ada, known by us so far. As illustrated in Figure 1, our library supports various symmetric primitives like block ciphers, modes of operation, hash functions and message authentication codes (MACs). Furthermore, it provides asymmetric algorithms like DSA, RSA, and elliptic curve Diffie-Hellman (ECDH). In comparison to the `libsparkcrypto` [33] the `libadacrypt` does not support SPARK[3], but `AUnit-3.4`[4] test suites. The statement coverage dithers between 68 and 100 percent depending on the package, which was measured using the coverage testing tool `gcov`[5]. In the next few months we aim to achieve a statement coverage of at least 95 percent for each package.

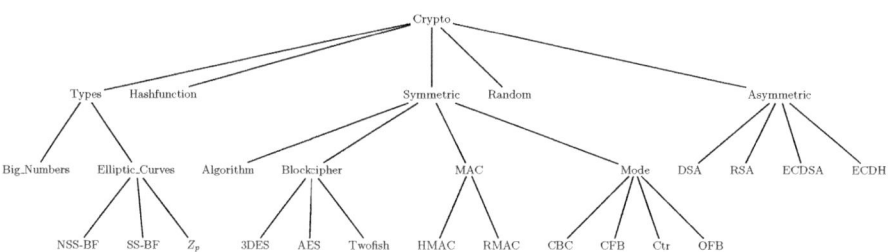

Fig. 1. A coarse package overview of the `libadacrypt`-0.2.0

The `libadacrypt`-0.2.0 runs only properly under GNU/Linux-based 32- and 64-bit operating systems, since the random generator is a wrapper for the Linux

---

[3] `http://libre.adacore.com/libre/tools/spark-gpl-edition/`, November 2011.
[4] `http://libre.adacore.com/libre/tools/aunit/`, November 2011.
[5] `http://gcc.gnu.org/onlinedocs/gcc/Gcov.html`, November 2011.

pseudo random number generator (PRNG) `/dev/random`. In the second half of 2012 a cryptographic secure PRNG will be included in this library to achieve a cross platform independent version.

The new ideas presented below will allow the library to support secure nonce handling and secure authenticated encryption. Our goal is to depict the foundations for a high level cryptographic secure channel API.

3   Handling Secure Authenticated Encryption (AE)

The security requirement for an AE scheme can be described as follows: *The ciphertext must not leak any information about the original plaintext, except for the plaintext length.* More formally: Let messages M_i be chosen by the adversary. Write $|M_i|$ for the bit length of a message M_i. Then it should be unfeasible to distinguish between the following two scenarios:

1. Encrypt the same plaintext $M_1 = M_2 = \ldots = M_n$ n-times.
2. Encrypt n different plaintexts $M_1, \ldots, M_n$ with $|M_1| = \ldots = |M_n|$.

If we tried to achieve this by a stateless deterministic encryption algorithm (like SIV [31], or BTM [22]), the first case would give n times the same ciphertext, while the second case would give n different ciphertexts. Thus a state-of-the-art encryption scheme must be probabilistic or stateful (or both). This has been formalized by Goldwasser and Micali [18] in the early 1980's. Rogaway proposed a unified point of view, by always defining a cryptographic scheme as a deterministic algorithm which is initialized by a user supplied state [28, 29, 30]. The initial state can consist of a nonce and an optional part denoted as associated data. A scheme supporting associated data is called *authenticated encryption with associated data scheme (AEAD)*. Among other things, usually the programmer of the AE scheme does not know in advance where her algorithm is being applied. It can be applied on an embedded system where the randomness is insufficient, since cryptographic applications need cryptographic secure random number generators (RNG) whose output is not predictable by any adversary, ever. In that case an internal state must be maintained for the AE scheme.

Off- and On-Line Encryption. An AE scheme is called on-line if any generated ciphertext block C_i only depends on the key K, the plaintext blocks $P_1, , \ldots, P_i$, and an optional nonce N. On-line encryption is the most natural way to encrypt any message, since application developers expect it to encrypt – in an on-line manner meaning – that the i-th ciphertext block can be written before the (i+1)-th plaintext block has to be read. This approach allows to encrypt files larger than available memory, because the message can be processed sequentially.

However, off-line encryption schemes require the entire message at once before generating the ciphertext. Therefore, the plaintext must be known in advance (or read more than once) which is an encumbrance to software architects. This violates the pretension of obvious efficiency considerations. In comparison to on-line encryption this approach requires at least available memory as big as the plaintext to encrypt.

3.1 Generic Composition

Assume a developer needs a secure AE scheme. Achieving the twofold goal of integrity and confidentiality by combining a secure encryption with a message authentication code is a non-trivial task. In general there are three methods to combine these two constructs.

Encrypt-and-Mac. Encrypt the plaintext and append a MAC of the plaintext. Variants of this method are used in the transport layer of the SSH protocol [36].

Mac-then-Encrypt. Append a MAC to the plaintext and then encrypt them together. Variants of this method are used in the SSL protocol [34].

Encrypt-then-Mac. Encrypt the plaintext to get a ciphertext and append a MAC of this ciphertext. Variants of this method are used in the IPsec protocol [23].

The *Encrypt-then-Mac* scheme is the only one, which does not show any weakness in both integrity and confidentiality [2]. Note, however, that this can fail trivially by key management errors. Firstly, [2] assume two independent keys for encryption and authentication. Secondly, if the encryption key has been updated and the authentication key has not, then *Encrypt-then-Mac* will decrypt a ciphertext into "authentic" random garbage (if the cryptosystem is good).

Conclusion: For the non-expert, it is surprisingly difficult to provide strong security by combining secure schemes for encryption and message authentication. A decent cryptographic library should provide an API for secure authenticated encryption schemes.

3.2 Nonce Problematic

Motivation. The motivation of using nonces is given by the security definition of an ideal AE scheme. Assume an adversary gets access to a set of (chosen) ciphertexts and cannot achieve any additional information about any plaintext than its length. This implies that an adversary seeing the encryptions of two (equal-length) plaintexts P_1 and P_2 cannot even decide if $P_1 = P_2$ or not.

Thus, encrypting the same plaintext twice must result in two different ciphertexts. A stateless deterministic AE scheme would fail – at least an user must provide is a fresh nonce $N \in \mathcal{N}$ for each encryption.

Nonce Length. Choosing the right nonce length depends on the application limitations. Normal computers like a desktop PC or a laptop do not have so strict memory limitations (in terms of non-volatile memory) as light weight systems like smart cards or RFID chips. Furthermore the nonce length can depend on the available bandwidth. Zenner showed lower bounds for the nonce length l in [38], which depend on the type of nonce generator used and the maximum number of nonces used in a given context.

```
with Ada.Finalization;
private with Crypto.Types.Mutexes;

generic
   type Block is private;

package Crypto.Types.Nonce_Generator is
   package Fin renames Ada.Finalization;

   type Nonce is abstract limited new Fin.Limited_Controlled with private;

   not overriding
   function Update(This : in out Nonce) return Block is abstract;

private
   type Nonce is abstract new Fin.Limited_Controlled with
      record
         Value : Block;
         Mutex : Crypto.Types.Mutexes.Mutex_Type;
      end record;
end Crypto.Types.Nonce_Generator;
```

Fig. 2. An abstract nonce generator package specification written in Ada 2012

Nonce Misuse. Users know that leaking the private key is a bad idea. But a nonce misuse can destroy their security just as well – often as a surprise for the layperson. Most "provably secure" nonce-based AE schemes actually assume *nonce-respecting adversaries.* This type of adversary has full control over the nonce, but cannot use the same nonce twice. If an application ever reuses the nonce, the security proof is not applicable to the application's setting any more. As it turns out, attacks are abundant in that case [14].

During the development of our cryptographic library (`libadacrypt`) we had to provide an API for nonce handling. This specification can be seen in Figure 2. Since a state of a nonce generator should never be copied, the type Nonce is declared as `limited`. As some nonce generators must support an initialization and finalization step during the usage of nonces, we decided to inherit the Nonce type from `Limited_Controlled`. To provide the opportunity of a thread safe realization we add a mutex to the abstract nonce type. The handling of the mutex remains to the developer of any implementations of this abstract class.

The function `Update()` of our interface returns the current new nonce and updates the internal state Value. The abstract class does not provide any getter or setter subprograms to ensure that the same value cannot be returned twice. In the following we present three realizations of nonce handling.

Random-Based Nonce Generator. When a random-based nonce generator is invoked, it outputs a random value of bit length n. This type of nonce generators does usually not depend on any initialization. In some cases initialization is needed (*e.g.,* open `/dev/random` on a Linux- or BSD-Kernel-based OS). If based on a secure random number generator this approach provides a negligible collision probability of about $\frac{q^2-q}{2^{n+1}}$ (birthday bound) where q is the total number of generated nonce values and n describes the bit length of the nonce value

[38]. Unfortunately not all embedded systems provide enough entropy to make a PRNG cryptographic secure.

Counter-Based Nonce Generator. A counter-based nonce generator is based on a persistent counter value which is increased after each invocation of the function `Update`. The constructor of a nonce counter object needs at least two parameters 1) a reference to the persistent counter and 2) a possible starting value, and works as follows: If the valid persistent counter already exists, it is used to initialize the object instead of the user provided starting value, otherwise it creates a persistent counter initialized by the starting value. This behavior ensures strong resistance against misuse. This nonce generator should be implemented using the Singleton pattern.

Counter+Random-Based Nonce Generator. This approach was introduced by Zenner as mixed solution 2 [38]. In this setting, the nonce value is split into two parts, where the l most significant bits contain the random value, and the remaining $n - l$ least significant bits cover the counter value. During the initialization the only user input required is the starting value for the counter part. The random value is generated by invoking a cryptographic secure PRNG. If we consider the size of the random part to be $n/2$, collision probability is given by the birthday bound $\frac{q^2-q}{2^{n/2+1}}$. This solution does not require non-volatile memory, since the random part is used to provide a certain amount of nonce reuse resistance.

3.3   Plaintext Leaking

Consider a scenario where Alice and Bob have established a secure channel based on an AE scheme upon an insecure channel. Furthermore, we consider an adversary capable to 1) eavesdrops all encrypted traffic on the secure channel, and 2) generates and inject chosen ciphertexts.

Note that all ciphertexts chosen by an adversary will most likely be invalid. Else the AE scheme would provide poor authenticity. But, a temporary would-be plaintext – or a part of it – may already have been decrypted at Bob's side, and Bob may use it, in spite of the authentication failure. A common real life example is the browser usage when an user accepts invalid certificates. A study from 2008 [11] showed that 1 out of 5 participants ignores security warnings.

Even if Bob is not so foolish to ignore an authentication failure, he may be tempted to process the already known part of the plaintext in parallel with decrypting the remaining part, to improve performance. He can later abort processing the plaintext, if authentication fails. As harmless as this may look for any non-cryptographer, this is likely to break almost any AE scheme. During the application processing of an invalid and most likely syntactically incorrect plaintext, error handling is usually been triggered, *e.g.*, an exception will be raised. This can leak information about unauthentic plaintexts to the adversary.[6]

Conclusions: A well designed API of a secure AE scheme should defend against leaking the (partial) decrypted ciphertext before the authenticity has been verified. Additionally, any error handling must avoid to give the adversary additional information, not foreseen by the designer of the cryptosystem.

4   An API for Authenticated Encryption Schemes

We designed the following API shown in Figure 3 for the `libadacrypt` which allows to implement an AE(AD) scheme. We choose a generic abstract class structure to realize our goal of providing an authenticated encryption scheme package for the `libadacrypt`. Hence, the user of the library must implement each abstract subprogram. The order of the given parameters of a subprogram can be seen as a recommendation for the usage in a specific implementation.

Encryption. The encryption of a given message consists of two steps. In the first step, the authenticated encryption scheme must be initialized with a nonce and a key. There exist three methods of realizing the key management.

1. The key is directly given as the input (line 12).
2. The key is computed using Diffie-Hellman key-exchange protocol with mutual authentication based on certificates [7] (line 15).
3. The key is computed from a password, hashed using a cryptographic secure hash algorithm like SHA-2 [27], Keccak [4] or Skein [13] (line 18).

Note, that in each case the procedure `Init_Encrypt` must invoke the function `Nonce.Update` to obtain a nonce for the ongoing encryption process. This makes nonce misuse difficult, even for sloppy developers.

The second and final step of the encryption phase is given by the procedure `Encrypt` itself (lines 22-25). We choose this generic approach – based on callback functions – to provide the user of the library different possibilities to realize the storage handling of the associated data (header), plain- and ciphertexts. Hence, the user of the API must provide a function `Read_Header` of type `Callback_Reader` (line 23). This type of function attempts to read up to B'Length bytes from a data source, writes those bytes to the byte array B, and returns the number of written bytes. Usually, this function wraps a `File_Type` from the `Ada.Direct_IO` package or an input stream from the `Ada.Streams.Stream_IO` package. If the authenticated encryption scheme does

---

[6] Error messages help developers and users to identify the proximate cause of a problem. But in the topic of security, error messages might provide an adversary with additional information. An example where the application provide the adversary with useful information is given by the attack of Bleichenbacher [5]. His attack exploited only the behaviour of some servers to signal an error if a decrypted plaintexts has been found invalid, according to some simple syntactic convention.

```
1   with Crypto.Types.Nonces;
2   with Crypto.Symmetric.Blockcipher;
3   generic
4      with package BC is new Crypto.Symmetric.Blockcipher(<>);
5      with package N  is new Crypto.Types.Nonces(BC.Block);
6   package Crypto.Symmetric.AE is
7      use Crypto.Types;
8      type AE_Scheme is abstract tagged limited private;
9      type Callback_Writer is access procedure (B : in Bytes);
10     type Callback_Reader is access function  (B : out Bytes) return Natural;
11
12     procedure Init_Encrypt(This    : out AE_Scheme;
13                            Key     : in BC.Key_Type;
14                            Nonce   : in out N.Nonce'Class) is abstract;
15     procedure Init_Encrypt(This          : out AE_Scheme;
16                            Certificate   : in X509;
17                            Nonce         : in out N.Nonce'Class) is null;
18     procedure Init_Encrypt(This          : out AE_Scheme;
19                            Password      : in String;
20                            Nonce         : in out N.Nonce'Class) is null;
21
22     procedure Encrypt(This             : in AE_Scheme;
23                       Read_Header      : in Callback_Reader;
24                       Read_Plaintext   : in Callback_Reader;
25                       Write_Ciphertext : in Callback_Writer) is abstract;
26
27     procedure Init_Decrypt(This          : out AE_Scheme;
28                            Key           : in BC.Key_Type;
29                            Nonce_Value   : in BC.Block) is abstract;
30     procedure Init_Decrypt(This          : out AE_Scheme;
31                            Certificate   : in X509;
32                            Nonce_Value   : in BC.Block) is null;
33     procedure Init_Decrypt(This          : out AE_Scheme;
34                            Password      : in String;
35                            Nonce_Value   : in  BC.Block) is null;
36
37     function Decrypt_And_Verify(This            : in AE_Scheme;
38                                 Read_Header     : in Callback_Reader;
39                                 Read_Ciphertext : in Callback_Reader;
40                                 Write_Plaintext : in Callback_Writer)
41                                 return Boolean is null;
42     function Decrypt_And_Verify(This                  : in AE_Scheme;
43                                 Read_Header           : in Callback_Reader;
44                                 Read_Ciphertext       : in Callback_Reader;
45                                 Write_Masked_Plaintext : in Callback_Writer;
46                                 Read_Masked_Plaintext  : in Callback_Reader;
47                                 Write_Plaintext        : in Callback_Writer)
48                                 return Boolean is abstract;
49  private
50     type AE_Scheme is abstract tagged limited record
51        Nonce_Value : BC.Block;
52     end record;
53  end Crypto.Symmetric.AE;
```

Fig. 3. API for secure authenticated encryption schemes

not support associated data the function Read_Header should always return zero. The parameter Read_Plaintext (line 24) is also of the type Callback_Reader and is needed to read the plaintext from a user specified data source. In addition, the user must provide a callback procedure named Write_Ciphertext of type Callback_Writer (line 25). This procedure takes an array of bytes as input and is responsible to write the encrypted plaintext bytes to its destination.

Decryption. The ciphertext decryption process is similar to the encryption process, with the exception that we provide two different Decrypt_and_Verify functions depending on the available volatile memory. The initialization phase, which is similar to the initialization phase of the encryption, can be seen in lines 27-35. Instead of a `Nonce` Type the procedures `Init_Decrypt` have nonce value from type `BC.Block` as parameter. Due to the fact that the output of a nonce object can be a random value which is unpredictable (cf. Section 3.2).

We start with the simple scenario where the decrypted plaintext candidates always fit into the secure volatile memory available. The user of our library can invoke the function `Decrypt_and_Verify` shown in lines 37-41. The function works as follows. At first, the ciphertext is decrypted and the plaintext candidate is stored locally. When the entire ciphertext has been read, either verification succeeds, the function starts to write the plaintext to its destination using the procedure `Write_Plaintext` and eventually returns `True`. Or the verification fails. Then the plaintext candidate is erased from local memory without writing anything to the plaintext destination, and the function returns `False`.

If you do not want to allocate local memory for the entire plaintext candidate, just follow the *Decrypt-Then-Mask* approach, where the plaintext candidate is "masked" (i.e., re-encrypted) before written to an user-defined temporary storage. Any "unmasking" only takes place when the verification succeeds. Accordingly, the function `Decrypt_and_Verify` in lines 42-48 has two additional parameters `Write_Masked_Plaintext` and `Read_Masked_Plaintext`. It works as follows:

1. Generating a temporary "masking" key[7].
2. Decryption: Alternate between calling `Read_Ciphertext`, decryption, "masking", and calling `Write_Masked_Plaintext`.
3. Verification: When the entire ciphertext has been read, check if it has been valid or not.
   (a) Valid: Alternate between calling `Read_Masked_Plaintext`, "unmasking", and calling `Write_Plaintext`. Erase the "masking" key and return `true`.
   (b) Not valid: Erase the "masking" key and return `false`.

The "masking" is actually realized by using the given block cipher in a secure (but un-authenticated) encryption mode like CBC using the "masking" key and an initial value based on the variable `Nonce_Value`.

Security Evaluation. As an authenticated encryption scheme is given as input to the procedures `Encrypt` and `Decrypt_and_Verify` the developer which uses the implementation of the given API does not have to fulfill the hard task of combining a secure encryption scheme and a message authentication code. The upcoming implementations of this package are provable secure AE schemes.

The decryption process, which stores the plaintext candidate in a temporary storage, avoids the problem of plaintext leaking discussed before. Hence, attacks like the Bleichenbacher attack mentioned before will not be possible anymore.

---

[7] There are two common ways to generate this key, either using a random value or derive the new key from hashing (parts of) the current state of the authenticated encryption scheme object using a cryptographically secure hash function.

Table 1. Crypto-Library Comparison

Name	Language	AE Support	Nonce Support	NRR	PLR
Botan-1.10.1 [25]	C++	Yes	Yes	Partial	No
Bouncy Castle-1.46 [19]	Java/C#	Yes	No	-	No
Crypto++ 5.6.1 [12]	C++	Yes	Yes	No	No
libadacrypt*	Ada	Yes	Yes	Yes	Yes
libsparkcrypto-0.1.1 [33]	SPARK	No	No	-	-
OpenSSL-1.0.0e [37]	C	No	No	-	-

NRR is the abbreviation for Nonce Re-use Resistance.
PLR is the abbreviation for Plaintext Leaking Resistance.

5   Comparison of Cryptographic Libraries

In this section, we examine common open source cryptographic libraries regarding to the support of authenticated encryption schemes and nonces. In coherence of any support, we check if those libraries contain any measurements that aid application developers to 1) avoid nonce misuse issues and 2) prevent plaintext leaking in terms of authenticated encryption schemes. The results of our comparison are given in Figure 1. Note, that libadacrypt* denotes the libadacrypt including our presented extensions.

The formally verified source code of the libsparkcrypto is proven correct using the SPARK toolset, but it only supports a limited amount of functionality, excluding authenticated encryption schemes and nonces. The famous OpenSSL library is widely used on the GNU/Linux environment, but does not support authenticated encryption schemes and nonces as well. Hence, in the following comparison we no longer consider libsparkcrypto and OpenSSL.

We defined that a nonce support exists if the source code of a library implies that the developers of those libraries are aware of the mentioned nonce issues. The Crypto++ has no countermeasures against nonce reuse, except the test if an unpredictable and random nonce is zero. However, Botan provides a class for nonces called OctetString which can be initialized with a PRNG. This helps against nonce reuse, but OctetString has a pitfall. It can be initialized with a constant value. Such a behaviour should be studiously avoided by a well designed nonce class.

None of the mentioned libraries support any resistance against plaintext leaking, except the libadacrypt*. Based on this result, we claim that the majority of developers of cryptographic libraries are not aware of the problematic nature of plaintext leaking.

6   Conclusion and Outlook

We have shown that the usage and the generation of an authenticated encryption scheme is a nontrivial task. Our solution leads to a less error prone but slightly non-intuitive implementation, due to the use of callback functions, especially in the Decrypt_And_Verify functions. We believe that this is better than a more intuitive API that lacks defences against nonce reuse and plaintext leakage – especially for high-assurance applications, a domain of Ada.

Using the API presented in the current paper, we plan to implement common block cipher based authenticated encryption schemes like *EAX, McOE, SIV, BTM* and *OCB*. Furthermore, we want to implement the nonce generators described by Zenner [38]. Finally, we have the intention to provide an easy-to-use high level API for a secure channel based on either file types or sockets.

References

[1] Adamson, A., Maurer, M., R.P.W., et al.: FlexiProvider (November 2011),
     http://www.flexiprovider.de/overview.html
[2] Bellare, M., Desai, A., Pointcheval, D., Rogaway, P.: Relations Among Notions
     of Security for Public-Key Encryption Schemes. In: Krawczyk, H. (ed.) CRYPTO
     1998. LNCS, vol. 1462, pp. 26–45. Springer, Heidelberg (1998)
[3] Bellare, M., Rogaway, P., Wagner, D.: The EAX Mode of Operation. In: Roy, B., Meier,
     W. (eds.) FSE 2004. LNCS, vol. 3017, pp. 389–407. Springer, Heidelberg (2004)
[4] Bertoni, G., Daemen, J., Peeters, M., Assche, G.V.: The Keccak SHA-3 submis-
     sion. Submission to NIST, Round 3 (2011)
[5] Bleichenbacher, D.: Chosen Ciphertext Attacks Against Protocols Based on the
     RSA Encryption Standard PKCS #1. In: Krawczyk, H. (ed.) CRYPTO 1998.
     LNCS, vol. 1462, pp. 1–12. Springer, Heidelberg (1998)
[6] Borisov, N., Goldberg, I., Wagner, D.: Intercepting Mobile Communications: The
     Insecurity of 802.11. In: MOBICOM, pp. 180–189 (2001)
[7] Boyko, V., MacKenzie, P.D., Patel, S.: Provably Secure Password-Authenticated
     Key Exchange Using Diffie-Hellman. In: Preneel, B. (ed.) EUROCRYPT 2000.
     LNCS, vol. 1807, pp. 156–171. Springer, Heidelberg (2000)
[8] C.C.C. (CCC). Analyse einer Regierungs-Malware (2011),
     http://www.ccc.de/system/uploads/76/original/
     staatstrojaner-report23.pdf
[9] Dworkin, M.: Recommandations for block cipher modes of operation. SP
     800-38a, U.S. DoC/National Institute of Standards and Technology (2001),
     http://csrc.nist.gov/CryptoToolkit/modes/
[10] Dworkin, M.: Special Publication 800-38C: Recommendation for block cipher modes
     of operation: the CCM mode for authentication and confidentiality. National Institute
     of Standards and Technology, U.S. Department of Commerce (May 2005)
[11] Egelman, S., Cranor, L.F., Hong, J.I.: You've been warned: an empirical study of
     the effectiveness of web browser phishing warnings. In: CHI, pp. 1065–1074 (2008)
[12] W.D., et al.: Crypto++ Library 5.6.1 - a Free C++ Class Library of Cryptographic
     Schemes (August 2010), http://www.cryptopp.com/
[13] Ferguson, N., Lucks, S., Schneier, B., Whiting, D., Bellare, M., Kohno, T., Callas,
     J., Walker, J.: The Skein Hash Function Family. Submission to NIST (2010)
[14] Fleischmann, E., Forler, C., Lucks, S.: McOE: A Foolproof On-Line Authenti-
     cated Encryption Scheme. Cryptology ePrint Archive, Report 2011/644 (2011),
     http://eprint.iacr.org/
[15] Forler, C., Barshun, A., M.R., et al.: Libadacrypt-0.2.0 (November 2011),
     https://github.com/cforler/Ada-Crypto-Library
[16] Fouque, P.-A., Joux, A., Martinet, G., Valette, F.: Authenticated On-Line En-
     cryption. In: Matsui, M., Zuccherato, R.J. (eds.) SAC 2003. LNCS, vol. 3006, pp.
     145–159. Springer, Heidelberg (2004)

[17] Gillmor, D.K.: Crypt-Nettle-0.3 (March 2011),
    http://search.cpan.org/~dkg/Crypt-Nettle-0.3
[18] Goldwasser, S., Micali, S.: Probabilistic Encryption. J. Comput. Syst. Sci. 28(2),
    270–299 (1984)
[19] Gustavsson, T., Kerr, C., E.T., et al.: The legion of the bouncy castle java cryp-
    tography apis (February 2011), http://www.bouncycastle.org/java.html
[20] Hotz, G.: Console Hacking 2010 - PS3 Epic Fail. In: 27th Chaos Communications
    Congress (2010),
    http://events.ccc.de/congress/2010/Fahrplan/attachments/
    1780_27c3_console_hacking_2010.pdf
[21] Iwata, T.: New Blockcipher Modes of Operation with Beyond the Birthday Bound
    Security. In: Robshaw, M. (ed.) FSE 2006. LNCS, vol. 4047, pp. 310–327. Springer,
    Heidelberg (2006)
[22] Iwata, T., Yasuda, K.: BTM: A Single-Key, Inverse-Cipher-Free Mode for Determin-
    istic Authenticated Encryption. In: Jacobson Jr., M.J., Rijmen, V., Safavi-Naini, R.
    (eds.) SAC 2009. LNCS, vol. 5867, pp. 313–330. Springer, Heidelberg (2009)
[23] Kent, S.: IP Encapsulating Security Payload (ESP). RFC 4303 (Proposed Stan-
    dard) (December 2005)
[24] Kohno, T.: Attacking and Repairing the WinZip Encryption Scheme. In: ACM
    Conference on Computer and Communications Security, pp. 72–81 (2004)
[25] Lloyd, J.: Welcome — Botan (July 2011), http://botan.randombit.net/
[26] McGrew, D.A., Viega, J.: The Security and Performance of the Galois/Counter
    Mode (GCM) of Operation. In: Canteaut, A., Viswanathan, K. (eds.) IN-
    DOCRYPT 2004. LNCS, vol. 3348, pp. 343–355. Springer, Heidelberg (2004)
[27] N.N.I. of Standards and Technology. FIPS 180-2: Secure Hash Standard (April
    1995), http://csrc.nist.gov
[28] Rogaway, P.: Authenticated-Encryption with Associated-Data. In: ACM Confer-
    ence on Computer and Communications Security, pp. 98–107 (2002)
[29] Rogaway, P.: Nonce-Based Symmetric Encryption. In: Roy, B., Meier, W. (eds.)
    FSE 2004. LNCS, vol. 3017, pp. 348–359. Springer, Heidelberg (2004)
[30] Rogaway, P., Bellare, M., Black, J., Krovetz, T.: OCB: a block-cipher mode of
    operation for efficient authenticated encryption. In: ACM Conference on Computer
    and Communications Security, pp. 196–205 (2001)
[31] Rogaway, P., Shrimpton, T.: A Provable-Security Treatment of the Key-Wrap
    Problem. In: Vaudenay, S. (ed.) EUROCRYPT 2006. LNCS, vol. 4004, pp. 373–
    390. Springer, Heidelberg (2006)
[32] Sabin, T.: Vulnerability in Windows NT's SYSKEY encryption. BindView Secu-
    rity Advisory (1999), http://marc.info/?l=ntbugtraq&m=94537191024690&w=4
[33] Senier, A.: Libsparkcrypto - A cryptographic library implemented in SPARK
    (September 2010), http://senier.net/libsparkcrypto/
[34] Wagner, D., Schneier, B.: Analysis of the SSL 3.0 Protocol. In: Proceedings of the
    2nd UNIX Workshop on Electronic Commerce, pp. 29–40 (1996)
[35] Wu, H.: The Misuse of RC4 in Microsoft Word and Excel. Cryptology ePrint
    Archive, Report 2005/007 (2005), http://eprint.iacr.org/
[36] Ylonen, T., Lonvick, C.: The Secure Shell (SSH) Transport Layer Protocol. RFC
    4253 (Proposed Standard) (January 2006)
[37] Young, E.A., Hudson, T.J.: OpenSSL: The Open Source toolkit for SSL/TLS
    (September 2011), http://www.openssl.org/
[38] Zenner, E.: Nonce Generators and the Nonce Reset Problem. In: Samarati, P.,
    Yung, M., Martinelli, F., Ardagna, C.A. (eds.) ISC 2009. LNCS, vol. 5735, pp.
    411–426. Springer, Heidelberg (2009)

Handling Synchronization Requirements under Separation of Concerns in Model-Driven Component-Based Development

Patricia López Martínez[1] and Tullio Vardanega[2]

[1] Computers and Real-Time Group, University of Cantabria, 39005 Santander, Spain
`lopezpa@unican.es`
[2] Department of Mathematics, University of Padua, 35121 Padova, Italy
`tullio.vardanega@math.unipd.it`

Abstract. In this paper we discuss how the concept of separation of concerns could be conveniently applied to improve the model-driven component-based development of real-time high-integrity systems. Interpreting Dijkstra's view in this regard, we seek separation of concerns between the specification of needs (expressed declaratively by the user as requirements and assumptions) and the conception of a demonstrable solution for them (which we want to implement automatically, in the spirit of model-driven development). We aim to enable software designers to specify the assumptions needed on the expected behavior of the system solely by attaching declarative attributes to the affected elements of the system model. We then want the underlying design environment to produce a solution that provably achieves that behavior at run time. We find this vision to fit very well in a component-based development as it naturally allows the declarative space to be confined to interfaces (for the outside view of components) and operations (for the inside view of them). To prove the viability of our vision we apply it to the handling of synchronization requirements as seen from the perspective of the calling component, which is acutely more challenging than from the standpoint of the provider component.

Keywords: Separation of Concerns, component-based development, synchronization, high-level data races.

1 Introduction

In the last few years Component-based Software Engineering (CBSE) [1] has emerged as a key paradigm for the improvement in the quality and the economy of the development of high-integrity real-time systems. However, the success of CBSE in this application domain has been disappointingly modest [2]. Although it is not clear whether as a cause or as a consequence of this failure, the lack of a real component market or effective repositories of reusable components is a serious impairment, without which the very essence of CBSE, i.e. easier and wider reuse, has little practical value.

M. Brorsson and L.M. Pinho (Eds.): Ada-Europe 2012, LNCS 7308, pp. 89–104, 2012.

Multiple causes may be identified for this lack. In this work we discuss about one of them in particular, which we consider especially important: the fact that the principle of Separation of Concerns (SofC) [3] is not properly considered in the development of reusable components. We argue that proper application of this principle is crucial for high-integrity real-time systems, where the satisfaction of non-functional requirements is a paramount concern.

The concept of SofC [3] was first intended as a means for mastering complexity in software development. The idea of SofC consists in applying a sort of "divide-and-conquer" strategy to the vast spectrum of problems to be addressed by software design. Separating the different aspects of a software design (functionality, performance, distribution, timing, etc.) enables separate and specialized reasoning about each of them, which is bound to contribute to improving the quality, the trust and the effectiveness of the overall design. Besides this general, commonly agreed definition of SofC, however, there is not much consensus about it when it comes to applying it at a more practical level; surely not in the high-integrity real-time scientific and industrial community that we know of.

In this paper, we discuss this issue and we offer our own interpretation of SofC for application to real-world industrial development. As a proof of concept, we plant our own definition onto a real component-based technology for high-integrity systems that constitutes the result of two former European R&D projects, ASSERT[1] and CHESS[2], and which has been defined considering support for SofC as one of its main principles. The vision and results presented in [4] and [5] constitute the basis for the research work outlined in this paper.

Among all the non-functional aspects that may affect high-integrity real-time systems, this paper discusses how synchronization can be configured and managed in an application following the proposed SofC approach. Accordingly, this paper is structured as follows. Section 2 introduces our view on how SofC should be applied to the development of real-time applications. Section 3 presents the main characteristics of the proposed real-time component-based technology and how it supports our interpretation of SofC. How synchronization requirements are addressed in the component model is detailed in Section 4. Detail insight into how atomic blocks can be obtained in the implementation is given in Section 5. Finally, Section 6 provides some conclusions and outlines future work.

2   Our View of Separation of Concerns

For a good and common understanding of the concept of SofC, the first thing that must be defined is the level of abstraction at which it is applied. Several approaches are focused on separating concerns, typically functional vs. non-functional concerns, from a low-level perspective, i.e. at the solution domain level [6].

---

[1] ASSERT: Automated proof-based Systems and Software Engineering for Real-Time systems. FP6 IST-004033 2004-2008. http://www.assert-project.net

[2] Composition with guarantees for High-Integrity Embedded Software Components Assembly, ARTEMIS Joint Undertaking grant nr. 216682. http://chees-project.ning.com

Our belief instead is that for drawing the maximum benefit from SofC, its principles must be applied at a higher level of abstraction, starting from the very first steps of the development process. In our view in fact, SofC must govern *all* of the development process and all the decisions that are taken in it, so that the subsequent lower-level use of SofC can become just a consequence of its earlier application at higher levels of abstraction.

2.1   Specification of Needs and the Solution

More specifically, we want to apply SofC between the specification of the needs of a system and the conception of the solution to them. The wisdom of this approach to separation may be also inferred from the following quote off the same essay where Dijkstra first introduced the concept of SofC: *"The task of "making a thing satisfying our needs" as a single responsibility is split into two parts "stating the properties of a thing, by virtue of which it would satisfy our needs" and "making a thing guaranteed to have the stated properties".* So, we want to clearly separate the responsibilities involved in the specification of needs, i.e. *stating the properties of a thing by virtue of which it would satisfy our needs,* from the responsibilities of the elaboration of a solution, i.e. *making a thing guaranteed to have the stated properties*, which at some point consists in building source code that provides and preserves the properties previously asserted.

The concept of "specification of needs" requires a clarification, since it may be understood to take place at different levels of abstraction. The first specification of the system needs, in the temporal sequence of normal development (also known as requirements specification) falls under the responsibility of the customer. This specification is usually made in some informal manner, without seeking any specific order or distinction between functional and non-functional requirements. Trying to apply SofC at this level seems to be scarcely attractive, partly owing to the distance of that stage from the time at which design decisions are actually made, and also due to the invincibly heterogeneous culture and working practice of customers.

The target of our approach, and also the one that Dijkstra obviously referred to, is the specification of needs made by the software designer. The duty of the software designer is thus ultimately to design an application that satisfies all the needs specified (or implied) by the customer, as well as any other relevant stakeholder. To that end, the designer must respond to these needs (regardless of how informally specified) with a formal set of decisions and properties. When applying a component-based approach, the software designer role represents the agent in charge of designing the application as a composition of instances of reusable components, which collaborate in meeting the given requirements.

Among all the aspects of the design that the software designer must deal with, some refer, rely, or build (for feasibility, tractability, provability, etc.) on well-known theories and techniques, for which proven solutions exist, which may and should be reused in the design, avoiding the error-prone task of implementing them again from scratch. In general, these aspects are transversal to the specifics of the application and tend to relate to non-functional properties: reliability, timing, concurrency, and synchronization among them. Of course, there will inevitably exist aspects of the system that exhibit many more factors of variability and novelty, which stem from domain-specific characteristics and for which reuse, if not an impediment tout-court would be simply ineffective. At the risk of some generalization, we maintain that those aspects more frequently cluster around the algorithmic (functional) parts of the system.

Thus, the idea we pursue is to try and apply a cost/benefit driven strategy to the design decisions made in the development process. Those aspects, for which leaving the responsibility of their design and implementation to the software designer is expected to incur a negative cost/benefit ratio, are encapsulated as isolated concerns and addressed by the reuse of consolidated "blue-print" solutions. The duty of the software designer in that case consists of selecting the most appropriate solutions, and adapting them to the system at hand. Interestingly, the adaptation should solely entail the assignment of instantiation values to a set of predefined properties. An MDE-based development scenario makes this possible. Applying Model-Driven Engineering (MDE) [7], a system is described by a set of complementary models, each of them defining its own set of property attributes, which the software designer must annotate with proper values. The solution will be automatically generated by model transformations based on that particular assignment.

2.2 The Role of Software Architecture

We contend that the key to our chosen interpretation of SofC between the specification of the needs and the solution critically rests on the role played by the *software architecture*. As other authors claim [8], the software architecture plays an essential role in generating software that guarantees certain properties. With a suitable definition of the software architecture:

- The software designer must be capable of formally specifying the system needs only by an appropriate assignment of a set of property attributes on the software architecture. Different views of the software architecture are used to configure or adapt proven solutions that implement the different concerns of the design. Applying an assume/guarantee terminology, the set of properties assigned represent the software designer assumptions on the final behavior of the system.
- A solution fulfilling the required properties at run-time will be generated based on the property attributes assigned to the software architecture, without requiring any additional intervention by the software designer. From an assume/guarantee perspective, the software architecture is responsible for guaranteeing the fulfillment of the assumptions made by the software designer.

3   SofC in a Component Model for High-integrity Systems

The above definition of SofC must be applied on a real component-based development process to prove its viability and usefulness. To that end, we rely on the component-based development methodology [4][5] that proceeds from the ASSERT and CHESS projects. The role of system designer is played there by the *software integrator*, which designs an application as a composition of reusable software components that are developed by *software suppliers*. The reusable components represent strictly functional, sequential code, and the software integrator is the authority in charge of assembling and configuring them to meet the functional and non-functional requirements set on the application (that is, set on the assembly of components as opposed to components taken in isolation). Hence, our interpretation of SofC applies to separating the way in which the software integrator specifies the system needs in the system model (formulated as an interconnected assembly of component instances) and the way in which a solution that satisfies them is generated.

Among all kinds of system needs that may matter for a high-integrity application, in this paper we focus on the non-functional requirements in the time domain. We therefore address the concern of building an application that exhibits predictable timing behavior, to which schedulability analysis can be applied to ascertain that the timing requirements set on the application are met.

The methodology we apply assumes a software reference architecture that warrants SofC, property preservation and correctness by construction to the development process. The four constituents of the architecture that guarantee those features are:

- A component model, which allows designing the software as a composition of reusable software units.
- A computational model, which relates the design entities of the component model, their execution needs and their extra-functional properties for concurrency, time and space, to a framework of analysis techniques which ensures that the architectural description is statically analysable in the dimensions of interest.
- A programming model, which ensures that the implementation of the design entities conforms to the semantics, the assumptions and the constraints of the computational model.
- A conforming execution platform, which actively preserves at run time the system and software properties asserted by static analysis.

From the point of view of applying SofC, we focus exclusively on the component model, which we see as the conceptual frame within which the software integrator must specify the system needs. The features of the component model are the only information that the software integrator must be aware of in system design. The other elements of our architecture concept guarantee that the needs specified by the software integrator in the component-based design of the system *can* be implemented.

SofC is implemented at the software integrator level (design level) by describing the software architecture using *design views*. For each identified primary concern, a specific view of the complete model of the system is provided to the system integrator. The currently supported views are depicted in Figure 1. These concern-specific views abstract and isolate those aspects of the software architecture that are strictly related with a designated concern, defining the property attributes that must be annotated with concern-specific values to determine the corresponding blue-print solution to the features needed in the system. The full set of views of the model fully specifies the system needs.

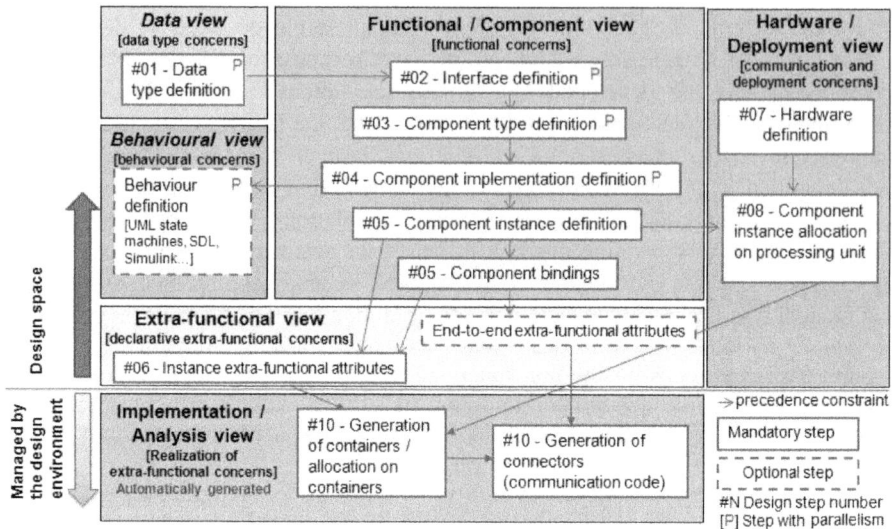

Fig. 1. SofC supported by design views in the development process

At the solution level, the component model enforces SofC by carefully allocating distinct concerns to distinct software entities: components, containers and connectors. Components are software units that comprise pure sequential code, and are candidates for software reuse. Containers are software wrappers, automatically generated by the design environment, which realize the declared non-functional attributes and warrant the preservation of the analysis results. Connectors are responsible for supporting the interactions between components at implementation level. The software integrator exclusively manages components in the design space. Containers and connectors are generated by the design environment. Hence, to apply our notion of SofC, the software integrator only needs to consider components.

Figure 1 depicts the design flow induced by the component model, expressed in terms of design steps, precedence relations, and allocation to design views. Definition of component types, component implementations and assemblies of component instances is allocated to the Functional/Component View as the involved entities include only functional concerns. For a detailed explanation of the involved steps the reader can refer to [4][5]. In this paper, we are focused on the Extra-functional view. It is the one in which the software integrator can annotate the system model with the extra-functional attributes that express the non-functional needs of the system. This view is actually split in several sub-views, one for each addressed non-functional concern of interest. In our case, we focus on the sub-views that have a bearing on the timing predictability of the system; hence the *concurrency view* and the *synchronization view*. Each operation provided by a component interface is marked as either immediate, viz. executed by the flow of control on the caller side, or deferred, viz. executed by a dedicated flow of control in the callee; and then it is further decorated (that is, annotated with property attributes) according to its chosen marking. In the concurrency view, deferred operations can be marked as either periodic, or sporadic or bursty[3]. In the synchronization view, immediate operations are marked as either protected or unprotected.

Figure 2 shows the example that we use in this paper to make our case. The left part of the diagram shows the *Controller* component type, which provides the implementation of a given control algorithm through its *controlPI* provided interface. The data on which the control is applied are accessed through the *ioRI* required interface. The algorithm specific computation is performed by accessing the *computeRI* required interface: this is a classic solution to make the component modular with respect to the specific control algorithm in use. *ControllerImpl* is a specific implementation of *Controller*. The right part of the figure depicts an assembly of component instances, annotated with extra-functional properties.

When the system model is completely annotated, it is used to generate the input required for the analysis of interest. The ensuing results are back propagated in the software integrator space to either confirm or refute the feasibility of his design. We recall that in our context *system design* means *decoration* of interfaces of component instances, and *assembly* of component instances. On a feasible system model, containers and connectors are automatically generated to implement the extra-functional attributes specified at instance level.

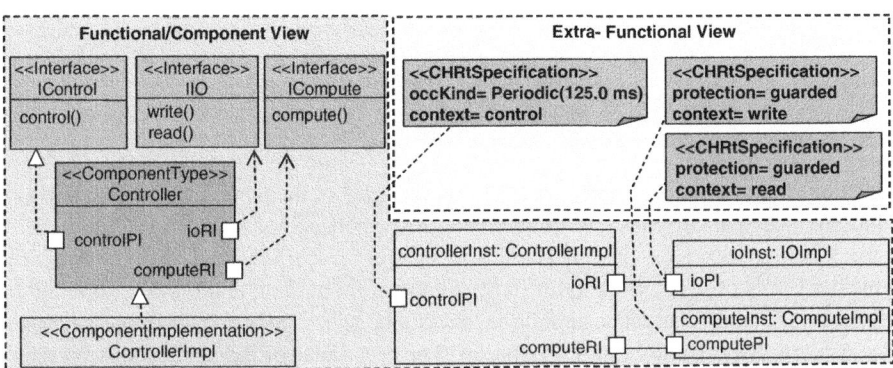

Fig. 2. Definition of components, assemblies and extra-functional properties

4   SofC Applied: Handling Synchronization Requirements

Synchronization is a very apparent instance of a low-level concern that is not (and need not be) explicitly addressed or specified in the customer needs. The customer only identifies the functions that must be implemented by the applications, without being concerned with the way the implementer will use internally concurrency so long as a functionally correct and timing predictable execution of the desired function is guaranteed. Synchronization is also the kind of concern which our notion of SofC is

---

[3] Bursty operations are used to model dense releases of sporadic jobs possibly followed by spans of inactivity, with a maximum number of activations allowed in a bounded interval.

perfectly fit for, since its handling rests on a well-known set of theories and algorithms, which can be reused without needing any reimplementation.

Looking at how SofC is applied to synchronization management in the component model requires addressing two complementary aspects:

- A formal definition of the synchronization viewpoint, i.e. defining the properties of the software architecture that are exposed to the software integrator to specify the needs (the assumptions) of the system from the synchronization point of view.
- Defining how synchronization is handled at the solution level, i.e. how the above properties map to the generated solution in a way that guarantees the assumptions specified at the design level. Within the MDE approach we use, this essentially translates to defining the transformation rules to be applied for the generation of the implementation code.

One important remark here is in order: synchronization is one particular design aspect that is *not* totally independent of other aspects of design, specifically, of concurrency. The amount and type of synchronization mechanisms required in a system depend directly on the level of concurrency of the system, i.e. on the number of concurrent threads of control that access shared data. This implies a relationship between the concurrency and the synchronization views of the software architecture; in fact, there is a precedence relation between them: synchronization should always be addressed once concurrency attributes have been fixed.

4.1   Synchronization Levels

The definition of the set of properties to be included in the synchronization viewpoint and the mechanisms used to implement the synchronization at the solution level completely depend on the provided support for synchronization. We define three distinct levels of synchronization: Individual operation; data; and block of operations. Each level entails distinct assumptions that can be specified at the design level as well as different ways of building the solution. The remainder of the paper focuses on how synchronization assumptions can be specified in the system model.

Per-operation protection is the option that is currently supported in the component model. It consists in protecting the entire execution of some of the operations provided by a component instance. Based on the customer needs, the components interfaces, and the expected concurrency, the software integrator assigns a *protected/ unprotected* nature to each operation provided by a component instance. The software integrator only assigns this property for immediate operations, i.e. those that are not to be executed by a thread of control on the side of the callee. This observation shows the degree of dependency between the synchronization and concurrency views, since, for a proper assignment of the protected nature of an operation, its concurrent nature should have been assigned first. This way of configuring synchronization in component-based systems is similar to the solution adopted in other component models, such as [9] and [10]. However, it is a coarse-grained approach, which could incur higher-than-desirable blocking times for a large fraction of the application tasks, since much code could be unnecessarily executed in a protected manner.

Per-data protection can be used to reduce the amount of code that is executed with mutual exclusion, hence reducing blocking-time penalties. Instead of protecting entire operations, this approach protects concurrent accesses to individual data within the component. The basic idea is to protect accesses to the internal state of the component (where the data are), which is comprised of the set of member attributes defined in the component type. Using this approach, the software integrator only has to assign the *protected/unprotected* nature to each single component instance as a whole, meaning that accesses to its internal data will be accordingly protected on an individual basis.

The main advantage of this approach over the previous one is that it leads to a code that avoids setting protections that are not really needed. Moreover, this option represents the standard way to prevent low-level data races [11]: all the threads that access to a shared variable acquire a lock to it prior to modification and release the lock after that. However, the guaranteed absence of low-level data races does not prevent the occurrence of high-level data races. Together with [11], by high-level data races we refer to sequences of operations in a program where each access to shared data is protected, but the program behaves incorrectly because operations that should be carried out atomically interleave with conflicting operations.

The two previous cases present the software integrator with different options to decorate individual instances in a component assembly with properties that represent the system needs or assumptions regarding synchronization. Our third level of synchronization support, *per-block-of-operations protection*, addresses the risk of high-level data races. It is in fact the absence of *atomicity* in blocks of operations [12] that may lead to high-level data races [11]. In this case, the intent is to protect the execution of end-to-end sequences of operations made within the component's code. These sequences do not fully map to any single provided service of a target component, since in that case they could be protected with the *per-operation* option.

The main motivation for supporting atomicity across blocks of operations in the component model is to guarantee at the solution level the assumptions about logical consistency of code that can be made at the client side, i.e., by the component supplier. A typical example is a control algorithm, notionally represented as a sequence of read-compute-write operations, all executed via the invocations of Required Interfaces of a component, in which consistency is strictly *assumed* between the read and write operations. If we only decorate instance-level provided interfaces, as we do with the two earlier cases, we *cannot* capture this kind of client-side assumptions over a sequence of calls to required interfaces.

A similar approach is taken in the RT-CCM component model [13], although it does not entirely satisfy our interpretation of SofC, since in RT-CCM the software supplier requires the design environment to provide specific mechanisms, such as locks or condition variables: the software supplier must therefore deal with synchronization and concurrency issues. Conversely, in the case in question, the software supplier only identifies segments of code that should be executed atomically from a *logical* perspective without getting involved with the solution that guarantees this assumption. It is important to clarify here that executing a sequence of operations atomically does not mean executing it in a non-preemptible manner, but with mutual exclusion guarantees across concurrent executions of the operations involved on it.

Some works address this kind of synchronization issues relying on assume-guarantee reasoning [14]. Techniques of this kind however base on premises that conflict with the opacity principle required in component-based development. They are based on establishing rely and guarantee assumptions on the internal state of the system, specifically on the state of the internal variables of the system, hence they need a complete knowledge of the underlying code. This is not possible in our case, where the client component manages the operations of its required interfaces, but does not know anything about the state of the provider components.

5   Supporting Atomic Blocks in the Component Model

Let us now present how we add support for per-block-of-operations protection in the component model. To do so requires defining a strategy for both:

- Formulating the client-side level assumptions. They will be formulated by means of decorations of the intra-binding component specifications that are associated to a component implementation. For each provided operation whose internal flow includes invocations on required interfaces, a component implementation includes a description of that flow, formulated as a UML Activity. Each such description constitutes an intra-component binding specification.
- Supporting atomicity at the solution level. A new set of transformation rules must be defined which, when applied by the transformation tools, leads to a solution (code) that supports the specified assumptions.

5.1   Formulating Assumptions about Atomic Blocks at the Client-Side Level

The software supplier that writes the code of a component implementation may detect fragments of code that use Required Interfaces that should be executed as an atomic unit for reasons of logical correctness or consistency. The implementer may thus write code *assuming* that the required level of atomicity will be guaranteed by the design environment. That information must be propagated to the design environment, which is responsible for producing an implementation that guarantees the assumption. That information decorates the corresponding intra-component binding specification, which is formulated as an UML *Activity* according to the following rules:

- The activity is defined as a sequence of *Actions*, which correspond to the execution of either blocks of code belonging to the component (modelled as *OpaqueAction* or *CallOperationAction* elements) or invocations made on the required ports (modelled as *CallOperationAction* elements).
- Modelling a sequence of actions that must be executed atomically requires them to be previously encapsulated in another *Activity*. Then, the invocation of this *Activity* is formulated by means of a *CallBehaviorAction* within the main *Activity*, and stereotyped as <<Atomic>>.

Let use the example in Figure 2 to clarify the approach. The implementation of the *control()* provided operation in *ControllerImpl* is written assuming an atomic execution of the sequence of *ioRI.read()*, *computeRI.compute()* and *ioRI.write()* operations. Figure 3 shows how this atomicity assumption is annotated by the component developer (the software supplier) in the Activity that constitutes the intra-component binding specification of the *control()* operation of *ControllerImpl*.

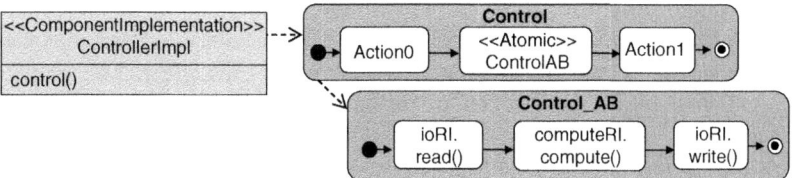

Fig. 3. Declaration of an atomic block in a component implementation

5.2   Guaranteeing Atomic Blocks in the Design Environment

The design environment has full responsibility for guaranteeing the correct execution of the blocks of code that have been annotated as <<Atomic>> by the component supplier, where "correct" means "satisfying the user assumption".

The software integrator is still in charge of defining an assembly of interconnected instances and assigning them a set of desired extra-functional properties. Based on the nature of the interfaces of the instances, the software integrator assigns the property attributes related with concurrency and synchronization, as seen from the perspective of their individual use (i.e. in the per-operation style). Conversely, the requirements related to the atomic nature of internal blocks of code in the components have to do with an *internal* assumption on the guarantees offered by the execution platform in the *combined* use of the required interfaces. The design environment, specifically the transformation tools, will generate a solution that guarantees these atomic executions but always in a totally opaque way from the software integrator point of view.

We now describe the approach we follow to provide atomic execution of internal blocks of code in the running example shown in Figure 2. Being an instance of *ControllerImpl*, *controllerInst* has an <<Atomic>> block, *controlAB*, declared inside its *control()* provided operation, which in this specific assembly corresponds to the sequence of invocations *ioInst.read()*, *computeInst.compute()* and *ioInst.write()*. Guaranteeing an atomic execution for a given sequence of operations (atomic block) is achieved by conceptually transforming the initial assembly into a new one, where the atomic block is provided as an individual provided operation of a new auxiliary component instance. The auxiliary instance decouples the client instance (the one that needs to execute the atomic block) from the server instances (those that provide the operations executed inside the atomic block). The new assembly for our example is shown in Figure 4, where *AuxInst* is the auxiliary instance. It provides the *AB1()* operation, which corresponds to the *ControlAB* atomic block. *AuxInst* is in charge of invoking the corresponding operations involved on *AB1()* (hence, in *ControlAB*) on *ioInst* and *computeInst* instances, which now are decoupled from *controllerInst*.

Annotating *AB1* operation as protected guarantees that it will be executed with mutual exclusion in the face of other invocations of it made on *AuxInst*.

The example in Figure 2 is a little deceiving: it involves only one thread executing the atomic block (the one that is generated owing to the periodic nature assigned to *controlInst.control*). Hence a consistent execution will always be guaranteed. We ought to complicate the example to ascertain the real benefits of introducing support for atomic blocks. A new instance, called *updateInst*, is added to the initial assembly, with its *update()* operation invoking operation *write()* on *ioInst*. Due to the extra-functional annotations, the invocation will be executed periodically by a new thread. In order to guarantee an atomic execution of *ControlAB*, and hence data consistency, invocations of *ioInst.write()* cannot interleave with executions of *ControlAB*. Thus, they must be implemented through the same auxiliary instance (*AuxInst*) and with mutual exclusion on the *AB1()* operation. Therefore, as we show in Figure 5, a new operation is added to *AuxInst*, called *AB2()*, which internally invokes *ioInst.write()*. Annotating *AB2()* as protected we guarantee that it will be always executed with mutual exclusion regarding *AB1()*, and hence we also guarantee a correct execution of *ControlAB* block (this follows from observing that, in force of the transformation rules currently in place, all the protected operations of a single component interface use one and the same protection mechanism).

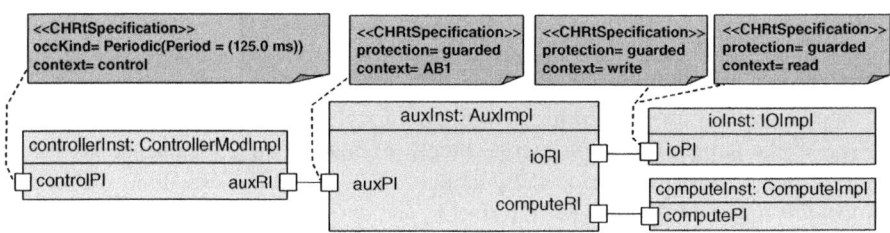

Fig. 4. Use of auxiliary instances to support atomic blocks

All in all, the general approach to support atomic blocks from the solution level standpoint involves restructuring the instance-level architecture of the system, i.e., the binding of component instances that form the system. The intent is that the sequences of operations marked as atomic blocks are executed with mutual exclusion guarantees against any potentially conflicting action, whether atomic blocks or singular operations. Of course, this modification of the structure is applied internally by the design environment, without making it explicit to the software integrator. Moreover, auxiliary instances have only been introduced here to explain the approach, but they need not be actually generated as part of the transformations that create the solution. Let us now look at the inside of the applied transformations. The user model, for example the one shown in right part of Figure 2, represents the PIM (Platform Independent Model) specification of the system. Our PIM is declarative on all non-functional aspects: the implementation decisions made by the software supplier only concern the internals of components. Automated transformation turns the PIM into a complete implementation model, normally known as PSM. The PSM (Platform

Specific Model) model is formulated using the MARTE profile [15]. Figure 6 depicts the PSM MARTE model that corresponds to the example in Figure 5. The main transformations applied are summarized in Table 1.

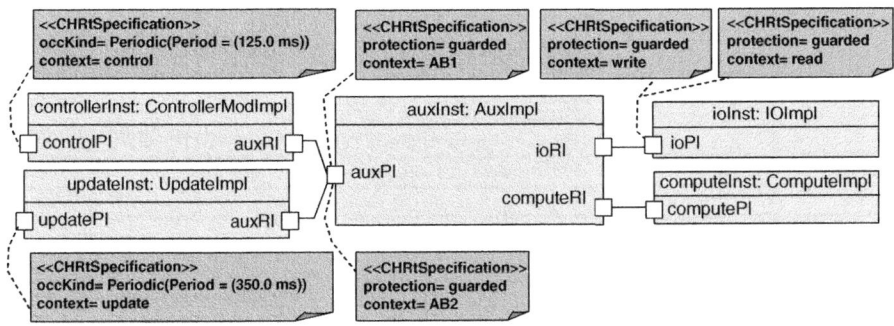

Fig. 5. Avoiding conflicts between atomic blocks and individual operations

The transformation engine continues on from this PSM to generate two distinct outputs: (1) an analysis model that is input to the MAST toolset [16], for applying schedulability analysis to the implementation model of the system; (2) the final code that guarantees the behavior specified in the implementation model.

Bearing in mind the structure of the underlying software architecture (introduced in Section 3), the well-formedness of output (1) is guaranteed by the fact that the PSM specification language strictly conforms to the computational model, the Ravenscar Computational Model (RCM) [17], which ensures that an implementation specification expressed in it is directly amenable to static analysis. We use the PSM MARTE to MAST transformation proposed in [18] for generating the MAST model that constitutes output (1). The results of the analysis are first propagated back onto the PSM model, and finally onto the PIM, where the software integrator can consult them. Typical results obtained from the analysis are optimal priorities for the deferred operations, priority ceilings for the protected operations, and worst-case execution times for the tasks. No information on the atomic blocks is back propagated to the software integrator since they are meant to stay completely opaque to that perspective and only remain an implementation artifact that satisfies the supplier's assumptions.

Once the system is ascertained to be schedulable, transformation (2) is applied to the PSM – annotated with the results of the analysis – to generate the source code of the system implementation. Referring again to the software architecture structure of the approach, the solution is built according to the programming model of choice. Adopting the Ada Ravenscar Profile [19] combined with a set of appropriate code archetypes [20] as programming model ensures that the generated code will satisfy the assumptions, semantics and constraints imposed by the RCM.

Table 1. Example of PIM to PSM transformations

Operation	Annotation	PSM Model element
control	Periodic (125ms)	<<ScheduableResource>> controllerInst_control_task
		<<SaEndToEndFlow>> controllerInst_control (arrivalPattern = Periodic(125ms), endToEndD = 125ms)
	Atomic	<<SaStep>> AB1 (sharedRes = ioInst, subUsages = [read, compute,write])
update	Periodic (75ms)	<<ScheduableResource>> updateInst_control_task
		<<SaEndToEndFlow>> updateInst_control (arrivalPattern = Periodic(75ms), endToEndD = 75ms)
read	Guarded	<<SaStep>> read (sharedRes = ioInst)
write	Guarded	<<SaStep>> write (sharedRes = ioInst)
compute	Concurrent	<<SaStep>> compute

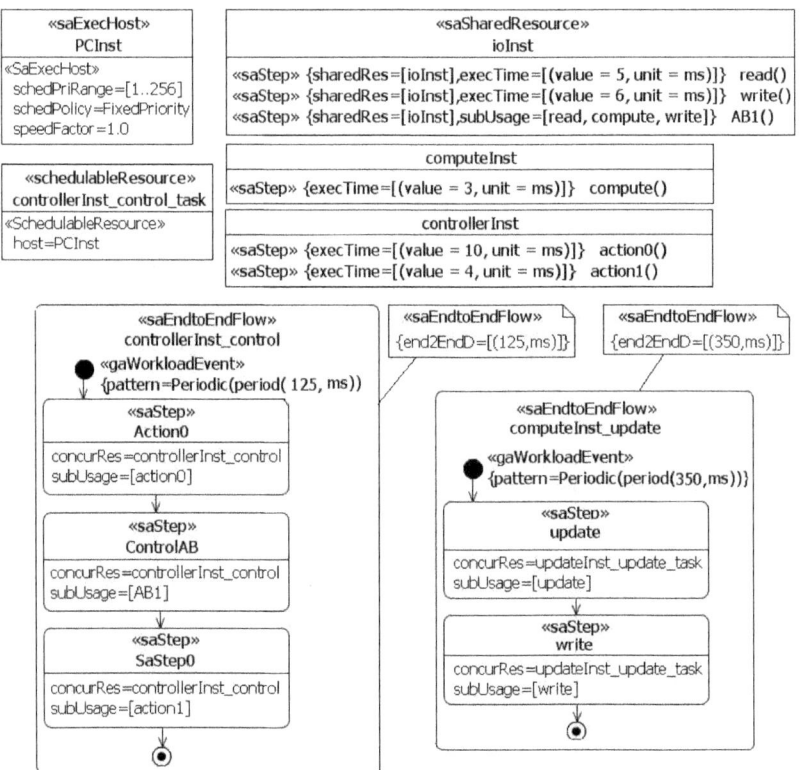

Fig. 6. PSM MARTE model of the example in Figure 5

6   Conclusions and Future Work

We argue that a more stringent application of Dijkstra's notion of separation of concerns (SofC) has potential for improving the quality and fitness of component-based development for high-integrity real-time systems. In this paper we see SofC particularly applied between the specification of the system needs in the non-functional domain, and the automatic elaboration of a solution that provably fulfills them. Used in conjunction with an MDE strategy, the proposed interpretation of SofC allows a software designer to operate declaratively by specifying system needs as values assigned to a certain set of proper attributes of designated elements of the system model. Appropriate transformations are then applied, which lead to a solution that guarantees the specified assumptions. As evidence of the benefit of the approach, the *same* specification of needs (hence the same system model) may result in *different* implementations, according to the transformation rules applied in code generation from the annotated system model.

The paper focused on applying SofC to handle synchronization requirements. With the proposed strategy, the design environment guarantees the assumptions made for the provider component, as well as for the client component. The former set of assumptions is formulated by the software integrator as decorations on the components interfaces; the latter are formulated by the software supplier as decorations of the component implementations with the intent of preventing the final implementation to exhibit high-level data races.

Currently we take a pessimistic approach: the synchronization mechanisms required to guarantee atomic executions and individual operations protection are *always* included, even they are not strictly necessary. This amounts to marking as protected *all* the provided operations of the auxiliary instances. As future work, a more optimized approach can be implemented, where only those synchronization mechanisms that are strictly required due to actual internal concurrency of the system are generated. Also as part of future work, we will look at a more challenging set of application problems that help us determine that the generated solutions are effectively free of high-level data races. Some features of the *per-block-of-operations protection* approach must be also evaluated and compared with the two other options, in terms of e.g., the footprint increase of the executable image and the increase in the blocking time incurred in the system.

Acknowledgements. The authors gratefully acknowledge Marco Panunzio who was the principal designer of the software architecture used in the paper as a proof of concept of the proposal.

This work has been funded in part by the Spanish Government under grants TIN2008-06766-C03-03 (RT-MODEL) and TIN2011-28567-C03-02 (HI-PARTES).

References

1. Szyperski, C.: Component Software: Beyond Object-Oriented Programming, 2nd edn. Addison-Wesley Professional, Boston (2002)
2. Panunzio, M., Vardanega, T.: On component-based development and high-integrity real-time systems. In: 15th IEEE Intl. Conf. Embedded and Real-Time Computing Systems and Applications. IEEE Press, Beijing (2009)
3. Dijkstra, E.W.: On the role of scientific thought. In: Dijkstra, E.W. (ed.) Selected writings on Computing: A Personal Perspective, pp. 60–66. Springer (1982)

4. Panunzio, M., Vardanega, T.: A Component Model Fit for Embedded Real-Time Systems. Submitted to REDS Special Issue of ACM Transactions on Embedded Computing Systems
5. Panunzio, M.: Definition, realization and evaluation of a software reference architecture for use in space applications. Ph.D. thesis. University of Padua, Italy (2011)
6. Mili, H., Sahraoui, H., Lounis, H., Mcheick, H., Elkharraz, A.: Understanding separation of Concerns. In: Early Aspects: Aspect-Oriented Requirements Engineering and Architecture Design, pp. 75–84 (2004)
7. Schmidt, D.C.: Model-Driven Engineering. IEEE Computer 39(2) (2006)
8. Wallnau, K.: Point/Counterpoint. IEEE Software 28(3) (2011)
9. Bondarev, E., de With, P., Chaudron, M.: Compositional Performance Analysis of Component-Based Systems on Heterogeneous Multiprocessor Platforms. In: Proc. 32th. Euromicro Conf. on Software Engineering and Advanced Applications. IEEE Press (2006)
10. Díaz, M., Garrido, D., Llopis, L., Rus, F., Troya, J.M.: UM-RTCOM: An analyzable component model for real-time distributed systems. J. Syst. Software 81 (2008)
11. Artho, C., Havelund, K., Biere, A.: High-level data races. Software Testing, Verification and Reliability 13, 207–277 (2003)
12. Flanagan, C., Qadeer, S.: Types for Atomicity. In: Workshop on Types in Language Design and Implementation. ACM Press (2003)
13. López Martínez, P., Barros, L., Drake, J.M.: Scheduling Configuration of Real-Time Component-Based Applications. In: Real, J., Vardanega, T. (eds.) Ada-Europe 2010. LNCS, vol. 6106, pp. 181–195. Springer, Heidelberg (2010)
14. Jones, C.B.: An approach to splitting atoms safely. In: 21st Annual Conference of Mathematical Foundations of Programming Semantics, MFPS XXI. Electronic Notes in Theoretical Computer Science, vol. 155, pp. 43–60 (2006)
15. Object Management Group, UML Profile for Modeling and Analysis of Real-Time and Embedded systems (MARTE), version 1.0, OMG doc. formal/2009-11-02 (2009)
16. González Harbour, M., Gutiérrez, J.J., Palencia, J.C., Drake, J.M.: MAST: Modeling and Analysis Suite for Real-Time Applications. In: 22nd. Euromicro Conf. Real-Time Systems. IEEE Press (2001)
17. Burns, A., Dobbing, B., Vardanega, T.: Guide for the Use of the Ada Ravenscar Profile in High Integrity Systems. Technical Report YCS-2003-348. University of York (2003)
18. Medina, J., García Cuesta, A.: From composable design models to schedulability analysis with UML and UML profile for MARTE. In: 3rd Workshop on Compositional Theory and Technology for Real-time Embedded Systems (2010)
19. Burns, A., Dobbing, B., Romanski, G.: The Ravenscar Tasking Profile for High Integrity Real-Time Programs. In: Asplund, L. (ed.) Ada-Europe 1998. LNCS, vol. 1411, pp. 263–275. Springer, Heidelberg (1998)
20. Panunzio, M., Vardanega, T.: Ada Ravenscar Code Archetypes for Component-Based Development. In: Brorsson, M., Pinho, L.M. (eds.) Ada-Europe 2012. LNCS, vol. 7308, pp. 1–17. Springer, Heidelberg (2012)

An Approach to Model Checking Ada Programs

José Miguel Faria[1,2], João Martins[1], and Jorge Sousa Pinto[1]

[1] HASLab/INESC TEC & Universidade do Minho, Portugal
[2] Critical Software, SA

Abstract. This paper describes a tool-supported method for the formal verification of Ada programs. It presents ATOS, a tool that automatically extracts from an Ada program a SPIN model, together with a set of desirable properties. ATOS is also capable of extracting properties from a specification annotated by the user in the program, inspired by the SPARK Annotation language. The goal of ATOS is to help in the verification of sequential and concurrent Ada programs, based on model checking.

1 Introduction

Critical systems differ from other classes of systems in that severe consequences may arise from a failure. The use of verification techniques (in particular formal ones) capable of ensuring high levels of reliability is highly recommended for these systems, in order to reduce the risk of failures as much as possible.

The tool presented in this paper and the associated formal verification technique address precisely this problem: they can be used to verify critical software systems at the implementation level, written in the Ada programming language [18]. Ada is considered one of the most suitable languages for the development of high-integrity software systems, which is mainly explained by its safe design, and the existence of clear guidelines for building this kind of system.

Model checking [11] stands among the most successful formal verification techniques. Given a model of a finite state system and a specification (typically given as a set of properties expressed as temporal logic formulas), the goal of model checking is to provide, in a fully automated way, a yes or no answer to the question "does the model satisfy the specification?". The application of model checking techniques to software is seen as very promising and has indeed led to the creation of a new research area, known as *software model checking* [10]. Software model checking is not simply the direct application of model checking to models of software systems; this application poses several challenges that software model checking tools must address (at least partially). Most notably:

Model construction: Manual model construction of software systems is an error-prone and time consuming process, due to the complexity of these systems. In addition, there is a gap between the semantics of programming languages like C, Ada, or Java, and the input languages of model checking tools. Programming languages have richer features, with more complex semantics, than modeling languages.

M. Brorsson and L.M. Pinho (Eds.): Ada-Europe 2012, LNCS 7308, pp. 105–118, 2012.
© Springer-Verlag Berlin Heidelberg 2012

State explosion: This is recognizably the biggest problem of model checking. In software model checking the problem can become even more serious due to the size of software systems, which leads to the generation of models with very large states spaces. Aggressive abstractions may have to be considered.

Property specification: Typically, properties are specified using some variant of temporal logic. This creates two difficulties: First, it requires some level of expertise for expressing the desired properties of the system. Second, the mapping of these properties to properties of the model may not be straight-forward, since the typical specification languages are designed to express properties of mathematical models rather than of source code.

Output interpretation: When a property does not hold in a given model, the model checker reports a counter-example: a trace providing evidence of the violation of the property. Large models can produce very long traces, and manually matching them with the source code can be a really hard job.

Our Approach. The ATOS tool introduced in this paper helps overcoming some of the obstacles in the application of model checking to verify sequential and concurrent Ada programs. Software model checking tools follow essentially one of two main approaches: either (i) they generate input models for (one or more) existing model checkers, or (ii) they include their own algorithms to check the correctness of the models. This is the case of well-known tools like BLAST[4].

ATOS follows the first approach: it relies on SPIN [9], a model checking tool focused on verifying the correctness of (models of) concurrent systems, which clearly matches our intents. The models are described in PROMELA, the SPIN modeling language, and the properties to be checked can be stated either as Linear Temporal Logic (LTL) [14] formulas or as PROMELA assertions. ATOS takes an Ada program and extracts from it a PROMELA model, which simulates the runtime behavior of the former. The specification of the generated models, and consequently of the Ada program, is stated through a set of desired properties of the model. These can be automatically inferred by ATOS or specified in the Ada program using an annotation language inspired by SPARK [2].

ATOS directly addresses the first and third challenges listed above: given an Ada program, it is capable of automatically extracting a PROMELA model from it, and also of inferring desirable properties directly from the program. Although at this stage the remaining two challenges have still not been considered, the translation of Ada programs into models of an advanced model checking tool like SPIN allows ATOS to profit from all of its abstraction techniques, which can be a great help in dealing with the state explosion problem. So it is fair to say that the second challenge is indirectly addressed to some extent.

The purpose of this paper is to report our initial results with the development of ATOS, and to illustrate its application. Section 2 explains how ATOS extracts PROMELA models from Ada programs. Section 3 then presents the ATOS specification mechanisms, used for expressing properties to be verified. Section 4 describes a non-trivial case study that we have used to validate our approach and tool: we verify a component of the MILS high-assurance architecture. Section 5 discusses related work; we conclude the paper in Section 6.

2   Model Extraction

The ATOS tool (fully implemented in Ada) is capable of translating a subset of the Ada language into PROMELA models. All the syntax and semantic information of Ada Programs required for the translation is provided by the Ada Semantic Interface Specification (ASIS) [5], a library that offers an excellent interface to the syntax trees of Ada programs (AST). The translation performed by ATOS requires only the main file of a program as input, even if this depends on other library units declared in separate files.

It would be extremely difficult to cover the entirety of Ada, so we have focused on a subset of the language. However, this is not a standard subset like SPARK or the Ravenscar profile, which have been proposed and used in the context of completely different approaches to verification from the one proposed in this paper (for instance, SPARK is targeted at flow analysis and deductive verification, based on theorem proving and user-provided contracts). There are restrictions required for our technique that do not make sense in SPARK, and vice-versa. The subset handled by ATOS consists of the following Ada declarations: subprograms (procedures and functions), packages, concurrency primitives (tasks, protected objects, and entries), variable declarations (including arrays and basic records), integer constants, and new integer types and subtypes. ATOS also supports most Ada statements, as well as the Ada inheritance mechanism. The translation details for most of these constructs are given next.

Encapsulation. Encapsulation is a well-known mechanism used by most programming languages, including Ada, which restricts and hides objects' data. This mechanism is not directly matched by the PROMELA semantics; nevertheless, it is partially assured by the ATOS translation. The encapsulation is guaranteed for variable declarations; all other declarations are required to use different names in order to avoid their redefinition along the extracted model.

ATOS preserves encapsulation of variables by declaring them globally in the model, prefixed with the name of their "parent entity". For example, a variable Var from task T is declared globally as T_Var. The variable renaming is performed automatically by ATOS. This solution was introduced to restore encapsulation lost due to difficulties in the use of local scopes in PROMELA, in particular the fact that PROMELA *processes* (used for encoding Ada tasks) do not allow the declaration of *inlines* inside their 'bodies'. Inlines are used, for example, to translate procedures and functions (see below), so this restriction forced them to be declared globally (i.e. without encapsulation) along with their variables.

Subprograms. Subprograms encompass functions and procedures, whose execution can be invoked through a procedure call. Subprogram parameters have modes (in, out, or in out) and can be passed either by copy or by reference. Parameters passed by reference are simply updated along the execution of the subprogram. A parameter passed by copy denotes a separate object from the actual parameter; information is transferred between the two at exactly two moments, immediately before and after the execution of the subprogram. To simulate this, ATOS creates an auxiliary variable for each, which is assigned with the value of the parameter before the beginning of the procedure execution. All occurrences of a parameter inside the procedure are replaced by the corresponding auxiliary variable. At the end of the subprogram's execution, the parameter is assigned with the value of this auxiliary variable.

There is no direct equivalent to an Ada procedure in PROMELA; ATOS translates procedures as `inlines`, a primitive that simply defines replacement code for a designated name, possibly with parameters. The procedure's statements are converted into inline statements, whereas the declarations are made global as explained before. The procedure's parameters are translated into inline parameters. However, unlike the original parameters, they do not have a type and an associated mode. This does not become a problem since the parameters' type and mode checking are guaranteed up-front by the Ada compiler (ATOS assumes the input Ada programs compile successfully).

Concurrency. The concurrency model of Ada is based on three main ingredients: tasks, protected objects, and shared data. Concurrent Ada programs may be executed on a single processor (interleaved) or on multiprocessors, and their behavior is defined by a scheduler, according to one of the scheduling policies available in the language. The SPIN concurrency model is different from Ada's: the behavior of SPIN models is defined simply by arbitrarily interleaving statements from different processes.

Tasks. The definition of an Ada task is divided in two parts: the *specification*, which describes the interface with other tasks, and a *body* that contains the code defining the task's behavior. A task can be declared either as a single task or as a type task. The first becomes active from the moment it is declared, whereas a type task simply creates a new type that can be instantiated later.

Each task of an Ada program is translated into a PROMELA process. Similarly to Ada tasks, PROMELA processes are the only primitive that can represent concurrent activities. Single tasks are converted into `active` `proctypes`, which become active from the moment they are declared. Type tasks are translated into PROMELA `proctypes`, which simply creates a new process type that can be instantiated later. However, ATOS creates a new type for each instantiation, due to encapsulation issues: because all the variables of an Ada program are declared globally, without encapsulation the variables of a task type would be the same for any number of instantiations. To overcome this, ATOS creates a new type and new declarations for each instantiation. Listings 1.1 and 1.2 illustrate the conversion of two instantiations from a task type T.

```
proctype T0(){
   . . .
}
```

```
proctype T1(){
   . . .
}
```

Listing 1.1. First instantiation of task type T

Listing 1.2. Second instantiation of task type T

Table 1. Correspondence between Ada predefined types and PROMELA types

Type Ada	Range Ada	Type PROMELA	Range PROMELA
boolean	false, true	bool	false, true
integer	$-2^{15} + 1..2^{15} - 1$	short	$-2^{15}..2^{15} - 1$
positive	$1..2^{15} - 1$	unsigned	$0..2^{n=15} - 1$
natural	$0..2^{15} - 1$	unsigned	$0..2^{n=15} - 1$

Each process has an associated ID number that univocally identifies its sent messages, and an associated channel through which it can receive messages from other processes.

Protected Objects. Protected objects are a structured mechanism that provides mutually-exclusive access to shared data. A protected object is relatively similar to a package, the main difference being the fact that all operations are mutually exclusive. The operations correspond to three different constructs: `procedures`, `functions`, and `entries`. Only one operation is allowed to start at each time, with the exception of functions, of which more than one can execute simultaneously.

If the operation is an `entry`, it must evaluate the barrier expression before executing: if the barrier is open the operation is executed; otherwise the task that is trying to execute the operation communicates to the corresponding protected object process that the barrier is closed, and is enqueued. Every time a process finishes the execution of a protected operation, it communicates this to the protected object process, which then activates the enqueued processes to test the entries' barriers before opening the "semaphore" again. Similarly to tasks, protected objects can be declared either as *single* or *type*, and are correspondingly translated to PROMELA processes as `active proctype` or `proctype`, respectively. In order to ensure the correct simulation of an Ada protected object, ATOS also creates two PROMELA channels associated to the process resulting from its translation: one for queuing the blocked entries and another for communicating with other processes.

The `procedure` and `function` operations are translated in the same way as any other procedures and functions. The only difference is that, in the beginning of the operation, there is a small piece of code that tries to acquire permission to execute. `Entries` are also translated similarly to procedures: they are converted to inlines, and their parameters to inline parameters. However, they include extra statements that test the barrier expression, and communicate the result to the protected object in order for the latter to know if it is closed or not.

Types and Variable Declarations. The Ada and PROMELA type systems are of course very different, with the former language offering a much more powerful and wider type system. Table 1 illustrates the correspondence between Ada predefined types and the PROMELA types defined by ATOS. The range of values that a PROMELA type can represent is always greater or equal to the corresponding Ada type range. As such, when corresponding types have different ranges, overflow errors could stay undetected in the model. For example, a variable with type short in PROMELA can represent the number -2^{15} (the target systems have a 16-bit architecture), which is not possible with the corresponding Ada type. This is easily avoided by adding an LTL formula asserting that a variable respects its range of values.

ATOS is capable of converting variables of the Ada predefined types listed in Table 1, as well as of new integer types and subtypes defined in an Ada program. ATOS also allows for the use of *range constraints* in variable declarations, and takes advantage of this range to reduce the size of variables. For example, the natural variable Readers with range 0..2 is declared as an unsigned with the smallest number of bits that can represent the upper bound of the range (2 bits in this case), instead of being declared as an unsigned with 15 bits.

Arrays. An array is a data structure that aggregates a list of elements, all of the same type; such structures exist both in Ada and PROMELA. However, Ada arrays are more powerful data structures, since Ada declarations allow for the use of complex expressions defining the array range. In PROMELA, the range of an array can only be defined as $0..N - 1$, where $N \in \mathbb{N}$ represents the number of elements. In Ada, the range of an array is defined as an interval N..M, where $N, M \in \mathbb{Z}$ and $N \leq M$, thus allowing for the definition of a lower and an upper bound for the range.

ATOS can convert all Ada array declarations, except for those having a predefined range, such as Character or Positive. In the conversion of an Ada array into a PROMELA array, ATOS firstly calculates the number of elements defined in the array as $Nr\_Of\_Arrays\_Elements = Upper\_Bound - Lower\_Bound + 1$. Given the number of elements, ATOS can now declare the array in PROMELA, but the translation work is not over yet, since PROMELA arrays can only be accessed for indexes between 0 and $Nr\_Elements - 1$. This problem is solved by calculating the difference between 0 (the lower bound of a PROMELA array) and the $Lower\_Bound$ of the Ada array; the calculated offset is then added to the value of any PROMELA array index every time the array is accessed.

Statements. The notion of statement or instruction is present in both Ada and PROMELA. ATOS is able to convert the following Ada statements: if, null, assignment, case, loop, exit, while loops, for loops, goto, procedure call, accept, selective accept, return, and entry call. As an example, the details of the translation of accept statements will now be given.

Accept statements are declared in the specification part of a task (as an entry declaration) and identify the interaction points of a task. They are translated by just mapping their semantics into PROMELA models. In PROMELA processes communicate through channels, so an accept statement is mapped simply as an execution point where a task is listening on a channel that will possibly receive a message from some other task, containing the sender identification and the parameters of the accept statement. The general PROMELA code corresponding to the translation of an accept statement is given below.

```
*AcceptName*  ?  *SenderID*,*Parameters*  ->
                 *Statements*
                 Processes[*SenderID*]  !  *AcceptName*
```

A sender task remains suspended until the requested task finishes the execution of the accept statement, after which it sends a message to the sender task in order to activate it again, following the Ada semantics.

Main Program. The concept of a *main* routine exists in Ada, despite not being identified with a special name as happens in other programming languages (like Java or C). The main of an Ada program is translated into a PROMELA `active proctype main`, which is parameterless. The process contains the corresponding Ada main subprogram statements, and possibly instantiations of task types. The process instantiations in PROMELA are performed inside other processes, because they are executed through the `run` statement rather than by a declaration as in Ada.

3   Property Specification

A model checker verifies whether a model enjoys a given property or set of properties. Hence, the specification of properties is a crucial step in the process. ATOS offers high level mechanisms for expressing properties of the extracted models, based both on (SPARK-inspired) annotations in the source code, and on automatic inference of properties from Ada programs.

Automatic Properties. ATOS is capable of inferring some temporal properties, which are then attached to the models. For instance, ATOS automatically adds the property stating *deadlock freedom*. Another example concerns the numeric types of PROMELA, which do not allow for a precise conversion from the Ada types. In order to overcome this problem, an LTL formula is automatically extracted checking if the upper and lower bounds of variables with such types are respected. The same mechanism is used to ensure that variables with a range constraint respect this range of values. The generic LTL formula for the verification of variable ranges is illustrated below. All names for LTL formulas start with RC and are suffixed with their creation number.

ltl RC0..N { [ ](*VarName* ≥ *Var_LowerBound* && *VarName* ≤ *Var_UpperBound*)}

Temporal properties. The specification of temporal properties in ATOS is restricted by the LTL temporal logic of SPIN. ATOS offers a high-level mechanism for the specification of temporal properties (as annotations in the code) based on the property patterns for LTL proposed in [6]. These consist of five basic patterns: *universal, absence, response, existence,* and *precedence.* These patterns in turn have variations that are defined in terms of five basic *pattern scopes:*

- a pattern holds *globally* along the program execution;
- a pattern holds *after* the first execution of a specified event;

- a pattern holds *before* the first execution of a specified event;
- a pattern holds *between* the occurrence of a designated event and the occurrence of another specified event;
- a pattern holds *after* the occurrence of a specified event and *until* the next occurrence of another event, or throughout the rest of the program execution if there is no further occurrence of that event before the end of the program.

In addition to using these sets of patterns, users can also specify their own temporal properties (writing the LTL expressions directly).

Asserts, Preconditions and Postconditions. These annotations, inserted in the source code, allow for the verification of conditions at a certain point during program execution, and are converted into PROMELA asserts. An annotation corresponding to an assertion can be specified anywhere in an Ada program where statements are allowed. Pre- and postcondition annotations (requirement 3, contained in Section 4, exemplifies the use of a postcondition annotation) are defined only in the body of the followings Ada constructs: functions, procedures and entries. Precondition statements appear at the beginning of the corresponding primitives; postconditions appear at the end.

Invariants. This mechanism allows for the specification of properties for checking whether a given logical expression is valid along the execution of an Ada procedure, function, or entry. An invariant annotation is given in the body of the relevant Ada routine (similarly to preconditions and postconditions), and may be annotated as follows:

$$- -\# \textbf{ invariant } \textit{Expression}$$

ATOS converts an invariant annotation into several LTL formulas, one for each task that possibly executes the Ada routine. ATOS generates LTL formulas equivalent to this pattern annotation:

$$\textit{Expression } \textbf{is\_true between } Q \textbf{ andOp } R$$

where Q (resp R) corresponds to the state whereupon begins (resp. ends) an operation execution. The invariant is verified if all LTL formulas are valid.

4   Case Study

As an example to illustrate the usefulness of ATOS, we adopted a prototype implementation of a MILS Message Router (MMR) system, extracted from [15]. Very briefly, an MMR controls the message flow between components in a MILS (Multiple Independent Levels of Security) architecture. This concept, developed by Rushby[16] and Alves-Foss [1], is a high-assurance security architecture based on the separation of components and on controlled information flow, using a separation kernel.

```
with Lbl_t , Msg_t ;

package Memory

is
   type Mem_Space_T is array (Lbl_t . Proc_Id ' First .. Lbl_t . Mem_Size) of
      Msg_t . Msg;
   Mem_Space : Mem_Space_T ;

   procedure Write( M:  in  Msg_t . Msg;  S:  in  Lbl_t . Pointer );

   function Read(S:  in  Lbl_t . Pointer)  return  Msg_t . Msg;

end Memory ;
```

Listing 1.3. The specification of package *Memory*

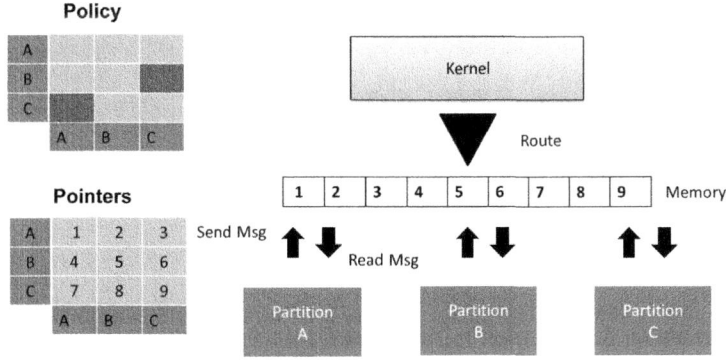

Fig. 1. The MMR system

Implementation. The MMR program is composed of six packages, which contain all the data structures and operations required for the simulation of an MMR system. As an example, the specification part of the package Memory is shown in Listing 1.3. The main data structures and operations of the MMR implementation are illustrated in Figure 1 and briefly described below:

– **Message:** A record structure composed by three fields: origin, dest and data (the latter is just a symbolic field).
– **Memory:** Represented as an array, where each position is a memory cell (or memory space), named Mem_Space in the source code. Each position contains a message, and belongs to a certain partition. All partitions have the same number of memory cells, equal to the number of system partitions. If the system has, say, three partitions, then each of these has three memory cells.
– **Pointers:** Used to indicate which memory spaces belong to each partition at a given moment. This data structure is represented as a square matrix, where each column contains the pointers to the memory space of a certain partition. The value of position (i, j) in the matrix Pointers points to a memory position belonging to the partition i.

- **Mailbox:** A data structure designed as a square matrix (named `Flags`), where each column represents the mailbox of a partition. The mailbox is simultaneously an *inbox* and an *outbox*, thereby the position (i, j) in the matrix indicates (through a boolean value) both if partition i has received a message from partition j and if partition i has sent a message to partition j. The two cases may be distinguished by inspecting the message information.
- **Policy:** The data structure which contains the partition information flow policy. This structure is once more a square matrix, named `Policy_Space` in the source code. Each matrix position contains a boolean value, indicating a communication permission: the contents position (i, j) states if the partition i can send information to the partition j.
- **System Operations:** The MMR system contains three main operations: `route`, `send message`, and `read message`. In order to avoid concurrency problems (precisely of the sort that ATOS is intended to detect) these three operations are declared within a protected object, which makes them mutually-exclusive. `route` is the procedure responsible for the message flow between partitions: it routes a message if the communication is authorized (i.e. the source partition is authorized to send information to the destination partition) or erases it, otherwise. The `send message` and `read message` operations simulate the processes of sending and receiving messages.

In order to test the MMR system a *main* subprogram was created, containing two `partition` tasks and one `kernel` task, with the following behavior:

- **Partition:** Sending and reading messages to/from other partitions. This behavior is repeated twice by each partition, with the restriction that a message cannot be sent from a partition to itself.
- **Kernel:** Routing the messages sent from partitions. This behavior is repeated twice by the kernel task.

Verification. Our verification of the MMR implementation, performed with ATOS, intends to assess its correctness according to several functional requirements. Some of these requirements were already identified in [15], but new ones are also taken into account. As an example, four of these requirements are described next, along with the program annotations that are used to express them.

1. **The information flow policy is immutable** – this requirement can be mapped to the code level by ensuring that no values of the policy matrix are modified once this data structure has been initialized. The specification of this property through an annotation is quite intuitive, using the following pattern property:

   `−− #property` *PolicyIsImmutable* **is_true after** *PolicyStatementsEnd*

   The expression *PolicyIsImmutable* is built by specifying the initial values of the `policy` matrix, which can be done by inspecting the `policy` package. In our present case, only partition 1 is allowed to send information to

AllowedMsg $\equiv$ $Flags \sim (x)(y)$ **and** $Policy\_Space(x)(y)->$
$(Mem\_Space(Pointers(y)(x)) = Mem\_Space \sim (Pointers~(x)(y))$
and $Flags(y)(x))$
NotAllowedMsg $\equiv$ $Flags \sim (x)(y)$ **and** **not** $Policy\_Space(x)(y)->$
$(Mem\_Space(Pointers(y)(x)) = DefMsg$ **and**
not $Flags(y)(x))$
NoAlterations $\equiv$ **not** $Flags \sim (x)(y)->$
$(Mem\_Space(Pointers(y)(x)) = DefMsg$ **and**
not $Flags(y)(x))$

Fig. 2. Correct message routing properties

partition 2, therefore all the other communications are forbidden. This may be specified by setting *PolicyIsImmutable* as follows:

PolicyIsImmutable $\equiv$ $Policy\_Space(1)(2)$ **and** **not** $Policy\_Space(x)(y)$

where $\{x, y\} \in \mathcal{P}$, $x \neq 1$ and $y \neq 2$, with $\mathcal{P}$ being the set of partition numbers. The specification of the expression *PolicyStatementsEnd* is trickier than the previous, because it requires the identification of a point in the program (the end of the package policy statements). To identify a certain point in an Ada program the primitive Label can be used: the label PolicyEnd is first added at the end of the policy statements. However, in SPIN it is not possible to refer to a label without identifying the process that reaches it. As such, and because all package statements are executed in main, the expression *PolicyStatementsEnd* is specified as follows:

PolicyStatementsEnd $\equiv$ $main@PolicyEnd$

2. **The memory space of a partition can only contain messages whose sender is authorized** — the mapping of this requirement to source code is performed by stating that if a partition x has received a message from a partition y, then the partition y must be authorized to send information to the partition x. This property should be valid along the whole program execution, and thereby is annotated as:

$--$ **#property** $(Flags(x)(y)$ **and** $Mem\_Space(Pointers(x)(y)).Dest = x$
$--$ **#** **and** $Mem\_Space(Pointers(x)(y)).Origin = y)->$
$--$ **#**$Policy\_Space(y)(x)$ **is_true globally**

where $\{x, y\} \in \mathcal{P}$ and $\mathcal{P}$ is the set of partition ID's.
3. **Messages are correctly routed** — this requirement tries to guarantee that the procedure Route behaves correctly. A correct routing behavior is defined through the verification of three distinct cases: (i) if there is a message and the communication is allowed, then the pointer of the memory position where the message is contained is swapped, and the inbox of the recipient partition

is activated (*AllowedMsg* in Figure 2); (ii) if there is a message but the communication is not allowed, then the message is erased, as well as the message indication in the sender's inbox (*NotAllowedMsg* in the same figure); (iii) all the mailbox slots that were not flagged should not produce unexpected modifications in the memory or in the mailbox of partitions (*NoAlterations* in the figure). From the conjunction of these different expected behaviors results a property that can then be annotated as a postcondition of Route:

−− **#post** *AllowedMsg* **and** *NotAllowedMsg* **and** *NoAlterations*

4. **The Kernel eventually executes the routing operation** – this requirement is mapped to the implementation level by stating that the kernel task eventually reaches the end of the Route procedure. A pattern property may be annotated specifying this requirement, as follows:

−− **#property** *KernelTask@RouteEnd* **becomes_true globally**

Beyond ensuring that the kernel task eventually executes the routing operation, this property also ensures that the precondition and postcondition of Route are asserted at least once. Observe that if the precondition of route contains the boolean value false but the model never reaches it, this error will not be detected in the model (even though SPIN outputs the unreachable code). This kind of error is very common, and can be easily detected by considering additional liveness properties similar to the above.

5   Related Work

Software model checking is a wide research area; several projects have been developed with the intention of applying model checking techniques to software. Among these, some have directly addressed the verification of Ada programs, namely Quasar [8] and Ada Translating Toolset [7]. Quasar also extracts models directly from Ada programs, but it uses Colored Petri Nets to represent the extracted models. The Ada Translating Toolset uses an intermediate representation of Ada programs before generating the corresponding models. The approach followed by ATOS and Quasar allows more accurate models to be extracted when compared to Ada Translating Toolset, since in the latter some program details are lost in the intermediate representation. However, since this representation stands closer to a model than the initial program, it has the advantage of allowing the easy generation of models for different model checkers.

A different application of model-checking has been followed by Asplund and Lundqvist [12], who have (manually) modelled Ada concurrency primitives using timed automata. Their goal is not to prove properties of arbitrary concurrent programs like the previous approaches, but instead to establish the correctness of an Ada Ravenscar runtime system, and checking general properties that should hold for *every* Ravenscar-compliant program.

Concerning the verification of Ada programs, and in particular concurrent Ada programs, the alternatives to the model checking approach are not abundant.

They are either based on symbolic execution, which is the case of Bakar Kiasan [3], or on logical deduction, which is the case of SPARK and RavenSPARK [17], the latter of which supports the verification of concurrent programs to some extent (RavenSPARK is a concurrent extension of SPARK following the principles of the Ada Ravenscar profile).

The major advantage of the ATOS approach (or any other based on model checking) with respect to the latter tools is the capability to state properties associated with *regions of code* rather than just single points. However, the latter approaches also have advantages, such as the absence of state explosion and the ability to resort to interactive proving when required. A current trend in the formal verification of software is to combine different techniques in the same tool or verification method; our view in developing ATOS is that it intends to be complementary, rather to replace the use of any of the above tools.

6   Conclusions

The tool presented in this paper provides mechanisms to extract models and property specifications from Ada programs and to export them to the SPIN model checker. Although the use of a modeling language to represent programming language features imposes some natural restrictions, the implemented model extraction covers a wide variety of Ada features, and generates models that are closely related to the original Ada programs. The presentation of both the tool and the case study in this paper are necessarily short; the reader is referred to [13] for further details.

Our initial results with the reported case study (and others) are quite promising. However, there is still a gap in the simulation of Ada programs, which is the absence of a scheduler (implemented in SPIN) that would approximate even more the behavior of concurrent programs. As a consequence of this all interleavings are considered, and thus false-positives may be found, corresponding to configurations that cannot in fact occur. This, and the development of mechanisms addressing other software model checking challenges (in particular state explosion and output interpretation) are left for future work.

Acknowledgements. This work was partially supported by the EVOLVE Project, "Iniciativa QREN, SI&IDT 1621", funded by "Programa Operacional FEDER", and by the FCT-funded project FAVAS (PTDC/EIA-CCO/105034/2008). The first author was also supported by the FCT grant SFRH/BDE/51049/2010.

References

1. Alves-Foss, J., Taylor, C., Oman, P.: A multi-layered approach to security in high assurance systems. In: Hawaii International Conference on System Sciences, vol. 9, p. 90302b (2004)

2. Barnes, J.: High Integrity Software: The SPARK Approach to Safety and Security. Addison-Wesley Longman Publishing Co., Inc., Boston (2003)
3. Belt, J., Hatcliff, J., Robby, Chalin, P., Hardin, D., Deng, X.: Bakar Kiasan: Flexible Contract Checking for Critical Systems Using Symbolic Execution. In: Bobaru, M., Havelund, K., Holzmann, G.J., Joshi, R. (eds.) NFM 2011. LNCS, vol. 6617, pp. 58–72. Springer, Heidelberg (2011)
4. Beyer, D., Henzinger, T.A., Jhala, R., Majumdar, R.: The software model checker BLAST: Applications to software engineering. Int. J. Softw. Tools Technol. Transf. 9, 505–525 (2007)
5. Bladen, J.B., Spenhoff, D., Blake, S.J.: Ada semantic interface specification (ASIS). In: Proceedings of the Conference on TRI-Ada 1991: Today's Accomplishments; Tomorrow's Expectations, TRI-Ada 1991, pp. 6–15. ACM, New York (1991)
6. Dwyer, M., Avrunin, G.S., Corbett, J.C.: Property specification patterns for finite-state verification. In: Proceedings of the Second Workshop on Formal Methods in Software Practice, pp. 7–15. ACM Press (1998)
7. Dwyer, M.B., Pasareanu, C.S., Corbett, J.C.: Translating Ada programs for model checking: A tutorial. Technical Report KSU-CIS-TR-98-12, Kansas State University (1998)
8. Evangelista, S., Kaiser, C., Pradat-Peyre, J.F., Rousseau, P.: Verifying linear time temporal logic properties of concurrent Ada programs with quasar. Ada Lett. XXIV, 17–24 (2003)
9. Holzmann, G.: The SPIN Model Checker: Primer and Reference Manual, 1st edn. Addison-Wesley Professional (2003)
10. Jhala, R., Majumdar, R.: Software model checking. ACM Comput. Surv. 41, 21:1–21:54 (2009)
11. Clarke Jr., E.M., Grumberg, O., Peled, D.A.: Model Checking. The MIT Press (1999)
12. Lundqvist, K., Asplund, L., Michell, S.: A Formal Model of the Ada Ravenscar Tasking Profile; Protected Objects. In: González Harbour, M., de la Puente, J.A. (eds.) Ada-Europe 1999. LNCS, vol. 1622, pp. 12–25. Springer, Heidelberg (1999)
13. Martins, J.: Formal verification of Ada programs: An approach based on model checking. Master's thesis, Universidade do Minho (2011), http://www.evolve-itea.org/public/publications.php
14. Pnueli, A.: The temporal logic of programs. In: Proceedings of the 18th Annual Symposium on Foundations of Computer Science, pp. 46–57. IEEE Computer Society, Washington, DC (1977)
15. Rossebo, B., Oman, P., Alves-foss, J., Blue, R., Jaszkowiak, P.: Using SPARK-Ada to Model and Verify a MILS Message Router. In: Proceedings of the International Symposium on Secure Software Engineering (2006)
16. Rushby, J.: The design and verification of secure systems. In: Eighth ACM Symposium on Operating System Principles (SOSP), Asilomar, CA, pp. 12–21 (December 1981); ACM Operating Systems Review 15(5)
17. SPARK Team. SPARK Examiner: The SPARK Ravenscar Profile (January 2008)
18. Tucker Taft, S., Duff, R.A., Brukardt, R.L., Plödereder, E., Leroy, P.: Ada 2005 Reference Manual. LNCS, vol. 4348. Springer, Heidelberg (2006)

Formal Modelling for Ada Implementations: Tasking Event-B

Andrew Edmunds, Abdolbaghi Rezazadeh, and Michael Butler

Department of Electronics and Computer Science, University of Southampton,
Southampton, UK
{ae2,ra3,mjb}@ecs.soton.ac.uk

Abstract. This paper describes a formal modelling approach, where
Ada code is automatically generated from the modelling artefacts. We introduce an implementation-level specification, Tasking Event-B, which is
an extension to Event-B. Event-B is a formal method, that can be used to
model safety-, and business-critical systems. The work may be of interest
to a section of the Ada community who are interested in applying formal
modelling techniques in their development process, and automatically
generating Ada code from the model. We describe a streamlined process, where the abstract modelling artefacts map easily to Ada language
constructs. Initial modelling takes place at a high level of abstraction.
We then use refinement, decomposition, and finally implementation-level
annotations, to generate Ada code. We provide a brief introduction to
Event-B, before illustrating the new approach using small examples taken
from a larger case study.

1 Introduction

Event-B [1] is a formal method that can be used in the rigorous development of
software systems. It may be used in by industry for business-, and safety-critical
systems; to increase confidence in the correctness of the system [2,3]. In this
paper we focus on the domain of multi-tasking, embedded control systems. Our
interest is the application of techniques, and provision of tools, for modelling
the systems, and generating code from the models. We illustrate the approach
using examples from a case study of an embedded Heater Controller, and we
use Ada 1995 [4] as the target language. To be able to link Event-B artefacts to
programming constructs we have devised an extension to Event-B called Tasking
Event-B. Tasking Event-B concepts are directly influenced by Ada constructs.
For instance, Ada tasks are modelled by AutoTask machines, and protected
objects are modelled by shared machines, in Tasking Event-B.

We continue with section 1.1 in which we discuss our motivation. Section 2
provides a brief introduction to the Event-B approach. Section 3 provides an
overview of the Tasking Event-B extension. In Section 4 we present more details
of Tasking features and the translation to Ada. Section 5 describes how we can
read/write directly to memory. Section 6 provides an overview of tooling issues,
and Section 7 provides a summary and discussion.

M. Brorsson and L.M. Pinho (Eds.): Ada-Europe 2012, LNCS 7308, pp. 119–132, 2012.
© Springer-Verlag Berlin Heidelberg 2012

1.1   Motivation

The Event-B method, and supporting tools [5], have been developed during the the EU DEPLOY [6] project. A number of the industrial partners, associated with the project, have been interested in the formal development of multi-tasking, embedded control systems. However, automatic generation from Event-B models, for these type of systems, was absent from the approach. We chose Ada as a basis for our approach, not only because of it's suitability for the application domain, but it also serves as a useful reference for our code generation constructs. Ada constructs match well with Event-B modelling elements, and this serves to simplify the translation to code. We do not, however, formally model all aspects of the implementation, e.g. time. We model the behaviour that relates to the control flow specified in the task bodies; for which we provide Event-B semantics. We developed a case study [7] of a Heating Controller to validate the code generation approach. The case study is an analogue of many embedded systems, where inputs from the environment are received and processed, and may have some effect in the environment caused by its outputs.

2   An Overview of Event-B

The Event-B method [1] was developed by J.R. Abrial, and uses set-theory, predicate logic and refinement to model discrete systems. The basic structural elements of Event-B models are contexts and machines. Contexts are used to describe the static aspects of a system, using sets and constants; the relationships between them are specified in the axioms clause. Machines are able to *see* Contexts; the content of a Context is visible and accessible to a machine. Machines are used to describe the dynamic aspects of a system, in the form of state variables, and guarded events, which update state. Safety properties are specified using the invariants clause. The invariants give rise to proof obligations, which are generated automatically by the tool; a large number of the proof obligations may be discharged without user intervention by auto-provers. Where auto-provers fail to discharge proof obligations, the user guides the interactive prover. They proceed by suggesting strategies, and sub-goals in the form of hypotheses, in the endeavour to complete the proof. Refinement is used to show that concrete models satisfy the safety properties of their abstract counterparts.

A fragment of an Event-B specification is shown in Fig. 1. The specification has variables, which are typed in the **invariant**. Invariants also describe desired safety properties. The event declares two parameters *tm1* and *tm2*. These are typed in the guard clause, following the **where** keyword. The third guard describes an enabling condition for the event. When the value of $avt < cttm2$ the event is enabled, and the updates described in the actions may take place. Actions may contain deterministic or non-deterministic assignments, or do-nothing (skip); but non-deterministic modelling constructs are removed by the time we reach the implementation level specification. In Fig. 1 the action assigns TRUE to the variable *hsc*.

```
                                    event TurnON_Heat_Source
     machine HCtrl_M0               any tm1 tm2
     sees HC_CONTEXT                where
     variables avt stm1 hsc cttm2...   tm1 ∈ ℤ
     invariants                        tm2 ∈ ℤ
        avt ∈ ℤ                        avt < cttm2
        stm1 ∈ ℤ                    then
           . . .                       hsc := TRUE
                                    end
```

Fig. 1. Example of Textual Event-B

3   An Overview of Tasking Event-B

Tasking Event-B is an extension to Event-B, but includes some restrictions to ensure the code is implementable. An Event-B operational semantics underpins the extension. As a means of verifying consistency between tasking Event-B and higher-level abstractions, the Tasking Event-B can be translated to a standard Event-B representation. Then using the Rodin tool we can show that this generated model refines the abstract development.

During the development, before the tasking Event-B stage, we use model decomposition to tackle complexity. The Rodin tool supports different approaches to decomposition; here we use shared event decomposition [8,9]. In section 4.1 we provide a more detailed picture of how an abstract model is decomposed into its sub-models. This decomposition approach results in a partitioning of the system whereby variables are distributed over decomposed machines. A machine has access to variables of another machine using pairs of synchronized events. Synchronized events allow machines to communicate using parameters; they model atomic access to variables residing in another machine. This synchronization approach is described in more detail in [10]. In order to keep track of the synchronizations, the Rodin tool produces a composition component [11] during the decomposition process.

In our approach controllers can be comprised of a number of tasks and, rather than allowing direct communication between controller tasks, we use a shared machine to encapsulate the shared data. This means that synchronizations are taking place between tasking machines and the shared machine. This structure is illustrated in Fig. 2, which describes the relationships between the components of an Event-B development, tasking Event-B and the generated Ada code. In the Tasking Event-B layer, machines are identified as AutoTask, Environ, or Shared. AutoTask Machines model *controller* tasks in the implementation level, and are implemented using Ada tasks. Shared Machines model encapsulated shared objects, and are implemented by protected objects. Environ Machines model the environment, and are implemented using Ada tasks.

An example of an AutoTask Machine, from our case study [7,12], is shown in Fig. 3. It is a descendant of the fragment shown in Fig. 1, following a number of refinement and decomposition steps. The machine of Fig. 3 is an implementation

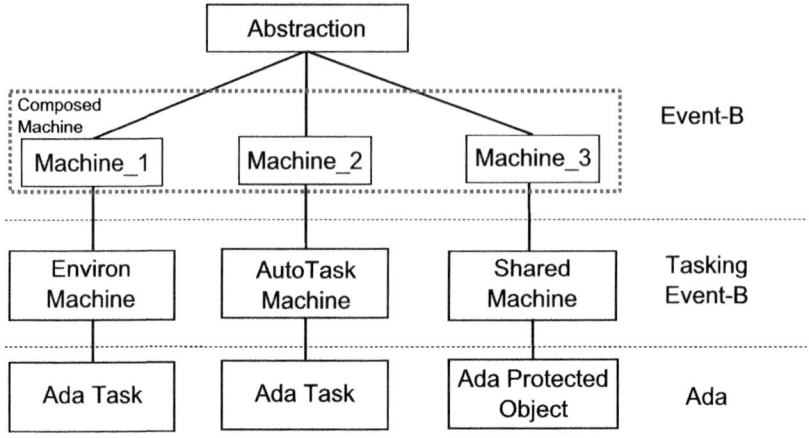

Fig. 2. Heating Controller Artefacts

level refinement, as indicated by the *autotask* annotation. As a convention, we prefix *event* names of the *environ machine* with **EN**, the *shared machine* with **SO**, and *temperature controller* with **TC**. We specify some tasking features such as the task type (e.g. periodic, triggered, one-shot, and repeating); the priority, and the task body. A main feature of the tasking level specification is the task body; this is used to specify flow control aspects of the task, with respect to the events that already reside in the machine. The task body may contain clauses, such as sequence, loop, and branch; and uses a programming-style syntax, e.g. ;, **do**, **if** and event names. Notice that there is no explicit use of a synchronization construct in the task body, we only refer to events that are local to the tasking machine. The code generator tool uses the composition component, mentioned previously, to find any synchronizations (if they exist) and then generates the implementations. Synchronizations between AutoTasks and the Shared machine are implemented using protected procedures. Synchronizations between Auto-Task and Environ machines are implemented as rendezvous, or direct memory access as required. A machine's events can model local (wrt the machine) state updates, subprograms, or branching and looping constructs. As indicated earlier, protected procedure calls are modelled using synchronized events in the task body; this is used when two machines communicate. If an event just updates local state, then updates are mapped to assignment clauses in the target, rather than incurring the overhead of a subprogram call. An *Output* construct is provided to allow text output to a console during simulation.

In the final, deployable system, inter-task communication can be prohibited. The main driver for this restriction is that we wish to generate safe multi-tasking code which is compliant with the Ravenscar subset of Ada [13]. We may relax this restriction, for environment tasks, to simulate the environment.

```
machine Temp_Ctrl_TaskImpl
is autoTask
refines Temp_Ctrl_Task
variables avt, cttm2, hsc, . . .

tasktype periodic(250)
priority 5
taskbody is
    . . .
    TCGet_Target_Temperature2;
    - - ||ₑ SOGet_Target_Temperature2
    if TCTurnON_Heat_Source
    else TCTurnOFF_Heat_Source;
    . . .
```

```
event TCTurnOn_Heat_Source
refines TurnOn_Heat_Source
when
    avt < cttm2
then
    hsc := TRUE
end

event TCGet_Target_Temperature2
refines Get_Target_Temperature2
any tm
where tm ∈ ℤ
then cttm2 := tm
end
```

Fig. 3. An Fragment of an AutoTask Machine

```
event SOGet_Target_Temperature2
refines Get_Target_Temperature2
any tm
where tm ∈ ℤ
        tm = cttm
then skip
end
```

Fig. 4. A Synchronizing Event in the Shared Object

4   Case Study

This section makes use of model and code fragments from a case study [7] to illustrate the translation from Tasking Event-B to Ada. We begin with some background to the case study, introducing the variables of the model. We will look at just one controller task, the temperature controller, which polls two temperature sensor values $ts1$ and $ts2$, in the environment. Their average value avt is calculated and displayed. If the average temperature is lower than the target temperature $cttm2$, the controller will turn on the heater source using Heat Source Switch $hsc := TRUE$, otherwise this switch will be turned off by the controller, $hsc := FALSE$. The status of the heater itself is monitored, and has an over-temperature ota alarm.

The development process starts with an abstract specification, followed by two successive refinements. We then decompose the model into two parts, one representing the environment, and the other representing the remainder of the system. The refinement process continues after the first decomposition in order to arrive at a concrete level suitable for implementation.

4.1   Event-B Development

At the top we show the most abstract model of the system where we specify
the system's main functionality, such as modelling the increase/decrease of the
target temperature, polling of the temperature sensors, calculation of the average
temperature, and activation of the heat source and alarms. In the first refinement
we introduce sensing and actuation. Sensing events model polling of the state of
the increase/decrease buttons, the temperature sensors, and the heater sensor.
Actuating events model the updates of target, and current temperature displays.
We also model actuation occurring as a result of controller decisions, such as
turning the heat on/off, and activating the various alarms. We decompose our
model in two stages; we first separate the controller subsystem, the part of the
system that should be implemented, from its surrounding environment. In the
second stage we decompose the controller subsystem; we identify three controller
tasks, and a protected object. The structure of the decomposition is visible in
the diagram in Fig. 5. Following decomposition we add an additional refinement,
the Tasking Event-B Layer. This refinement layer is used for our implementation
level specification. It is necessary to use refinement here, since the automatically
generated files (from the decomposition tool) cannot be modified.

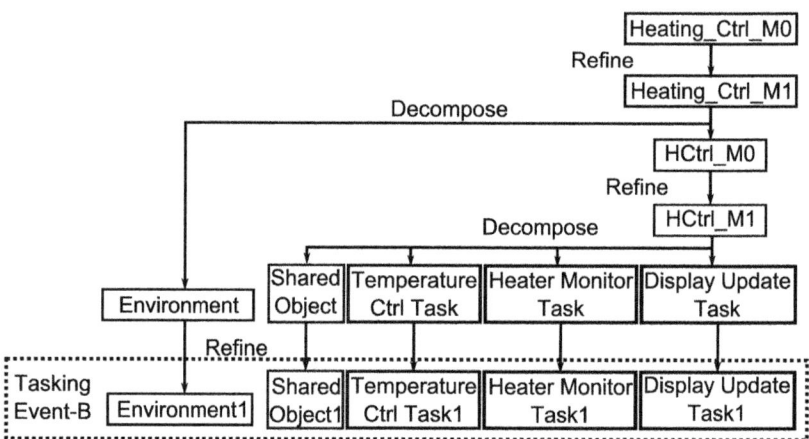

Fig. 5. The Development Approach

4.2   Guiding Code Generation with Tasking Event-B

In the previous step we decomposed into five machines; one modelling the environment, one modelling each of the three controller tasks, and one modelling
the protected object. We should now add the Tasking Event-B annotations to
guide code generation. The first step is to use annotations to identify the machines as being an AutoTask, Environ or Shared machine. With Environ, or
AutoTask machines, we also add a task body specification. The task body is
used to constrain the Event-B model, in such a way that it can be implemented

using programming constructs, such as sequence, branch and subprogram calls. The generated code is viewed as an implementation of a schedule of events.

In the discussion that follows, we use the temperature control task event *Temp_Ctrl_TaskImpl* from Fig. 3, as an example. We describe how we use Tasking Event-B to specify implementation details, that is, how the controller interacts with the environment. The full task body of the *Temp_Ctrl_TaskImpl* AutoTask is shown in Fig. 6, it includes a brief description of the activities performed. In (1) the temperature controller uses the TCSense_Temperatures event; in (2) the average temperature is calculated, and so on. The comment identifies the synchronizing event, which is presented here for clarity. The task body gives rise to the Ada code show in Fig. 7. We will look at the translated code in more detail, later in the section.

```
TCSense_Temperatures;                          - -(1)(‖ₑ ENSense_Temperatures)
TCCalculate_Average_Temperature;               - -(2)
TCDisplay_Current_Temperature;                 - -(3)(‖ₑ ENDisplay_Current_Temperature)
TCGet_Target_Temperature2;                     - -(4)(‖ₑ SOGet_Target_Temperature2)
if TCTurnON_Heat_Source end                    - -(5)
    else TCTurnOFF_Heat_Source end;
TCSet_Heat_Source_State;                        - -(6)(‖ₑ SOSet_Heat_Source_State)
TCActuate_Heat_Source;                          - -(7)(‖ₑ ENActuate_Heat_Source)
if TCSwitchOn_OverHeat_Alarm end               - -(8)
    else TCSwitchOff_OverHeat_Alarm end;
TCActuate_OverHeat_Alarm;                       - -(9)(‖ₑ ENActuate_OverHeat_Alarm)
```

    - -(1) poll the $ts1$ and $ts2$ temperature sensors.
    - -(2) calculate the average temperature.
    - -(3) update ctd, the displayed temperature.
    - -(4) get the target temperature from the protected object.
    - -(5) branching choice: set the heater on or off flag in the task.
    - -(6) set the heat source active flag in the protected object.
    - -(7) update $ahsa$, the activate heat source flag.
    - -(8) a branching choice: set activate overheat alarm flag in the task.
    - -(9) update $aota$, the activate overheat alarm flag.

Fig. 6. The Temp_Ctrl_TaskImpl Task Body

The development proceeds by adding annotations to events. In Fig. 8 we see the *sensing* annotation being used to indicate that an event is used in a sensing role. The *sensing* keyword is used with both the *TCSense_Temperatures* and *ENSense_Temperatures* events. This indicates that the events model polling of the environment; the *actuating* keyword is similar, except that it indicates that events update values is the environment. Now, returning to the translated code, arising from clause (1) of Fig. 6. It results in the following Ada program statement:

Envir1Impl.ENSense_Temperatures(stm1, stm2);

```
task body Temp_Ctrl_TaskImpl is
   ...
   procedure TCCalculate_Average_Temperature is
   begin
      avt := ((stm1 + stm2) / 2);
   end;
   begin
   ...
   Envir1Impl.ENSense_Temperatures(stm1, stm2);              -- (1)
   TCCalculate_Average_Temperature;                          -- (2)
   Envir1Impl.ENDisplay_Current_Temperature(avt);           -- (3)
   shared_object1implInst.SOGet_Target_Temperature2(cttm2);  -- (4)
   if(avt < cttm2) then                                      -- (5)
      hsc := TRUE;
   else
      hsc := FALSE;
   end if;
   shared_object1implInst.SOSet_Heat_Source_State(hsc);      -- (6)
   Envir1Impl.ENActuate_Heat_Source(hsc);                    -- (7)
   if(avt > Max) then                                        -- (8)
      ota := TRUE;
   else
      ota := FALSE;
   end if;
   Envir1Impl.ENActuate_OverHeat_Alarm(ota);                 -- (9)
   ...
end Temp_Ctrl_TaskImpl;
```

Fig. 7. Implementation of Temp_Ctrl_TaskImpl Task Body

```
event TCSense_Temperatures is sensing        event ENSense_Temperatures is sensing
refines TCSense_Temperatures                 refines ENSense_Temperatures
any t1 t2                                     any t1 t2
when                                          when
   t1 ∈ ℤ                                        t1 ∈ ℤ
   t2 ∈ ℤ                                        t2 ∈ ℤ
then                                             t1 = ts1
   stm1 := t1                                     t2 = ts2
   stm2 := t2                                  then
end                                              skip
                                              end
```

Fig. 8. Synchronization of a Sensing Event

Envir1Impl is the name of the environment task, and *ENSense_Temperatures* is the name of the task entry. The entry call implements a pair of synchronized events. In the most abstract model (not shown in this paper) *stm*1 keeps track of the sensed temperature, *ts*1, using an assignment *stm*1 := *ts*1. In the decomposition, the two temperature sensing events synchronize to achieve the same result; this is implemented as an entry call. We now describe the relationship between the implementation and the model. The variable *stm*1, appears in the action of the *TCSense_Temperatures* event, see Fig: 8. In the translation, the event parameter, *t*1 is replaced by the variable, *stm*1, and passed as an actual parameter in the entry call. The entry is implemented as an Ada *accept* statement in the *Envir1Impl* task, see Fig. 9. The monitored variable *ts*1 appears in the guard of the *ENSense_Temperatures* event, of Fig: 8, and translates to an **out** parameter in the entry signature. Note that in this case the event guard is translated to an assignment in the implementation. When returning from the entry call, the value held by the *out* parameter is assigned to the actual parameter; that is, *stm*1 := *t*1, in our example. Since *t*1 = *ts*1 we have *stm*1 := *ts*1, as required.

```
accept ENSense_Temperatures(t1: out Integer; t2: out Integer) do
    t1 := ts1;
    t2 := ts2;
end ENSense_Temperatures;
```

Fig. 9. Implementation of ENSense_Temperatures

The translation of events of shared machines is similar, except that we implement the machines as protected objects with procedures. The translation of synchronized events is otherwise the same, with respect to the mapping of event parameters to subroutine parameters.

5   Writing Directly to Memory Locations

So far we have described an approach which facilitates interation with the environment using rendezvous. However, we also provide an alternative approach, where the developer specifies some memory locations to read from, and write to. We provide a feature which allows developers to annotate event parameters with address information; using the *addr* keyword. Use of the *addr* address keyword is shown in Fig. 10. We specify a memory location, and its number base. In the example, *t*1 is given the address *ef*14 in base 16. We can see, on the right of the figure, the generated Ada code. The parameter *t*1 has been mapped to the integer variable declaration t1: Integer. The address of the variable has been set using the following statement, the **pragma** Atomic(t1) statement is used to indicate that any access to *t*1 must occur atomically. In the *TCSense_Temperatures* procedure implementation of Fig. 10, the variable *t*1 appears on the right-hand side of the assignment. When the statement is executed, the value is read from the memory location accessed by $t1$, and assigned to $stm1$. This approach does differ from the entry approach described in the previous section. Entry calls are atomic, whereas we are using non-atomic statements. For this reason the environment must be responsible for ensuring that the implementation of sensing events with multiple read actions, and actuating events with multiple write actions, are performed atomically (we do not envisage mixing sensing and actuating in a single event).

```
                                     task body Temp_Ctrl_TaskImpl is
                                         stm1 : Integer := 0;
                                         stm2 : Integer := 0;
                                         . . .
                                     procedure TCSense_Temperatures is
                                         t1 : Integer;
event TCSense_Temperatures               for t1'Address
is sensing                                   use System'To_Address(16#ef14#);
refines TCSense_Temperatures             pragma Atomic(t1);
any                                      t2 : Integer;
    addr(16,ef14) t1                     for t2'Address
    addr(16,ef18) t2                         use System'To_Address(16#ef18#);
when                                     pragma Atomic(t2);
    t1 ∈ ℤ                           begin
    t2 ∈ ℤ                               stm1 := t1;
then                                     stm2 := t2;
    stm1 := t1                       end;
    stm2 := t2                           . . .
end                                  begin
                                         loop
                                             delay until nextTime;
                                             TCSense_Temperatures;
                                             . . .
                                         end loop;
                                     end Temp_Ctrl_TaskImpl;
```

Fig. 10. Addressed Variables: Specification and Implementation

Using a combination of the approaches described in this paper, we can simulate interaction with the environment in the early stages of development, using entry calls.. Later in the development we can choose to read from, and write to, memory directly. To do this we simply add the address information to the relevant variables. We also have the option of the environment simulation reading from, and writing to memory.

6   Tooling

The Rodin tool [5], based on the Eclipse Platform [14], is a complete development environment for Event-B. We have extended the methodology and tools to add implementation level specification, using Tasking Event-B. Tasking Event-B and the code generators are fully integrated into the Rodin toolset, see Fig 11. When a development is ready for translation to code we have a simple pop-up menu with translation options. The code generators use the Tasking Event-B model, and a two-step process, see Fig. 12. The first step generates a Common Language Model (CLM); the CLM is an abstraction of commonly used software constructs. The abstract tasks and shared objects of the CLM are then used in the translation to Ada. The Ada translator generates the main procedure file, and specification and body files, in a directory ready for compilation. We have been successfully compiling and executing the generated code, using the GPS

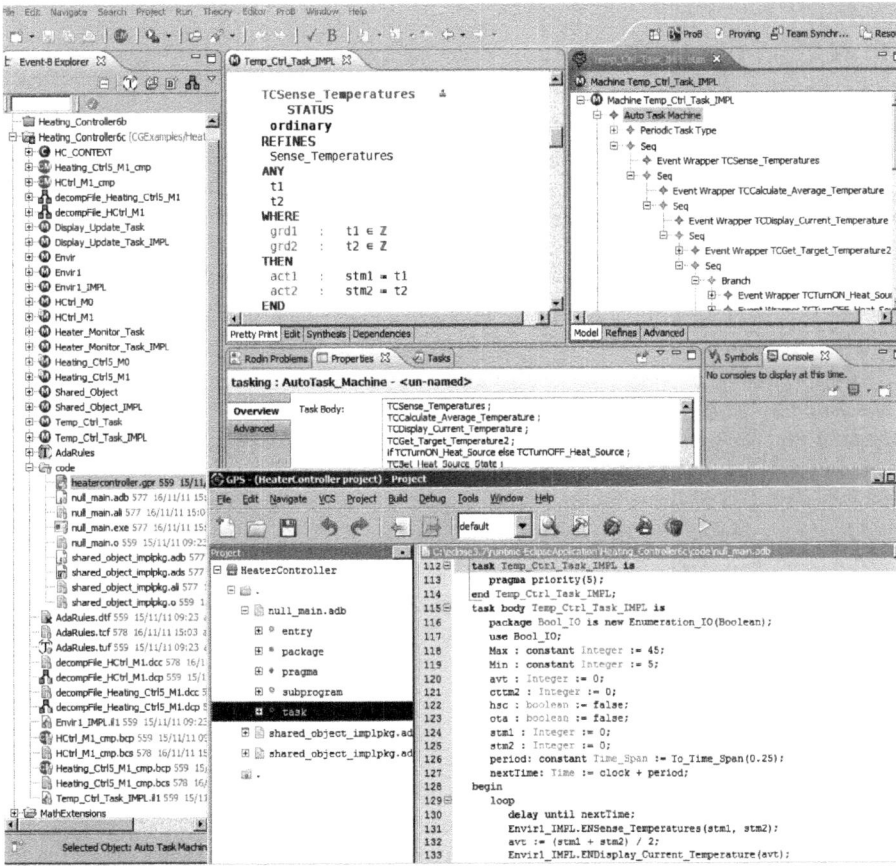

Fig. 11. Code Generation Tools

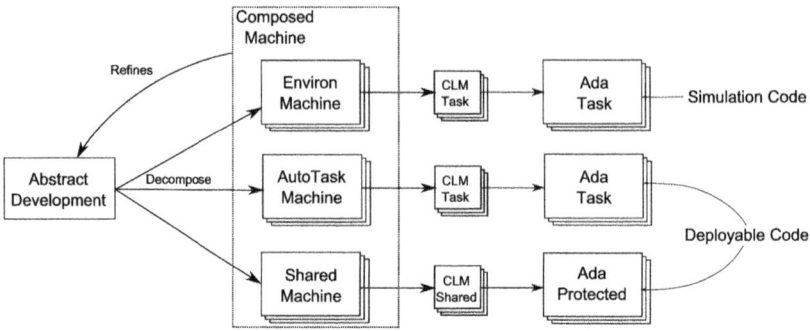

Fig. 12. Two-Step Code Generation

tool from AdaCore [15]. The only additional effort has been the creation of the project file; this may also be automated in the future.

7   Conclusions

In this paper we have described our methodology and tools for linking Event-B, through the use of the Tasking Event-B extension, to Ada code. We relate the Event-B modelling artefacts to their Ada counterparts; and, using the case study, we explain the relationship between the modelling abstraction and implementation in more detail. We have explained how Event-B is augmented with Tasking Event-B annotations, these are used to guide the code generator to produce code. For example, annotations identify the role of the machines in the implementation; a machine may be an AutoTask machine, Environ machine or Shared machine. AutoTask and Environ machines have a task body in which we are able to specify flow of control. This is done through the use of the sequence, branch and loop constructs. We make use of the tool-driven decomposition approach, to structure the development. This allows us to partition the system in a modular fashion, reflecting Ada implementation constructs. Decomposition is also the mechanism for breaking up complex systems to make modelling and proof more tractable. As part of the specification we indicate which of the events take part in sensing and actuating roles; we describe the relationship between event parameters, and their role in the implementation of sensing and actuating events. We extend the sensing and actuating features to allow specification of direct reads from, and writes to memory.

In a wider context, the work we have undertaken is to improve the approach for modelling of, and providing implementations for, multi-tasking embedded control systems. In this sense the case study can be seen as representative of the style of interactions, using sensing and actuation, in a domain where controllers are continuously monitoring and reacting to the environment. This work provides a basis for future developments in our sphere of interest, and will continue in the Advance project [16], and others. The Tasking Event-B control flow language has been given Event-B semantics, although we do not formalize every aspect of Tasking Event-B, such as modelling timing, or priority. With regard to modelling time, several projects are under way, investigating timing related issues [17]. We can use the Tasking Event-B model to generate an Event-B model of the implementation, using the Event-B semantics. We can show that this model refines the abstract development, thus showing that the properties of the abstract development are satisfied.

7.1   Related Work

The closest comparable work is that of Classical-B's code generation approach [18] using B0 [19]. B0 consists of concrete programming constructs, these map to programming constructs in target programming languages. B0 can be translated to Ada, but there is no support for concurrency. Code generation of B to embedded systems was carried out in [20], where the implementation results in sequential code. Some consideration is given, in [21], to the use of an Event-B-like syntax for analysis of multi-tasking programs. By comparison, we use the task body for scheduling, rather than taking a purely interrupt driven approach; we have yet to incorporate modelling of interrupts in Tasking Event-B.

VDM++ [22] may be used to generate code, it is an object-oriented extension to VDM-SL formal specification language. It has been used to model real-time systems, see [23]. The paper describes a controller and environment model similar to our own. They define an abstract operational semantics to describe additional modelling features, whereas we use Event-B semantics. They model time, and asynchronous communication, whereas we do not address these issues in the work presented here. However, the specification of timing properties is of great interest to us; and work has been done to address the issue in Event-B such as [24], or more recently [17]. Scade [25] is an industrial tool for formally modelling embedded systems. It provides a graphical approach to specification, and has a certified code generator. It has a similar control flow approach to that of UML-B statemachines [26].

References

1. Abrial, J.R.: Modeling in Event-B: System and Software Engineering. Cambridge University Press (2010)
2. Russo, A.: Formal Methods in Industry: The State of Practice of Formal Methods in South America and Far East (2009)
3. Metayer, C., Clabaut, M.: DIR 41 Case Study. In: [27], p. 357
4. Taft, T., Tucker, R., Brukardt, R., Ploedereder, E. (eds.): Consolidated Ada reference manual: language and standard libraries. Springer-Verlag New York, Inc., New York (2002)
5. RODIN Project, http://rodin.cs.ncl.ac.uk
6. The DEPLOY Project Team: Project Website, http://www.deploy-project.eu/
7. Edmunds, A., Rezazedah, A.: Event-B Wiki: Development of a Heating Controller System, http://wiki.event-b.org/index.php/
Development_of_a_Heating_Controller_System

8. Butler, M.: Decomposition Structures for Event-B. In: Leuschel, M., Wehrheim, H. (eds.) IFM 2009. LNCS, vol. 5423, pp. 20–38. Springer, Heidelberg (2009)
9. Silva, R., Pascal, C., Hoang, T., Butler, M.: Decomposition Tool for Event-B. Software: Practice and Experience (2010)
10. Edmunds, A., Butler, M.: Tasking Event-B: An Extension to Event-B for Generating Concurrent Code. In: PLACES 2011 (2011)
11. Silva, R.: Towards the Composition of Specifications in Event-B. In: B 2011 (2011)
12. Edmunds, A., Rezazedah, A.: Event-B Project Archives: Tasking Event-B Tutorial. University of Southampton, http://deploy-eprints.ecs.soton.ac.uk/304/
13. Burns, A., Dobbing, B., Vardanega, T.: Guide for the use of the Ada Ravenscar Profile in high integrity systems. Ada Lett. XXIV, 1–74 (2004)
14. The Eclipse Project: Eclipse - an Open Development Platform, http://www.eclipse.org/
15. AdaCore: GNAT Programming Studio, http://www.adacore.com/home/
16. The Advance Project Team: The Advance Project, http://www.advance-ict.eu
17. Sarshogh, M., Butler, M.: Specification and Refinement of Discrete Timing Properties in Event-B. In: AVoCS 2011 (2011)
18. Abrial, J.: The B Book - Assigning Programs to Meanings. Cambridge University Press (1996)
19. ClearSy System Engineering: The B Language Reference Manual (Version 4.6 edn.)
20. Bert, D., Boulmé, S., Potet, M., Requet, A., Voisin, L.: Adaptable Translator of B Specifications to Embedded C Programs. In: Araki, K., Gnesi, S., Mandrioli, D. (eds.) FME 2003. LNCS, vol. 2805, pp. 94–113. Springer, Heidelberg (2003)
21. Stoddart, B., Cansell, D., Zeyda, F.: Modelling and Proof Analysis of Interrupt Driven Scheduling. In: Julliand, J., Kouchnarenko, O. (eds.) B 2007. LNCS, vol. 4355, pp. 155–170. Springer, Heidelberg (2006)
22. CSK Systems Corporation: (The VDM++ Language Manual)
23. Verhoef, M., Larsen, P.G., Hooman, J.: Modeling and Validating Distributed Embedded Real-Time Systems with VDM++. In: Misra, J., Nipkow, T., Sekerinski, E. (eds.) FM 2006. LNCS, vol. 4085, pp. 147–162. Springer, Heidelberg (2006)
24. Degerlund, F., Grönblom, R., Sere, K.: Code Generation and Scheduling of Event-B Models (2011)
25. Berry, G.: Synchronous Design and Verification of Critical Embedded Systems Using SCADE and Esterel. In: Leue, S., Merino, P. (eds.) FMICS 2007. LNCS, vol. 4916, p. 2. Springer, Heidelberg (2008)
26. Snook, C., Butler, M.: UML-B: A Plug-in for the Event-B Tool Set. In: [27], p. 344
27. Börger, E., Butler, M., Bowen, J.P., Boca, P. (eds.): ABZ 2008. LNCS, vol. 5238. Springer, Heidelberg (2008)

Augmenting Formal Development
with Use Case Reasoning

Alexei Iliasov

Newcastle University, UK

Abstract. State-based methods for correct-by-construction software development rely on a combination of safety constraints and refinement obligations to demonstrate design correctness. One prominent challenge, especially in an industrial setting, is ensuring that a design is adequate: requirements compliant and fit for purpose. The paper presents a technique for augmenting state-based, refinement-driven formal developments with reasoning about use case scenarios; in particular, it discusses a way for the derivation of formal verification conditions from a high-level, diagrammatic language of use cases, and the methodological role of use cases in a formal modelling process.

1 Introduction

Use cases are a popular technique for the validation of software systems and constitute an important part of requirements engineering process. It is an essential part of the description of functional requirements of a system. There exists a vast number of notations and methods supporting the integration of use cases in a development process (see [8] for a structured survey of use case notations). With few exceptions, the overall aim is the derivation of test inputs for the testing of the final product. We propose to exploit use cases in the course of a stepwise formal development process for the engineering of correct-by-construction systems. We build upon the previous work to add the notion of use case refinement. The results open a way for some interesting methodological and tooling advances such as use case driven model refinement and the automation of use case construction via the mechanisation of use refinement rules.

In this work, we more carefully study the meaning of writing a use case for a formal specification. Previously, we have stated that the semantics of a model with a use case is simply the collection of all the theorems that must be demonstrated for the model correctness and the consistency of the use case and the model. This fits well into the picture of a proof-based semantics. However, from the discussions with the industrial partners of the IST Deploy Project [11], we have realised that the answer is not entirely satisfactory. It does not relate to the concepts familar from requirements engineering stage and does not provide a ground to judge about the appropriateness of the technique in an application to a given problem. We thus consider another form of semantics to supplement the existing proof semantics.

M. Brorsson and L.M. Pinho (Eds.): Ada-Europe 2012, LNCS 7308, pp. 133–146, 2012.

MACHINE M
  SEES Context
  VARIABLES v
  INVARIANT $I(c, s, v)$
  INITIALISATION $R(c, s, v')$
  EVENTS
    E_1 = **any** vl **where** $g(c, s, vl, v)$ **then** $S(c, s, vl, v, v')$ **end**
    $\ldots$
END

Fig. 1. Event-B machine structure

2   Background

The section briefly introduces modelling method Event-B and its extension for expressing use cases.

2.1   Event-B

The basis of our discussion is a formalism called Event-B[2]. It belongs to a family of state-based modelling languages that represent a design as a combination of state (a vector of variables) and state transformations (computations updating variables).

An Event-B development starts with the creation of a very abstract specification. A cornerstone of the Event-B method is the stepwise development that facilitates a gradual design of a system implementation through a number of correctness-preserving *refinement* steps. The general form of an Event-B model (or *machine*) is shown in Figure 1. Such a model encapsulates a local state (program variables) and provides operations on the state. The actions (called *events*) are characterised by a list of local variables (parameters) vl, a state predicate g called *event guard*, and a next-state relation S called *substitution* or event *action*.

Event guard g defines the condition when an event is *enabled*. Relation S is given as a generalised substitution statement [1] and is either deterministic ($x := 2$) or non-deterministic update of model variables. The latter kind comes in two notations: selection of a value from a set, written as $x :\in \{2, 3\}$; and a relational constraint on the next state v', e.g., $x :\mid x' \in \{2, 3\}$.

The **INVARIANT** clause contains the properties of the system, expressed as state predicates, that must be preserved during system execution. These define the *safe states* of a system. In order for a model to be consistent, invariant preservation is formally demonstrated. Data types, constants and relevant axioms are defined in a separate component called *context*.

Model correctness is demonstrated by generating and discharging *proof obligations* - theorems in the first order logic. There are proof obligations for model consistency and for a refinement link - the forward simulation relation - between the pair of *abstract* and *concrete* models. More details on Event-B, its semantics, method and applications may be found in [2] and also on the Event-B community website[5]. A concise discussion of the Event-B proof obligations is given in [7].

2.2   The Use Case Extension of Event-B

The approach to use case reasoning is based on our previous work on a graphical notation for expressing event ordering constraints [10,9]. The extensions is realised as a plug in to the Event-B modelling tool set - the Rodin Platform [13] - and smoothly integrates into the Event-B modelling process. It provides a modelling environment for working with graph-like diagrams describing event ordering properties. In the simplest case, a node of such graph is an event of the associated Event-B machine; an edge is a statement about the relative properties of the connected nodes/events. There are three main edge kinds: **ena**, **dis** and **fis**. Mathematically, they are defined as follows as relations over Event-B events.

$$U = \{f \mapsto g \mid \varnothing \subset f \subseteq S \times S \wedge \varnothing \subset g \subseteq S \times S\}$$
$$\mathbf{ena} = \{f \mapsto g \mid f \mapsto g \in U \wedge \operatorname{ran}(f) \subseteq \operatorname{dom}(g)\}$$
$$\mathbf{dis} = \{f \mapsto g \mid f \mapsto g \in U \wedge \operatorname{ran}(f) \cap \operatorname{dom}(g) = \varnothing\}$$
$$\mathbf{fis} = \{f \mapsto g \mid f \mapsto g \in U \wedge \operatorname{ran}(f) \cap \operatorname{dom}(g) \neq \varnothing\}$$

where $f \subseteq S \times S$ is a relational model of an Event-B event (mathematically, an event is a next-state relation). These definitions are converted into *consistency* proof obligations. For instance, if in a use case graph there appears an edge connecting events b and h one would have to prove the following theorem (see [10] for a justification).

$$\forall v, v', p_b \cdot I(v) \wedge G_b(p_b, v) \wedge R_b(p_b, v, v') \Rightarrow \exists p_h \cdot G_h(p_h, v') \tag{1}$$

A use case diagram is only defined in an association with one Event-B model, it does not exist on its own. The use case plug in automatically generates all the relevant proof obligations. A change in a diagram or its Event-B model leads to the re-computation of all affected proof obligations. These proof obligations are dealt with, like all other proof obligation types, by a combination of automated provers and interactive proof. Like in the proofs of model consistency and refinement, the feedback from an undischarged use case proof obligation may often be interpreted as a suggestion of a diagram change such as an additional assumptions or assertion - predicate annotations on graph edges that propagate properties along the graph structure. The example in the next section demonstrates how such annotations enable the proof of a non-trivial property.

The use case tool offers a rich visual notation. The basic element of a diagram is an event, visually depicted as a node (in Figure 2, f and g represent events). Event definition (its parameters, guard and action) is imported from the associated Event-B model. One special case of node is skip event, denoted by a grey node colour (Figure 2, 5). Event relations **ena**, **dis**, **fis** are represented by edges connecting nodes ((Figure 2, 1-3)). Depending on how a diagram is drawn, edges are said to be in *and* or *or* relation (Figure 2, 7-8). New events are derived from model events by strengthening their guards (a case of symmetric assumption and assertion) (Figure 2, 6). Edges may be annotated with constraining predicates inducing assertion and assumption derived events (Figure 2, 4).

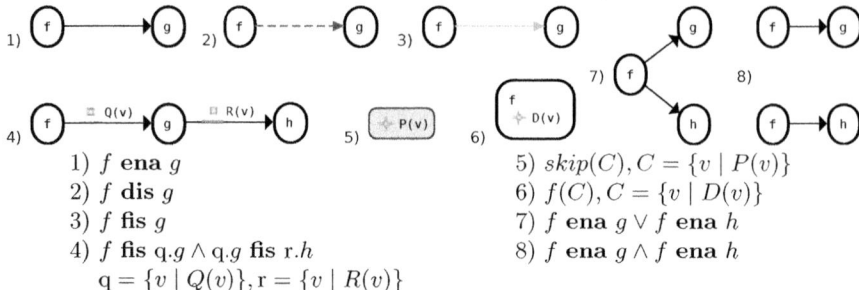

1) f **ena** g

2) f **dis** g

3) f **fis** g

4) f **fis** q.$g \land$ q.g **fis** r.h
   $\quad$ q $= \{v \mid Q(v)\}$, r $= \{v \mid R(v)\}$

5) $skip(C), C = \{v \mid P(v)\}$

6) $f(C), C = \{v \mid D(v)\}$

7) f **ena** $g \lor f$ **ena** h

8) f **ena** $g \land f$ **ena** h

Fig. 2. A summary of the core use case notation and its interpretation

Not shown on Figure 2 are nodes for the initialisation event start (circle), implicit deadlock event stop (filled circle) and nodes for container elements such as loop (used in the coming example). To avoid visual clutter, the repeating parts of a diagram may be declared separately as diagram *aspects*[10]. Aspects are used in the diagrams from Sections 5.4 and 5.6.

2.3   Small Example

As an illustration of what constitutes a use case we consider a small example concerned with the construction of a function computing the greatest common devisor (GCD) of two numbers. The properties characterise the GCD function $gcd \in \mathbb{N} \times \mathbb{N} \to \mathbb{N}$.

$$\forall a, b \cdot a, b \in \mathbb{N} \land a > b \Rightarrow gcd(a, b) = gcd(a - b, b)$$
$$\forall a, b \cdot a, b \in \mathbb{N} \land b > a \Rightarrow gcd(a, b) = gcd(a, b - a)$$
$$\forall a \cdot a \in \mathbb{N} \Rightarrow gcd(a, a) = a$$

The Event-B part of the example is a simple and abstract model. It defines four variables and four operations on these variables.

MACHINE gcd
$\quad$**VARIABLES** $x1, x2, y1, y2$
$\quad$**INVARIANT** $x1 \in \mathbb{N} \land x2 \in \mathbb{N} \land y1 \in \mathbb{N} \land y2 \in \mathbb{N}$
$\quad$**EVENTS**
$\quad\quad$copy1 $=$ **begin** $y1 := x1$ **end**
$\quad\quad$copy2 $=$ **begin** $y2 := x2$ **end**
$\quad\quad$sub1 $ =$ **when** $y1 > y2$ **then** $y1 := y1 - y2$ **end**
$\quad\quad$sub2 $ =$ **when** $y1 < y2$ **then** $y2 := y2 - y1$ **end**
END

With a use case diagram we prove that this Event-B model contains the behaviour that the realises the GCD function. More specifically, the following use case digram makes a provable statement that, starting with some two positive numbers, a certain sequence of event executions results in the computation of the GCD of the numbers.

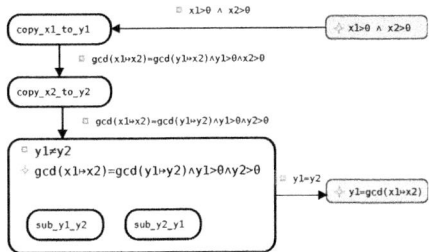

In the diagram above, rounded rectangles are events, arrows represent **ena** edges. Grey rectangles are assertions or, depending upon the view point, assumptions. The large rounded box is a structured a loop. It contains two events as a loop body (semantically, a choice of the two events) and is annotated with a loop condition and invariant. The only constraint that must be provided by a user is the loop invariant $gcd(x1 \mapsto x2) = gcd(y1 \mapsto y2) \wedge y1 > 0 \wedge y2 > 0$. All other edge constraints are then filled in automatically by a modelling assistant. It is certainly not difficult to prove the same property as a refinement link to one step computation of gcd. There is, however, a distinct advantage in using a graphical notation to formulate properties of event orderings, especially if these are interpreted as use case scenarious.

3   Use Case Semantics

It is possible to define the trace semantics of an Event-B machine. This is useful for us since a use case already resembles a record of event sequences. The traces of Event-B machine M are defined in the following way. Consider set S of finite sequences of event identifiers, $S = \mathbb{P}(seq(L))$; here L is set of event identifiers for machine M. Take some sequence $s \in S$; using event declarations from machine M one can convert s into a relation $r(s) \subseteq \Omega \times \Omega$ where Ω is the universe of machine states. Ω is the set of all safe states of a machine: $\Omega = \{v \mid I(v)\}$ where $I(v)$ is the machine invariant. Let $\langle \rangle$, $\langle e \rangle$ and $s \frown t$ signify, correspondingly, an empty sequence, a sequence containing sole element e and sequence concatenation; the procedure to obtain $r(s)$ is then the following.

$$r(\langle \rangle) = \mathrm{id}(\Omega)$$
$$r(t \frown \langle e \rangle) = [e]_R \circ r(t) \qquad (2)$$

where $[e]_R$ is a relational interpretation of an event $e \in L$ and $\circ$ is the relations composition operator: $(f \circ g)(x) = g(f(x))$. Let G_e, F_e and u_e be, respectively, the guard, the body and parameters of event L. Then $[e]_R \equiv \{v \mapsto v' \mid \exists u_e \cdot (G_e(v, u_e) \wedge F_e(v, u_e, v'))\}$. As a special case, the relational form of initialisation is $[\mathrm{INIT}]_R \equiv \mathrm{id}(init)$ where $init \subseteq \Omega$ is the set of vectors of initial values for machine variables; also, the relational form of skip (a stuttering step event of a machine) is $[\mathrm{skip}]_R \equiv \mathrm{id}(\Omega)$. Let us examine sequences s from S. Some of them prescribe event orderings that may not be realised because of the restrictions expressed in event guards; that is, relation $r(s)$ is empty. Some sequences initiate with an event other that initialisation; we shall reject such sequences as we do not know their meaning. What is left is the following set; it defines the traces of machine M:

$$tr(M) = \{s \mid s \in S \wedge t \in S \wedge s = \langle \text{INIT} \rangle \frown t \wedge r(s) \neq \varnothing\} \tag{3}$$

An important property of machine traces is that between any two machine events one could observe, in differing traces, any finite number of implicit skip events. That is, if there is a trace where a is followed by b there must also be a trace where a is followed by skip and then b; another trace where there are two skip's, three skip's and so on. See Chapter 14 in [2] for an explanation why these events are necessary. We record this observation in the following statement.

$$\forall s, t \cdot s \frown t \in tr(M) \Leftrightarrow s \frown \langle \text{skip} \rangle \frown t \in tr(M) \tag{4}$$

The meaning of a use case may now be stated in much clearer terms: *a use case specification defines a set of traces that are guaranteed to be among the traces of a machine*. To justify this claim we first define the traces of a use case and then show that each such trace is to be found in the traces of a machine.

A use case is understood to be a graph $U = (V, E)$ where a node is a tuple $(h, C) \in V$ of an event identifier $h \in L$ and a constraining predicate $C = C(v, u_L)$[1]. For some node $q = (h, C)$, its relational interpretation is $[q]_U \equiv \{v \mapsto v' \mid \exists u_h \cdot G_h(v, u_h) \wedge C(v, u_h) \wedge F_h(v, u_h, v')\}$. For any such node there is a corresponding event:

$$\forall q \cdot q \in V \Rightarrow (\exists e \cdot e \in L \wedge [q]_U \subseteq [e]_R) \tag{5}$$

It is not difficult to see why it is the case. As a witness for the bound variable e we take z such that $\{z\} = \text{prj}_1[\{q\}]$[2]. It trivially holds that $\text{prj}_1[V] \subseteq L$ and thus $z \in L$. Supposing $q = (h, C)$ it then follows that $z = h$ (since, by the definition of projection, $\{h\} = \text{prj}_1[\{(h, C)\}]$). Finally, condition $[q]_U \subseteq [e]_R$ holds as it is evident from the definitions of $[q]_U$ and $[e]_R$.

The link between use case nodes and machine traces may be lifted to event sequence. Consider set $\mathcal{U}$ of all the paths of graph U. From Condition 5 it follows that $\forall u \cdot u \in \mathcal{U} \Rightarrow \text{prj}_1[\text{ran}(u)] \subseteq L$, where $\text{ran}(u)$ is a set of values, nodes from V, contained in sequence u. Let P be a function mapping a sequences of graph nodes into a sequence of event identifiers; P does this by simply removing the constraining predicate C from each element of the first sequence. From Condition 5 and the statement above it then follows that $\forall u \in \mathcal{U} \Rightarrow P(u) \in S$.

Let us now consider what are the edges E of a use case graph. Set E is partitioned into three subsets, one for each kind of event relation: $E = E_e \oplus E_d \oplus E_f$. In the discussion we focus exclusively on E_e edges. Other edges do not contribute yet to the trace semantics. Let us consider subgraph $U^+ = (V, E_e)$.

---

[1] On a use case diagram, predicate C appears in an event node under event name with a star-like icon.

[2] prj_1 is the first projection of a cartesian product.

We claim that each P-projected path u from the set of paths $\mathcal{U}^+$ of the sub-graph is also found among the traces of machine M.

$$\forall u \in \mathcal{U}^+ \Rightarrow P(u) \in tr(M) \tag{6}$$

For $P(u)$ to be an element of $tr(M)$ it must satisfy the following three criteria (see Definition 3): $P(u)$ must be in S, the first element must the initialisation event and relational interpretation of $P(u)$, $r(P(u))$ must be a non-empty relation. The first condition has been discussed above. The second one we take as an assumption, that is, a use case graph containing paths that do not start with initialisation event is considered to be ill-formed. Since, from the Event-B semantics, set $init$ is known to be non-empty, the are only two reason why $r(P(u))$ could be empty: either there is an event in L that is mapped into an empty relation or there is an instance of relational composition of two non-empty relations yielding an empty relation. The former case, an empty relation, is impossible due to the requirement of event feasibility that, for every machine event $e \in L$, guarantees that there is a non-empty set of next states for this event: $I(v) \wedge G_e(v, u_e) \Rightarrow \exists v' \cdot F_e(v, u_e, v')$. Juxtaposition of this property with the definition of $[e]_R$ implies that for every event $e \in L$ it holds that $[e]_R \neq \varnothing$.

The latter case is also impossible due to the properties of a use case diagram. Let us consider two events, a and b, such that a **ena** b, in other words, there is an edge in graph U^+ connecting nodes $(a, \_)$ and $(b, \_)$. As a reminder, **ena** $= \{f \mapsto g \mid f \subseteq \Omega \times \Omega \wedge g \subseteq \Omega \times \Omega \wedge \mathrm{ran}(f) \subseteq \mathrm{dom}(g)\}$. Since $\mathrm{ran}([a]_R) \subseteq \mathrm{dom}([b]_R)$, relation $[b]_R \circ [a]_R$ is defined for all the values for which $[a]_R$ is defined: $\mathrm{dom}([b]_R \circ [a]_R) = \mathrm{dom}([a]_R)$. This generalises to any number of events: $\mathrm{dom}([e_n]_R \circ \cdots \circ [e_1]_R) = \mathrm{dom}([e_1]_R)$ where e_1 **ena** $e_2 \wedge \cdots \wedge e_{n-1}$ **ena** e_n. Set $\mathrm{dom}([e_1]_R)$ is not empty since, as discussed above, feasible events cannot yield empty relations. Predicate e_1 **ena** $e_2 \wedge \cdots \wedge e_{n_1}$ **ena** e_n is a characterisation of some path $u \in \mathcal{U}^+$ such that $P(u) = \langle e_1, \ldots, e_n \rangle$. Since $\mathrm{dom}(r(u))$ is not empty, it follows that $r(u)$ is not empty for an arbitrary path $u \in \mathcal{U}^+$ and the third criteria of Condition 6 is satisfied.

To summarise, by traces $tr(U)$ of a use case U we understand the set of all sequences $\{P(u) \mid u \in \mathcal{U}^+\}$ where $\mathcal{U}^+$ is set of paths (all starting with event INIT) of a subgraph U^+ constrained to edges **ena**. Condition 6 can be stated in the following, equivalent form.

$$tr(U) \subseteq tr(M) \tag{7}$$

Hence, a use case defines a set of traces that are also the traces of a machine. The crucial property that we have relied upon is that for some two events connected in a use case by an edge of **ena** kind it holds that a **ena** b. The property is translated into a condition on the actions and guards of the two events as given in the Definition 1. By discharging all such conditions for a use case scenario one establishes Property 7.

For practical reasons, it is necessary to deal with complex nodes that do not directly correspond to machine events. One important kind is the class of container elements. These appear due to an hierarchical organisation of large use cases and are also required to describe loops with a loop invariant. Inside a container element one finds event nodes and, possibly, other containers. To obtain traces of a use case with container elements, such use case must be first flattened. The flattening proceeds from inside so that the procedure is always applied to a container that does not contain other containers.

4   Co-refinement of Machines and Use Cases

With a trace semantics one defines refinement by stating that the traces of a refined model are contained in the traces of the abstract model. For Event-B this is stated with the following equivalence.

$$M \sqsubseteq N \Leftrightarrow \mathit{ff}[tr(N)] \subseteq tr(M) \tag{8}$$

where $\mathit{ff}(s)$ a mapping function such that $\forall i \cdot i \in \mathrm{dom}(s) \Rightarrow \mathit{ff}(s)(i) = \mathit{f}(s(i))$. Map f translates an event identifier from N into some event identifiers in M. The map may be partitioned into two parts $\mathit{f} = \mathit{f}_n \cup \mathit{f}_r$ where f_n maps all the new events of N into the skip event of M and f_r maps refined events of N into their abstract counterparts in M. f_r is defined explicitly in a model as a part of refined event declarations.

The Event-B refinement is known to satisfy Definition 8[7]. In fact, Event-B refinement is a stronger relation and takes into the account the notions of convergence and enabledness. For this reason, it would be ill-advised to consider trace refinement as a sole criterion of machine refinement.

Conditions 7 and 8 provide a basis for the definition of use case refinement. Assume there is use case U associated with machine M, $tr(U) \subseteq tr(M)$, and another use case W, $tr(W) \subseteq tr(N)$ associated with machine N refining M, $\mathit{ff}[tr(N)] \subseteq tr(M)$. Obviously, traces of W are found in traces of M but the relationship between U and W is not certain. Let us first see what kind of relationship we are looking for. Intuitively, N does the some thing as M but in a better way (note this does not follow from Condition 8 which allows N to do less of the same thing). The same principle transfers to use cases. What is expressed in an abstract use case U must be realised in a satisfactory way by concrete use case W. Consider the following illustration. If there is some phenomenon x in U is must be also present, perhaps in differing form, in W. If x is an event the requirement translates to not forgetting to include in W refined versions of abstract events used in U; x may be a complex phenomenon describing a situation where, for instance, event a is followed by event b. In W such a phenomenon may be portrayed literally, by including x as it is defined in U. It could also appear transformed where a and b are replaced by refined version a' and b'. Further, due to Condition 4, if x exists in U there also exists x_1 in U such that between a and b there is one skip event. This means that x' may be formed as a' followed by some new event e and then by b'. Since new event e is mapped into skip it would match phenomenon x_1, that is, $x = \mathit{ff}(x_1)$.

To summarise, the notion of use case refinement is expressed as the equality of abstract and concrete use case under the mapping ff.

$$U \sqsubseteq W \Leftrightarrow U = \mathit{ff}[W] \wedge tr(U) \subseteq tr(M) \wedge tr(W) \subseteq tr(N) \wedge M \sqsubseteq N \qquad (9)$$

The notion of use case refinement embeds the notions of use case/machine consistency and machine refinement: one must not discuss use case refinement in detachment from machines they characterise.

5   Case Study

With the case study we illustrate the role of a use case in a formal development. We show how one can formulate a simple scenario to characterise an abstract design and then evolve it hand in hand with the detalisation of a functional model. Thus, at each development stage not only we attend to the issue of correctness but also give an argument for the adequacy of the constructed design.

The problem we study is the construction of control logic for a sluice mechanism. The sluice is placed between areas of greatly differing pressures making it unsafe to operate a simple door. The major components of the sluice are two doors that are tightly sealed when closed, a middle chamber where the pressure may be controlled by the means of a pump, and six buttons placed on the walls as depicted in the diagram below.

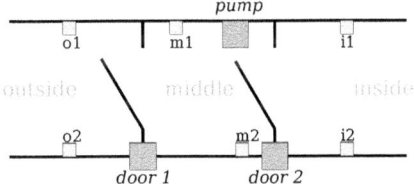

In the diagram, $i1, i2, m1, m2, o1, o2$ are buttons. They all have the same functionality and no fixed purpose; however, it is permitted to produce a note for a sluice use that would describe the meaning of the buttons and operational steps required to use the sluice. The following is a brief summary of the system requirements. Consult [4] for the complete list.

SYS the purpose of the system is to allow a user to safely travel between inside or outside areas
ENV4 six buttons, two per each area, are used to interact with a user;
ENV5 at any moment, there is at most one human operator in the system
SAF1 a door may be open only if the pressures in the locations it connects are equalised;
SAF2 at most one door is open at any moment;
SAF3 pressure may only be changed when the doors are closed;

The key use case of the requirements document may be summarised as follows: *when a user is in the inside (outside) area, it is possible for the user to safely travel to the outside (inside) area by interacting with the system only by pressing the buttons.*

5.1 Abstract Model

The development starts with a high level abstraction that depicts the whole system as a single, conceptual 'door'. The model, although trivial, makes two important statements: the system does not terminate; a closed 'door' eventually opens and vice versa. The following is the complete Event-B model of the initial abstraction.

MACHINE m0
  VARIABLES *door*
  INVARIANT *door* $\in$ DOOR
  INITIALISATION *door* := CLOSED
  EVENTS
    open = **when** *door* = CLOSED **then** *door* := OPEN **end**
    close = **when** *door* = OPEN **then** *door* := CLOSED **end**
END

A use case of the model resembles a simple automata where a system, once initialised, forever cycles between the only two states.

All the subsequent use cases merely provide a more detailed description of the same phenomenon.

5.2 First Refinement

The first refinement explains the meaning of the abstract 'door' by relating its states to the states of two physical doors of the system. The following predicates explain the conenction between the doors.

$$door1 = \text{CLOSED} \wedge door2 = \text{CLOSED} \Rightarrow door = \text{CLOSED}$$
$$door1 = \text{OPEN} \vee door2 = \text{OPEN} \Rightarrow door = \text{OPEN}$$
$$\neg(door1 = \text{OPEN} \wedge door2 = \text{OPEN})$$

The last condition expresses safety requirement **SAF2**. The abstract 'door' is now removed from the model and the behaviour is expressed in the terms of the two new doors. The following events describe how the first door opens and closes. The events for the second door are symmetric.

open1 = **when** *door1* = CLOSED $\wedge$ *door2* = CLOSED **then** *door1* := OPEN **end**
close1 = **when** *door1* = OPEN **then** *door1* := CLOSED **end**

The new use case is constructed mostly automatically by asking the tool to refine the abstract use case.

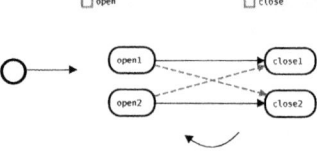

The light grey boxes depict the split refinement of abstract events open and close, as prescribed by the ff map computed from the definition of concrete Event-B model. The tool would not know what to do about edges and thus, to be on the safe side, it simply puts new events into containers. The edges piercing the container boundary were manually as were the disabling edges. The latter highlight the fact that these are the impossible event connections.

5.3   Second Refinement

In this step, a simple concept of user is introduced. The model expresses that for a user to arrive at a location he must first travel through an open door connecting the location with the middle area. We are not concerned yet with how a user arrives at the middle area. A new variable, $userstate \in$ USER appears and is manipulated by the following events.

move_in = **when** $userstate \neq$ IN $\wedge door2 =$ OPEN **then** $userstate :=$ IN **end**
move_out = **when** $userstate \neq$ OUT $\wedge door1 =$ OPEN **then** $userstate :=$ OUT **end**
appear = **begin** $userstate :\in$ USER **end**

The appear event models the fact that a user may leave the system and another user may appear at either location. In the following use case we identify two important states (the system is fully ready and the user is inside (outside)) around which much of the system evolution revolves.

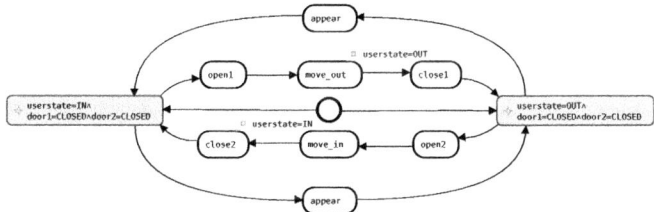

The diagram is an artificial composition of three simpler use cases: a use case for the intialisation, another for the appear event and the main loop use case. Also note the use assertion to propagate the information about user position through events close1 and close2.

5.4   Third Refinement

A more detailed user model is introduced by keeping track of the direction in which a user is supposed to travel. This allows us to relate the state when a user is in the middle area to the abstract notions of a user being inside or outside. Abstract variable $userstate \in \{$IN, OUT$\}$ is replaced with concrete variables $user \in \{$INS, OUTS, MID$\}$ and $dir \in \{$INW, OUTW$\}$.

$$user = \text{INS} \Rightarrow userstate = \text{IN}$$
$$user = \text{OUTS} \Rightarrow userstate = \text{OUT}$$
$$user = \text{MID} \wedge dir = \text{INW} \Rightarrow userstate = \text{OUT}$$
$$user = \text{MID} \wedge dir = \text{OUTW} \Rightarrow userstate = \text{IN}$$

At this point the use case naturally splits into two symmetric cases, one for each direction of travel. The loop of the previous use case is unfolded for the two complete travel scenarious.

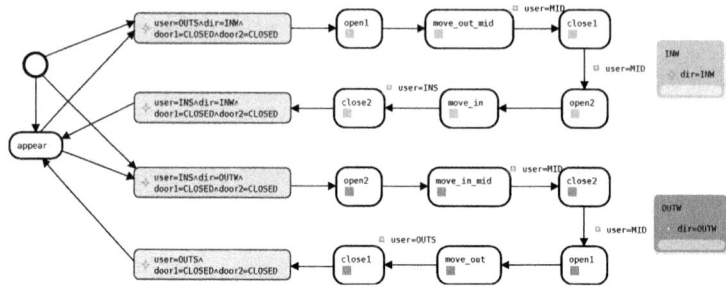

The two boxes to right of the diagram are aspects. They define conditions shared by a large proportion of the diagram. In this case, the conditions state the direction of use travel. The aspect weaving is indicated by small colour-coded square in an event node.

5.5 Fourth, Fifth and Sixth Refinements

The fourth refinement introduces a more detailed door model to account for doors that may get stuck when partially open: $dsns1 \in$ FULLY_CLOSED .. FULLY_OPEN. It replaced the abstract notion of door: $dsns1 = $ FULLY_CLOSED $\Leftrightarrow door1 = $ CLOSED. In the fifth refinement there appears a model of the pump device to control the middle area pressure. The pump is controlled by flag $pump \in PUMP$ and the pressure sensor $pressure \in PRESSURE\_LOW .. PRESSURE\_HIGH$ reports the current pressure. We are now able to express the remaining safety conditions, **SAF1** and **SAF3**.

$$dsns1 \neq \text{FULLY\_CLOSED} \vee dsns2 \neq \text{FULLY\_CLOSED} \Rightarrow pump = \text{PUMP\_OFF}$$
$$\neg stop = \text{TRUE} \wedge dsns1 \neq \text{FULLY\_CLOSED} \Rightarrow pressure = \text{PRESSURE\_HIGH}$$

The sixth refinement gets rid of variables *user* and *dir* and, instead, detects user position and intention using the six available buttons. It is a fairly intricate data refinement step that may be accomplished in more than one way and still satisfy the requirements.

5.6 Seventh Refinement

The concluding step adds a use case diagram as a final check of the model is adequacy. It is also a direct encoding of the informal use case mentioned earlier. The following diagram is a fragment refining the part of the previous use case starting with event open2 and ending with event close1. There are ways to cut such diagrams into smaller, self-contained parts[10].

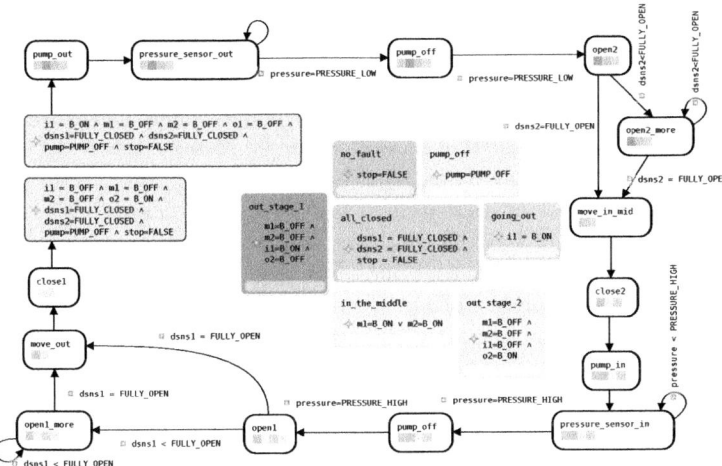

Proof Statistics. The proof statistics in terms of generated proof obligations is shown below. The numbers represent the total number of proof obligations, the number of automatically and manually proved ones, the number use case derived obligations, the percentage of manual effort and the proportion use case proof obligations.

Step	Total	Manual	Use case	Manual, %	Use case, %
m1	6	0	**6**	0%	100%
m2	26	0	**7**	0%	27%
m3	15	0	**12**	0%	80%
m4	48	7	**18**	14%	37%
m5	48	4	0	8%	0%
m6	48	4	0	8%	0%
m7	71	1	0	1%	0%
m8	15	3	**15**	20%	100%
Overall	277	19	**58**	7%	21%

Among the 19 manual proofs, 3 are due to use case proof obligations. The Event-B and use case models together with formal proofs may be found in [4]. Identical values for $m5$ and $m6$ are correct.

6   Conclusion

In this work we have presented an approach that, as we believe, makes Event-B more industry friendly by offering a formal counterpart of a well established informal concept. The approach should make it easier to integrate Event-B into an existing development process where use cases are already a part of the requirements engineering process. A hand-in-hand development of use cases and functional specification provides a degree of assurance that a development evolves in the right direction.

The most closely related work is a study of liveness-style theorems for the Classical B [3]. The work introduces a number of notation extensions to construct proofs about 'dynamic' properties of models - properties that span over several event executions. Like in a use case diagram, the formulation of reachability property requires spelling out a path that would lead to its satisfaction. One advantage of our approach is in the use of graphs to construct complex theorems from simple ones and the propagation of properties along the graph structure. The latter results in interactive modelling/proof sessions where proof feedback leads to small, incremental changes in the diagram.

There are a number of approaches [14,12,6] on combining process algebraic specification with event-based formalisms such as Event-B and Action Systems. The fundamental difference is that our technique does not introduce behavioural constraints and is simply a high-level notation for writing certain kind of theorems. It would be interesting to explore how explicit control flow information present in a process algebraic model part may affect the applicability and the practice of the proposed approach.

References

1. Abrial, J.-R.: The B-Book. Cambridge University Press (1996)
2. Abrial, J.-R.: Modelling in Event-B. Cambridge University Press (2010)
3. Abrial, J.-R., Mussat, L.: Introducing Dynamic Constraints in B. In: Bert, D. (ed.) B 1998. LNCS, vol. 1393, pp. 83–128. Springer, Heidelberg (1998)
4. The door controller model. Event B/Use case specification (2011), http://iliasov.org/usecase/doorctr.zip
5. Event-B. Community web site (2011), http://event-b.org/
6. Fischer, C., Wehrheim, H.: Model-Checking CSP-OZ Specifications with FDR. In: Araki, K., Galloway, A., Taguchi, K. (eds.) IFM 1999: Proceedings of the 1st International Conference on Integrated Formal Methods, London, UK, pp. 315–334. Springer (1999)
7. Hallerstede, S.: On the Purpose of Event-B Proof Obligations. In: Börger, E., Butler, M., Bowen, J.P., Boca, P. (eds.) ABZ 2008. LNCS, vol. 5238, pp. 125–138. Springer, Heidelberg (2008)
8. Hurlbut, R.R.: A survey of approaches for describing and formalizing use cases. Technical report, Expertech, Ltd. (1997)
9. Iliasov, A.: Augmenting Event-B Specifications with Control Flow Information. In: NODES 2010 (May 2010)
10. Iliasov, A.: Use Case Scenarios as Verification Conditions: Event-B/Flow Approach. In: Troubitsyna, E.A. (ed.) SERENE 2011. LNCS, vol. 6968, pp. 9–23. Springer, Heidelberg (2011)
11. Industrial deployment of system engineering methods providing high dependability and productivity (DEPLOY). IST FP7 project, http://www.deploy-project.eu/
12. Butler, M., Leuschel, M.: Combining CSP and B for Specification and Property Verification. In: Fitzgerald, J.S., Hayes, I.J., Tarlecki, A. (eds.) FM 2005. LNCS, vol. 3582, pp. 221–236. Springer, Heidelberg (2005)
13. The RODIN platform, http://rodin-b-sharp.sourceforge.net/
14. Treharne, H., Schneider, S., Bramble, M.: Composing Specifications Using Communication. In: Bert, D., Bowen, J.P., King, S., Waldén, M. (eds.) ZB 2003. LNCS, vol. 2651, pp. 58–78. Springer, Heidelberg (2003)

Formal Goal-Oriented Development of Resilient MAS in Event-B

Inna Pereverzeva[1,2], Elena Troubitsyna[2], and Linas Laibinis[2]

[1] Turku Centre for Computer Science
[2] Åbo Akademi University
Joukahaisenkatu 3-5, 20520 Turku, Finland
{inna.pereverzeva,elena.troubitsyna,linas.laibinis}@abo.fi

Abstract. Goal-Oriented Development facilitates structuring complex requirements. To ensure resilience the designers should guarantee that the system achieves its goals despite changes, e.g., caused by failures of system components. In this paper we propose a formal goal-oriented approach to development of resilient MAS. We formalize the notion of goal and goal achievement in Event-B and propose the specification and refinement patterns that allow us to guarantee that the targeted goals are reached despite agent failures. We illustrate our approach by a case study – development of an autonomous multi-robotic system.

Keywords: Event-B, formal modelling, refinement, goal-oriented development, multi-agent system.

1 Introduction

Goal-Oriented Development [5] has been recognised as an useful framework for structuring and specifying complex system requirements. In goal-oriented development, the system requirements are defined in terms of goals – the functional and non-functional objectives that a system should achieve. Often changes in system operational environment, e.g., caused by failures of agents – independent system components of various types – might hinder achieving the desired goals. Hence, to ensure system resilience [7], i.e., guarantee its dependability in spite of the changes, we need formally verify reachability of the targeted goals. Traditionally, such a verification is undertaken by abstracting implementation up to requirements level and model-checking satisfiability of goals. However, such an approach suffers from a state explosion that is especially prohibitive for such applications as multi-robotic systems [15].

In this paper we propose a formal development approach that ensures goal reachability "by construction". Our approach is based on refinement in Event-B. Event-B [2] is a formal top-down development approach to correct-by-construction system development. The main development technique – refinement – allows us to ensure that a concrete specification preserves globally observable behaviour and properties of abstract specification. Verification of each refinement step is done by

M. Brorsson and L.M. Pinho (Eds.): Ada-Europe 2012, LNCS 7308, pp. 147–161, 2012.

proofs. The Rodin platform [11] automates modelling and verification in Event-B. Currently Event-B is actively used within EU project DEPLOY [4] to model dependable systems from various domains.

We formalise goal-oriented development by defining a set of specification and refinement patterns. Our formalisation reflects the main concepts of the goal-oriented engineering. In particular, we demonstrate how to define system goals at different levels of abstraction and guarantee goal reachability while specifying collaborative agent behaviour. Moreover, we propose refinement patterns that allow the system to dynamically reallocate goals from failed agents to healthy ones and per se, guarantee resilience. A development of an autonomous multi-robotic system illustrates application of the proposed patterns. We believe that our approach offers a scalable technique for development and formal verification of complex resilient multi-agent systems (MAS).

The paper has the following structure. In Section 2 we briefly present our modelling framework – Event-B. In Section 3 we present the set of specification and refinement patterns that facilitate goal-oriented development in Event-B. In Section 4 we present a case study – development of an autonomous multi-robotic system by refinement. In Section 5 we overview the related work, discuss the presented approach and outline the directions for the future research.

2   Formal Modelling and Refinement in Event B

In this section we present our formal development framework – Event-B. The Event-B formalism is an extension of the B Method [1]. It is a state-based formal approach that promotes the correct-by-construction development paradigm and formal verification by theorem proving. Event-B has been specifically designed to model and reason about parallel, distributed and reactive systems.

2.1   Modelling in Event-B

In Event-B, a system model is specified using the notion of an *abstract state machine* [2]. An abstract state machine encapsulates the system state represented as a collection of model variables, and defines operations on this state, i.e., it describes the dynamic *behaviour* of the modelled system. A machine may also have the accompanying component, called *context*. A context might include user-defined carrier sets, constants and their properties, which are given as a list of model axioms. In Event-B, the variables are strongly typed by the constraining predicates called **invariants**. Moreover, the invariants specify important properties that should be preserved during the system execution.

The dynamic behaviour of the system is defined by the set of atomic **events**. Generally, an event can be defined as follows:

$$\mathbf{evt} \; \hat{=} \; \mathbf{any} \; vl \; \mathbf{where} \; g \; \mathbf{then} \; S \; \mathbf{end}$$

where vl is a list of new local variables (parameters), g is the event **guard**, and S is the event **action**. The guard is a state predicate that defines the conditions under which the action can be executed, i.e., when the event is *enabled*. If several events are enabled at the same time, any of them can be chosen for execution non-deterministically. If none of the events is enabled then the system deadlocks. In general, the action of an event is a parallel composition of deterministic or non-deterministic assignments.

2.2   Event-B Refinement

Event-B employs a top-down refinement-based approach to system development. Development starts from an abstract system specification that non-deterministically models the most essential functional requirements. In a sequence of refinement steps we gradually reduce non-determinism and introduce detailed design decisions. In particular, we can replace abstract variables by their concrete counterparts, i.e., perform data refinement. In this case, the invariant of the refined machine formally defines the relationship between the abstract and concrete variables. Via such a *gluing* invariant we establish a correspondence between the state spaces of the refined and the abstract machines.

Often a refinement step introduces new events and variables into the abstract specification. The new events correspond to the stuttering steps that are not visible at the abstract level, i.e., they refine implicit *skip*. To guarantee that the refined specification preserves the global behaviour of the abstract machine, we should demonstrate that the newly introduced events *converge*. To prove it, we need to define a *variant* – an expression over a finite subset of natural numbers – and show that the execution of new events decreases it. Sometimes, convergence of an event cannot be proved due to a high level of non-determinism. Then the event obtains the status *anticipated*. This obliges the designer to prove at some later refinement step, that the event indeed converges.

Each refinement step requires to verify a number of proof obligations that ensure that the refined specification adheres to its abstract counterpart [2]. The verification efforts, in particular, automatic generation and proving of the required proof obligations, are significantly facilitated by the Rodin platform [11].

Refinement and proof-based verification of Event-B offers the designers a scalable support for the development of such complex systems as multi-agent systems (MAS). MAS are decentralised distributed systems composed of agents asynchronously communicating with each other. Agents are computer programs acting autonomously on behalf of a person or organisation, while coordinating their activities by communication [9]. MAS are increasingly used in various critical applications such as factories, hospitals, rescue operations in disaster areas, etc. In the next section we show how refinement process can facilitate modelling MAS and reasoning about goal reachability.

3   A Formal View of Goal-Oriented Multi-agent System

3.1   Patterns for Goal-Oriented Development

The goal-oriented engineering facilitates structuring complex system requirements in terms of *goals* – objectives that the system should meet [5]. In this paper we focus on modelling functional goals, i.e., the goals defining objectives of the services that the system should deliver. We propose a number of *specification and refinement patterns* that interpret essential activities of goal-oriented engineering in terms of Event-B refinement.

A pattern in Event-B is an abstract machine that defines a generic modelling solution that can be reused in similar developments via instantiation. Usually, an Event-B pattern contains abstract types, constants and variables. The context of such a model constraints the instantiation by defining the properties that should be satisfied by concrete instantiations of abstract data structures. The invariant properties of a pattern, once proven, remain valid for all instantiations.

The aim of defining a pattern is to capture experience gained in modelling a certain problem. To illustrate how patterns are defined, let us now present a pattern that allows the designers to explicitly define goals while modelling a system in Event-B. We call it *Abstract Goal Modelling Pattern*.

3.2   Abstract Goal Modelling Pattern

Let $GSTATE$ be an abstract type defining the system state space[1]. Moreover, let *Goal* be a non-empty proper subset of $GSTATE$ that abstractly defines the given system goals. We say that the system has achieved the desired goals if its current state belongs to *Goal*. Both $GSTATE$ and *Goal* are the abstract types. Together with their properties they are defined in the model context as follows:

$$Goal \neq \varnothing \quad \text{and} \quad Goal \subset GSTATE.$$

Let us note that $GSTATE$ and *Goal* are generic parameters of the initial pattern. During a system development, we should supply their concrete instantiations that satisfy the properties shown above.

While modelling a system in Event-B, we should ensure that the system under development achieves the desired goal. We can formally express this by requiring that the system terminates in a state belong to *Goal*. The machine M_AGM is defined according to the *Abstract Goal Modelling Pattern*:

```
Machine M_AGM                              Reaching_Goal ≙
Variables gstate                               status anticipated
Invariants gstate ∈ GSTATE                     when
Events                                             gstate ∈ GSTATE \ Goal
   Initialisation ≙                            then
      begin                                        gstate :∈ GSTATE
         gstate :∈ GSTATE \ Goal             end
   end
```

The dynamic behaviour of the system is abstractly modelled by the event Reaching_Goal. The system terminates when Reaching_Goal becomes disable, i.e., when a state satisfying *Goal* is reached.

The event Reaching_Goal has the status *anticipated*. Hence, in the machine M_AGM goal reachability is postulated rather than proved. However, it also obliges us to prove (at some refinement step) that the event or its refinements

---

[1] In fact, it is sufficient to consider the states that our goal depends on.

converge. Therefore, while refining a concrete specification defined according to *Abstract Goal Modelling Pattern*, we will be forced to prove goal reachability.

Let us assume that we have a collection of Event-B patterns: P_1, P_2, ..., P_n that refine each other in the following way:

$$P_1 \text{ is refined by } P_2 \text{ ... is refined by } P_n.$$

Such a refinement chain expresses a generic development by refinement. Abstract data structures of all the involved patterns become generic parameters of the development. Each pattern abstractly defines a solution for specifying a certain modelling aspect. Therefore, each refinement step has a rationale behind it – its meta-level description. We use it to formulate modelling aspects that the refinement transformation aims at defining. The result of refinement transformation is called a refinement pattern.

Next we propose several refinement patterns that allow us to implement the ideas of goal-oriented engineering in Event-B refinement. We start from defining *Goal Decomposition Pattern*.

3.3   Goal Decomposition Pattern

The main idea of goal-oriented development is to decompose the high-level system goals into a set of subgoals. This is an iterative process that aims at building the hierarchy of system goals. Essentially, subgoals define intermediate stages of the process of achieving the main goal.

The purpose of *Goal Decomposition Pattern* is to explicitly model subgoals in the system specification. While defining this pattern, we should ensure that high-level goals remain achievable. Hence our refinement pattern should reflect the relation between the high-level goals and subgoals. Moreover, it should ensure that high-level goal reachability is preserved and can be defined via reachability of lower-layer subgoals.

In this paper we assume that subgoals are independent of each other. This means that reachability of any subgoal does not affect reachability of another one. Moreover, while a certain subgoal is reached, it remains reached, i.e., the system always progresses towards achieving its goals. Formally, it can be expressed as a stability property with respect to some state predicate P:

$$Stable(P) \iff \text{ "once } P \text{ becomes true it remains true".}$$

In Event-B, stability properties can be easily expressed by introducing auxiliary variables for storing the previous value of the state and then formulating stability properties as the invariant properties of the form:

$$P(prev\_state) = TRUE \implies P(state) = TRUE.$$

To express a goal decomposition in terms of Event-B, let us define a corresponding refinement pattern. We present it by the machine M_GD. The new pattern allows us to introduce a number of subgoals into our system model and express their reachability. Moreover, the refinement relation between patterns allows us to express reachability of the main goal via reachability of its subgoals.

Let us assume for simplicity, that system goal *Goal* is achieved by reaching three subgoals. The subgoals are defined as corresponding variables of the M_GD machine:

$Subgoal_1$, $Subgoal_2$, and $Subgoal_3$. The goal independence assumption allows us to partition high-level goal state space $GSTATE$ into three non-empty subsets: $SG\_STATE1, SG\_STATE2, SG\_STATE3$. We define the subgoals as follows:

$$Subgoal_i \neq \varnothing \quad \text{and} \quad Subgoal_i \subset SG\_STATEi, \; i \in 1..3.$$

To establish a relationship between the new state spaces SG_STATEi, $i \in 1..3$, of the M_GD machine and the abstract state space of M_AGM machine we define the following function:

$$State\_map \in SG\_STATE1 \times SG\_STATE2 \times SG\_STATE3 \rightarrowtail GSTATE,$$

where $\rightarrowtail$ designates a bijection function. Essentially it partitions the original goal state space into three independent parts.

To postulate that the main goal is reached if and only if all three subgoals are reached, we add an axiom into the context of the M_GD machine:

$$\forall sg1, sg2, sg3 \cdot \; sg1 \in Subgoal_1 \wedge sg2 \in Subgoal_2 \wedge sg3 \in Subgoal_3$$
$$\Leftrightarrow \; State\_map(sg1 \mapsto sg2 \mapsto sg3) \in Goal.$$

Refinement performed according to the *Goal Decomposition Pattern* is an example of the Event-B data refinement. We replace the abstract variable *gstate* with the new variables $gstate_i \in SG\_STATEi$, $i \in 1..3$. The new variables model the state of the corresponding subgoals. The following gluing invariant allows us to prove data refinement:

$$gstate = State\_map(gstate1 \mapsto gstate2 \mapsto gstate3).$$

Essentially the M_GD machine decomposes the Reaching_Goal event of the M_AGM machine into three similar events Reaching_SubGoal$_i$, $i \in 1..3$:

```
Machine M_GD
Reaching_SubGoal_i ≙ refines Reaching_Goal
  status anticipated
  when
      gstate_i ∈ SG_STATEi \ Subgoal_i
  then
      gstate_i :∈ SG_STATEi
  end
  ...
```

Let us observe that we can easily verify that the following stability property holds for the pattern M_GD:

$$Stable(gstate_1 \in Subgoal_1) \wedge Stable(gstate_2 \in Subgoal_2) \wedge Stable(gstate_3 \in Subgoal_3).$$

The proposed *Goal Decomposition Pattern* can be repeatedly used to refine subgoals into the subgoals of finer granularity until the desired level of details is reached.

3.4   Agent Modelling Pattern

Our elaborated *Abstract Goal Modelling* and *Goal Decomposition* patterns allow us to specify the system goal(s) at different levels of abstraction. In multi-agent systems, (sub)goals are usually achieved by system agents. Agents are independent entities that are capable of performing certain tasks. In general, the system might have several types of agents that are distinguished by the type of tasks that they are capable of performing. Our next refinement pattern – *Agent Modelling Pattern* – allows us to model agents and associate them with goals.

We introduce the set $AGENTS$ that abstractly defines the set of system agents. In this refinement pattern we also introduce a concept of agent *eligibility*. An agent is *eligible* if it is capable of achieving a certain task (subgoal). We define the non-empty sets EL_AG1, EL_AG2, and EL_AG3 of the agents eligible to achieve each particular subgoal.

Agent might fail while trying to achieve a certain subgoal. Then it is removed from the dynamic set of the eligible agents represented by the variable $elig_i$: $elig_i \subseteq EL\_AGi,\ i \in 1..3$.

A goal is achieved if there is at least one eligible agent associated with it. This is formulated as the corresponding invariant property in our pattern:

$$elig_1 \neq \varnothing \ \text{and}\ elig_2 \neq \varnothing \ \text{and}\ elig_3 \neq \varnothing.$$

The dynamic part of the *Agent Modelling Pattern* is defined in the machine M_AM. Since we assumed that the agents can fail, the goal assigned to the failed agent cannot be reached. To reflect this assumption in our model, we refine the abstract event Reaching_SubGoal$_i$ by two events Successful_Reaching_SubGoal$_i$ and Failed_Reaching_SubGoal$_i$, $i \in 1..3$, which respectively model successful and unsuccessful reaching of the subgoal by some eligible agent:

```
Machine M_AM
Successful_Reaching_SubGoalᵢ ≙ refines Reaching_SubGoalᵢ
   status convergent
   any ag
   when
        gstateᵢ ∈ SG_STATEi \ Subgoalᵢ ∧ ag ∈ eligᵢ
   then
        gstateᵢ :∈ Subgoalᵢ
   end
Failed_Reaching_SubGoalᵢ ≙ refines Reaching_SubGoalᵢ
   status convergent
   any ag
   when
        gstateᵢ ∈ SG_STATEi \ Subgoalᵢ ∧ ag ∈ eligᵢ ∧ card(eligᵢ) > 1
   then
        gstateᵢ :∈ SG_STATEi \ Subgoalᵢ ‖ eligᵢ := eligᵢ \ {ag}
   end
```

In the guard of the event Failed_Reaching_SubGoal$_i$ we restrict possible agent failures by postulating that at least one agent associated with the subgoal remains operational: $card(elig_i) > 1$, $i \in 1..3$. This assumption allows us to change the event status from anticipated to convergent. In other words, we are now able to prove that, for each subgoal, the process of reaching it eventually terminates. To prove the convergence we define the following variant expression:

$$card(elig_1)\ +\ card(elig_2)\ +\ card(elig_3).$$

When an agent fails, it is removed from a corresponding set of eligible agents $elig_i$. This in turn decreases the value of $card(elig_i)$ and consequently the whole variant expression. On the other hand, when an agent succeeds in reaching the goal, all the events become disabled, thus ensuring system termination as well.

In practice, the constraint to have at least one operational agent associated with our model can be validated by probabilistic modelling of goal reachability, which is planned as a future work. Let us also note that for multi-robotic systems with many homogeneous agents this constraint is usually satisfied.

3.5   Agent Refinement Pattern

Above we have defined the notion of agent eligibility quite abstractly. We establish the relationship between subgoals (tasks) and agents that are capable of achieving them. Our last refinement pattern, *Agent Refinement Pattern*, aims at unfolding the notion of agent eligibility. Here we define the agent eligibility by introducing agent attributes – *agent types* and *agent statuses*. An eligible agent will be an operational agent that belongs to a particular agent type.

We define an enumerated set of agent types $AG\_TYPE = \{TYPE1, TYPE2, TYPE3\}$ and establish the correspondence between abstract sets of eligible agents and the corresponding agent types by the following axioms:

$$\forall ag \cdot ag \in EL\_AGi \Leftrightarrow atype(ag) = TYPEi, \ i \in 1..3.$$

An agent is eligible to perform a certain subgoal if it has the type associated with this subgoal.

An agent might be operational or failed. To model the notion of agent status we define an enumerated set $AG\_STATUS = \{OK, KO\}$, where constants OK and KO designate operational and failed agents correspondingly.

Below we present an excerpt from the dynamic part of the *Agent Refinement Pattern* – the machine M_AR. We add a new variable $astatus$ to store the dynamic status of each agent:

$$astatus \in AGENTS \rightarrow AG\_STATUS.$$

Moreover, we data refine the variables $elig_i$. The following gluing invariants relate them with the concrete sets:

$$elig_i = \{a \mid a \in AGENTS \wedge atype(a) = TYPEi \wedge astatus(a) = OK\}, \ i \in 1..3.$$

In our case, the dynamic set of agents eligible to perform a certain subgoal becomes a set of active agents of the particular type. The event Failed_Reaching_SubGoal$_i$ is now refined to take into account the concrete definition of agent eligibility. The event also updates the status of the failed agent.

```
Machine M_AR
Successful_Reaching_SubGoal_i ≙ refines Successful_Reaching_SubGoal_i
   any ag
   when
       gstate_i ∈ SG_STATEi \ Subgoal_i ∧ astatus(ag) = OK ∧ atype(ag) = TYPE_i
   then
       gstate_i :∈ Subgoal_i
   end
Failed_Reaching_SubGoal_i ≙ refines Failed_Reaching_SubGoal_i
   any ag
   when
       gstate_i ∈ SG_STATEi \ Subgoal_i ∧ astatus(ag) = OK ∧ atype(ag) = TYPE_i ∧
       card({a|a ∈ AGENTS ∧ atype(a) = TYPE_i ∧ astatus(a) = OK}) > 1
   then
       gstate_i :∈ SG_STATEi \ Subgoal_i ∥ astatus(ag) := KO
   end
```

Further refinement patterns can be defined to model various fault tolerance mechanism. However, in this paper instead of building further the collection of patterns, we will demonstrate how to instantiate and use the described patterns in a concrete development.

4   Case Study: A Multi-robotic System

4.1   A Case Study Description

As a case study we consider a multi-robotic system. The goal of the system is to coordinate identical robots to get a certain area cleaned. The area is divided into several zones, which can be further divided into a number of sectors. Each zone has a base station – a static computing and communicating device – that coordinates the cleaning of the zone. In its turn, each base station supervises a number of robots by assigning cleaning tasks to them.

A robot is an autonomous electro-mechanical device – a special kind of a rover that can move and clean. The base station may assign a robot a sector – a certain area in the zone – to clean. As soon as the robot receives a new cleaning task, it autonomously travels to this area and starts to clean it. After successfully completing its mission, it returns back to the base station to receive a new order. The base station keeps track of the cleaned sectors. A robot may fail to clean the assigned sector. In that case, the base station assigns another robot to perform this task. To ensure that the whole area is eventually cleaned, each base station in its turn should ensure that its zone is eventually cleaned.

The system should function autonomously, i.e., without human intervention. Such kind of systems are often deployed in hazardous areas (nuclear power plants, disaster areas, mine fields, etc.). Hence guaranteeing system resilience is an important requirement. Therefore, we should formally demonstrate that the system goal is achievable despite possible robot failures.

Next, we will show how to develop a multi-robotic system by refinement in Event-B and demonstrate how to rely on the patterns proposed in Section 3 to formally specify the system behaviour to ensure reachability of the overall system goal.

4.2   Pattern-Driven Refinement of a Multi-robotic System

In this section we will describe our formal development of a multi-robotic system in Event-B. The development is concluded via instantiation of the proposed patterns, with the goal decomposition pattern being applied twice in a row.

Abstract Model. The initial model defined by the machine MRS_Abs specifies the behaviour of a multi-robotic system according to the *Abstract Goal Modelling Pattern*. We apply this pattern by instantiating abstract variables with the concrete values and specifying events that model system behaviour.

The state space of the initial model is defined by the type $BOOL$. The value TRUE corresponds to the situation when the desired goal is achieved (i.e., the whole territory is cleaned), while FALSE represents the opposite situation.

Similarly to the pattern machine M_AGM, the machine MRS_Abs contains an event, CleaningTerritory, that models system behaviour. It abstractly represents the process of cleaning the territory, where a variable $completed \in BOOL$ models the current state of the system goal. This event is constructed according to the pattern event Reaching_Goal by taking all the instantiations into account, as shown below:

```
Machine AbsMRS
Variables completed
Invariants completed ∈ BOOL
Events
   ...
CleaningTerritory ≙
   status anticipated
   when
        completed = FALSE
   then
        completed :∈ BOOL
   end
```

The system continues its execution until the whole territory is cleaned, i.e., as long as $completed$ stays FALSE. At this level of abstraction, the event CleaningTerritory has the *anticipated* status. In other words, similarly to the abstract pattern, we delay the proof that the event eventually converges to subsequent refinements. It is easy to see that the machine AbsMRS is an instantiation of the pattern machine M_AGM, where the abstract type $GSTATE$ its replaced with $BOOL$, the constant $Goal$ is instantiated with a singleton set {TRUE}, and the variable $gstate$ is renamed into $completed$.

First Refinement. Our initial model specifies system behaviour in a highly abstract way. It models the process of cleaning the whole territory. The goal of the first refinement is to model the cleaning of the territory zones. Refinement is performed according to the *Goal Decomposition Pattern*.

In the first refinement step resulting in the machine MRS_Ref1, we augment our model with representation of subgoals. The whole territory is divided into n zones, $n \in \mathbb{N}$ and $n \geq 1$. We associate the notion of a *subgoal* with the process of *cleaning a particular zone*. Thus a subgoal is achieved when the corresponding zone is cleaned. A new variable $zone\_completed$ represents the current subgoal status for every zone. The value TRUE corresponds to the situation when the certain zone is cleaned:

$$zone\_completed \in 1..n \to BOOL.$$

The refined model MRS_Ref1 is built as an instantiation of the *Goal Decomposition Pattern* machine M_GD, where the subgoal states are defined as elements of the variable $zone\_completed$, i.e.,

$$gstate_i = zone\_completed(i), \text{ for } i \in 1..n.$$

This observation suggests the following gluing invariant between the initial and the refined models:

$$completed = TRUE \Leftrightarrow zone\_completed[1..n] = \{TRUE\}.$$

The invariant can be understood as follows: the territory is considered to be cleaned if and only if its every zone is cleaned.

The pattern events Reaching_SubGoal$_i$ correspond to a single event CleaningZone:

```
Machine MRS_Ref1
CleaningZone ≙ refines CleaningTerritory
  status anticipated
  any zone, zone_result
  when
      zone ∈ 1..n ∧ zone_completed(zone) = FALSE ∧ zone_result ∈ BOOL
  then
      zone_completed(zone) := zone_result
  end
```

Second Refinement. In our development of a multi-robotic system we should apply the goal decomposition pattern twice, until we reach the level of "primitive" goals, i.e., the goals for which we define the classes of agents eligible for execution of these goals.

Every zone in our system is divided into k sectors, $k \in \mathbb{N}$ and $k \geq 1$. A robot is responsible for cleaning a certain sector. We associate the notion of a *subsubgoal* (or simply *task*) with the process of *cleaning a particular sector*. The task is completed when the sector is cleaned. A new variable *sector_completed* represents the current task status for every sector:

$$sector\_completed \in 1..n \to (1..k \to BOOL).$$

The refined model is again built as an instantiation of the *Goal Decomposition Pattern*, where the subsubgoal states are defined as the elements of the variable *sector_completed*, i.e.,

$$gstate_{ij} = sector\_completed(i)(j), \text{ for } i \in 1..n, \ j \in 1..k.$$

A gluing invariant expresses the relationship between subgoals and tasks:

$$\forall zone \cdot zone \in 1..n \Rightarrow (zone\_completed(zone) = TRUE \Leftrightarrow$$
$$sector\_completed(zone)[1..k] = \{TRUE\}).$$

The invariant postulates that any zone is cleaned if and only if its every sector is cleaned. The abstract event CleaningZone is refined by the event CleaningSector. The subsubgoal will be achieved if this section is eventually cleaned:

```
Machine MRS_Ref2
CleaningSector ≙ refines CleaningZone
  status anticipated
  any zone, sector, sector_result
  when
      zone ∈ 1..n ∧ sector ∈ 1..k ∧ sector_completed(zone)(sector) = FALSE ∧
      sector_result ∈ BOOL
  then
      sector_completed(zone) := sector_completed(zone) ⩤ {sector ↦ sector_result}
  end
```

Now we have reached the desire level of granularity of our subgoals. In the next refinement step (the machine MRS_Ref3) we are going to augment our model with an abstract representation of agents.

Third Refinement. The next refined model of our development is constructed according to the refinement *Agent Modelling Pattern*. As a result, we introduce the abstract set $AGENTS$, and its subset $ELIG$ containing the eligible agents for executing the tasks. A new variable $elig$ represents the dynamic set of (currently available) eligible agents. Following the proposed pattern, we should also guarantee that there will be at least one eligible agent for cleaning the sector. This property is formulated as an additional invariant: $elig \neq \varnothing$.

Moreover, according to the pattern, we need abstractly introduce agent failures. This is achieved by refining the abstract event CleaningSector by two events SuccessfulCleaningSector and FailedCleaningSector, which respectively model successful and unsuccessful execution of the task by some eligible agent:

```
Machine MRS_Ref3
SuccessfulCleaningSector ≘ refines CleaningSector
  status convergent
  any zone, sector, ag
  when
      zone ∈ 1..n ∧ sector ∈ 1..k ∧
      sector_completed(zone)(sector) = FALSE ∧ ag ∈ elig
  then
      sector_completed(zone) := sector_completed(zone) ⩤ {sector ↦ TRUE}
  end
FailedCleaningSector ≘ refines CleaningSector
  status convergent
  any zone, sector, ag
  when
      zone ∈ 1..n ∧ sector ∈ 1..k ∧ sector_completed(zone)(sector) = FALSE ∧
      ag ∈ elig ∧ card(elig) > 1
  then
      sector_completed(zone) := sector_completed(zone) ⩤ {sector ↦ FALSE}
      elig := elig \ {ag}
  end
```

Following the proposed pattern, we add in the event FailedCleaningSector the guard $card(elig) > 1$ to restrict possible agent failure in task performance. Let us also note that for multi-robotic systems with many homogeneous agents this constraint is not unreasonable. This assumption allows us to prove the convergence of the goal-reaching events, i.e., to prove that the process of cleaning the territory eventually terminates.

Fourth Refinement. Finally, the *Agent Refinement Pattern* for introducing agent types and their statuses is applied to produce the last refined model of our multi-robotic system. In this refinement step we explicitly define the agent types – robots and base stations. We partition our abstract set $AGENTS$ by disjointed non-empty subsets RB and BS, that represent robots and base stations respectively. In this case study robots perform the cleaning task. Hence our abstract set of eligible agents is completely represented by robots: $ELIG = RB$. Robots might be active or failed. We introduce the enumerated set $STATUS$, which in our case has two elements $\{active, failed\}$.

At previous refinement step we have modelled agent faults while performing their tasks in a very abstract way. Now we will specify them more concretely. We assume that only robots may fail in our multi-robotic system. Their dynamic status is stored in the variable rb_status:

$$rb\_status \in RB \rightarrow STATUS.$$

The abstract variable $elig$ is now data refined by the concrete set:

$$elig = \{a|a \in AGENTS \wedge atype(a) = RB \wedge rb\_status(a) = active\}.$$

The concrete events are also built according to the proposed pattern. For instance, the event FailedCleaningSector can now be specified as follows:

```
Machine MRS_Ref4
FailedCleaningSector ≙ refines FailedCleaningSector
  any zone, sector, ag
  when
      zone ∈ 1..n ∧ sector ∈ 1..k ∧ sector_completed(zone)(sector) = FALSE ∧
      ag ∈ RB ∧ card({a|a ∈ RB ∧ rb_status(a) = active}) > 1
      rb_status(ag) = active
  then
      sector_completed(zone) := sector_completed(zone) ⩤ {sector ↦ FALSE}
      rb_status(ag) := failed
  end
```

An overview of the development of an autonomous multi-robotic system according to the proposed specification and refinement patterns is shown in the Fig. 1.

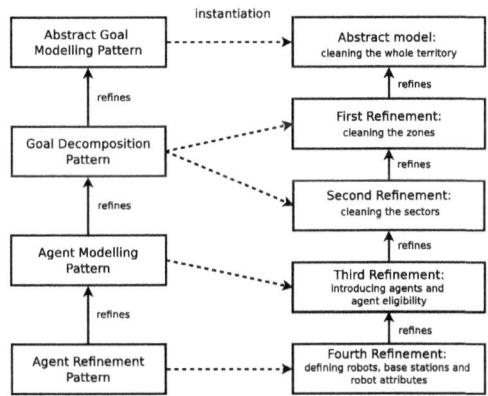

Fig. 1. Overview of the development

5   Conclusions

5.1   Discussion

In this paper we have proposed a formal goal-oriented approach to development of resilient MAS. We have demonstrated how to rigorously define goals in

Event-B and ensure goal reachability by refinement. We have defined a set of modelling and refinement patterns that describe generic solutions common to formal modelling of MAS. Rigorous modelling of the impact of agent failures on goal achieving allowed us to propose a dynamic goal reallocation mechanism that guarantees system resilience in presence of agent failures. We have illustrated our approach by a case study – development of an autonomic multi-robotic system.

While modelling the behaviour of a multi-robotic system, we have shown that refinement process allows us also to discover restrictions that we have to impose on system behaviour to guarantee its resilience. In our case, the goal was achievable only if at least one robot remains healthy. Feasibility of such a restriction can be checked probabilistically based on the failure rates of robots. In our future work we are planning to integrate stochastic reasoning in our formal development. Moreover, it would be also interesting to experiment with different schemes for goal decomposition and dynamic goal reallocation.

5.2   Related Work

Our approach is different from numerous process-algebraic approaches used for modeling MAS. Firstly, we relied on proof-based verification that does not impose restrictions on the size of the model, number of agents, etc. Secondly, we adopted a system's approach, i.e., we modeled the entire system and extracted the specifications of its individual components by decomposition. Such an approach allows us to ensure resilience by enabling goal reallocation at different architectural levels. Furthermore, by incrementally increasing complexity of our models, we have successfully managed to cope both with complexity of requirements and verification.

Formal modelling of MAS has been undertaken by [13,12,14]. The authors have proposed an extension of the Unity framework to explicitly define such concepts as mobility and context-awareness. Our modelling pursued a different goal – we aimed at formally guaranteeing that the specified agent behaviour achieves the defined goals. Formal modelling of fault tolerant MAS in Event-B has been undertaken by Ball and Butler [3]. They have proposed a number of informally described patterns that allow the designers to add well-known fault tolerance mechanisms to the specifications. In our approach, we implemented goal reallocation to guarantee goal reachability that can be also considered as a goal-specific fault tolerance.

The foundational work on goal-oriented development has been done by van Lamsweerde [5]. The original motivation behind the goal-oriented development was to structure the requirements and derive properties in the form of temporal logic formulas that the system design should satisfy. Over the last decade the goal-oriented approach has received several extensions that allow the designers to link git with formal modelling [6,8,10]. These works aimed at expressing temporal logic properties in Event-B. In our work, we have relied on goals to facilitate structuring of system behaviour but derived system specification that satisfies the desired properties by refinement.

References

1. Abrial, J.R.: The B-Book: Assigning Programs to Meanings. Cambridge University Press (2005)
2. Abrial, J.R.: Modeling in Event-B. Cambridge University Press (2010)
3. Ball, E., Butler, M.: Event-B Patterns for Specifying Fault-Tolerance in Multi-agent Interaction. In: Butler, M., Jones, C., Romanovsky, A., Troubitsyna, E. (eds.) Methods, Models and Tools for Fault Tolerance. LNCS, vol. 5454, pp. 104–129. Springer, Heidelberg (2009)
4. EU-project DEPLOY: http://www.deploy-project.eu/
5. van Lamsweerde, A.: Goal-oriented requirements engineering: A guided tour. In: Requirements Engineering, pp. 249–263 (2001)
6. Landtsheer, R.D., Letier, E., van Lamsweerde, A.: Deriving tabular event-based specifications from goal-oriented requirements models. In: Requirements Engineering, p. 200 (2003)
7. Laprie, J.: From dependability to resilience. In: 38th IEEE/IFIP Int. Conf. On Dependable Systems and Networks, pp. G8–G9 (2008)
8. Matoussi, A., Gervais, F., Laleau, R.: A Goal-Based Approach to Guide the Design of an Abstract Event-B Specification. In: 16th International Conference on Engineering of Complex Computer Systems, pp. 139–148. IEEE (2011)
9. OMG Mobile Agents Facility (MASIF): http://www.omg.org
10. Ponsard, C., Dallons, G., Philippe, M.: From Rigorous Requirements Engineering to Formal System Design of Safety-Critical Systems. ERCIM News (75), 22–23 (2008)
11. Rodin: Event-B Platform: http://www.event-b.org/
12. Roman, G.-C., Julien, C., Payton, J.: A Formal Treatment of Context-Awareness. In: Wermelinger, M., Margaria-Steffen, T. (eds.) FASE 2004. LNCS, vol. 2984, pp. 12–36. Springer, Heidelberg (2004)
13. Roman, G.C., Julien, C., Payton, J.: Modeling Adaptive Behaviors in Context UNITY. Theoretical Computure Science 376, 185–204 (2007)
14. Roman, G.C., McCann, P., Plun, J.: Mobile UNITY: Reasoning and Specification in Mobile Computing. ACM Transactions of Software Engineering and Methodology, 250–282 (1997)
15. Vain, J., Tammet, T., Kuusik, A., Juurik, S.: Towards scalable proofs of robot swarm dependability. In: BEC 2008, pp. 199–202 (2008)

Choices, Choices: Comparing between CHOC'LATE and the Classification-Tree Methodology

Pak-Lok Poon[1,*], Tsong Yueh Chen[2], and T.H. Tse[3]

[1] School of Accounting and Finance, The Hong Kong Polytechnic University, Hung Hom, Kowloon, Hong Kong
afplpoon@inet.polyu.edu.hk
[2] Faculty of Information and Communication Technologies, Swinburne University of Technology, Hawthorn 3122, Australia
tychen@swin.edu.au
[3] Department of Computer Science, The University of Hong Kong, Pokfulam, Hong Kong
thtse@cs.hku.hk

Abstract. Two popular specification-based test case generation methods are the choice relation framework and the classification-tree methodology. Both of them come with associated tools and have been used in different applications with success. Since both methods are based on the idea of partition testing, they are similar in many aspects. Because of their similarities, software testers often find it difficult to decide which method to be used in a given testing scenario. This paper aims to provide a solution by first contrasting the strengths and weaknesses of both methods, followed by suggesting practical selection guidelines to cater for different testing scenarios.

Keywords: Choice relation framework, classification-tree methodology, software testing.

1 Introduction

The set of test cases used in software testing, usually known as a *test suite*, should be comprehensive and effective so that any software failure can be revealed [8]. Thus, test suite generation remains a core issue in testing [21]. In general, test cases can be generated according to the program code or the specification. The former approach is known as *code-based* or *white-box* testing while the latter approach is known as *specification-based* or *black-box* testing.

Traditionally, code-based testing received more attention in the literature [9,15]. In contrast, specification-based testing is relatively less extensively studied, even though its advantages have been widely known [20]. Among various specification-based methods, two popular ones are the choice relation framework and the classification-tree methodology [5,6,7,10,12,14,18,22]. Both of these methods are considered to be useful because they can be applied to *informal* specifications that are primarily written in a narrative language. Both of them come with associated tools. The ***CHOiCe reLATion***

---

* Corresponding author.

M. Brorsson and L.M. Pinho (Eds.): Ada-Europe 2012, LNCS 7308, pp. 162–176, 2012.

framEwork (***CHOC'LATE***) [7,18] is an extension of the category-partition method [17] by incorporating formal concepts and practical techniques such as choice relations and their automatic deductions and consistency checks. The *Classification-Tree Methodology* (***CTM***) was originally developed by Grochtmann and Grimm [10] and was extended into an integrated classification-tree methodology by Chen et al. [6]. In this paper, for ease of presentation, we will refer to both the (original) classification-tree method and the (extended) integrated classification-tree methodology as CTM.

In general, CHOC'LATE and CTM are input domain partitioning methods [11,16]. The set of all possible inputs (known as the *input domain*) is divided into subsets (called *subdomains*) according to the specification such that all the elements in each subdomain have essentially the same type of behavior. Test cases are then selected from each subdomain instead of from the entire input domain. In this way, the resulting test suite may better represent the behavior of the software under test.

Despite the growing popularity of CHOC'LATE and CTM, software testers often find it difficult to decide which of them should be used in a given testing scenario, partly because of the similarities among both methods as explained above. This paper aims to provide a solution by first contrasting the strengths and weaknesses of the two methods, followed by suggesting practical selection guidelines to cater for different testing scenarios.

The rest of the paper is structured as follows: Section 2 gives an overview of CHOC'LATE and CTM, and discusses their applicability. Section 3 contrasts the strengths and weaknesses of the two methods in several important aspects. Section 4 then provides guidelines to help the tester decide whether CHOC'LATE or CTM should be used in a given testing scenario. Section 5 discusses some work related to CHOC'LATE and CTM. Finally, Section 6 summarizes the paper.

2   Overview of CHOC'LATE and CTM

2.1   CHOC'LATE

First, let us outline a few fundamental concepts for the understanding of CHOC'LATE [7,18]. A parameter is an explicit input to a system, while an environment condition is a state of the system. A *category* is a property specified in a parameter or an environment condition that affects the execution behavior of the software under test. For an admission system for a master degree program in accounting, an example of a category is the GMAT score. The possible values associated with a category are partitioned into disjoint subsets known as *choices*. An example of a choice is the set of GMAT scores below 650. Given a category P, P_x is used to denote a choice in P. When there is no ambiguity, we will simply write P_x as x.

A test frame is a set of choices. For instance, a test frame for the qualifications of a master degree applicant is {Qualified Accountant$_{yes}$, GMAT Score$_{<650}$}. A test frame is said to be *complete* if, when an element is selected from every choice in that test frame, a standalone test case can be formed. Suppose the admission system for the master degree program in accounting requires all applicants to state whether they are qualified accountants. Then, {Qualified Accountant$_{yes}$, GMAT Score$_{<650}$} is a complete test frame but {GMAT Score$_{<650}$} is incomplete.

Given any choice x, its *relation* with another choice y (denoted by $x \mapsto y$) must be one of the following: (a) x is *fully embedded* in y (denoted by $x \sqsubset y$) if and only if every complete test frame that contains x also contains y. (b) x is *partially embedded* in y (denoted by $x \sqsubseteq y$) if and only if there are some complete test frames that contain both x and y while there are also others that contain x but not y. (c) x is *not embedded* in y (denoted by $x \not\sqsubset y$) if and only if there is no complete test frame that contains both x and y. These three types of choice relations are exhaustive and mutually exclusive, and hence $x \mapsto y$ can be uniquely determined [5,7,18].

CHOC'LATE generates a test suite using the following procedure:

(1) Decompose the specification into individual *functional units* that can be tested separately.
(2) Define the categories according to the specification of each functional unit. Partition each category into choices.
(3) Construct a *choice relation table* that captures the constraint (formally known as the *choice relation*) between every pair of choices.
(4) Specify the *preferred maximum number of test frames* $\overline{M}$ and the *minimal priority level* $\underline{m}$. Construct a *choice priority table* that captures the *relative priority levels* (denoted by $r(x)$) of individual choices x. The *lower* the value of $r(x)$, the *higher* will be the priority for x to be used for test frame generation. Any choice x with $r(x) \leqslant \underline{m}$ will always be selected for inclusion as part of a test frame, no matter whether the number of generated test frames exceeds $\overline{M}$.
(5) There are two associated algorithms in CHOC'LATE: one for constructing test frames and the other for extending them. Use the algorithms to generate complete test frames. Form test cases from the complete test frames.

Example 1 (Test Suite Generation by CHOC'LATE)
The following is a university admission system (ADMIT) for a master degree program in accounting:

ADMIT captures the following types of information about an applicant in order to determine their eligibility for the program: (a) whether the applicant is a *qualified accountant*, that is, holder of a professional accounting qualification such as CPA; (b) if yes, whether the professional qualification is obtained locally or overseas; and (c) the GMAT score if known. Preference will be given to applicants with a professional accounting qualification, particularly obtained locally. To cater for the situation that an applicant is about to take or has just sat for the GMAT examination, ADMIT allows an applicant to apply for the program before knowing the GMAT score. However, if such an applicant is given a provisional offer, a GMAT score of 650 or above must be obtained before the program starts.

We describe how CHOC'LATE generates a test suite $TS_{ADMIT}(CHOC)$ for ADMIT:

(1) Because of the simplicity of ADMIT, the specification can be treated as one functional unit in its entirety. No decomposition is needed.
(2) The categories and choices are defined according to ADMIT and shown in Table 1.

Table 1. Categories and choices for ADMIT

Categories	Associated Choices
Qualified Accountant	Qualified Accountant$_{yes}$, Qualified Accountant$_{no}$
Professional Qualification	Professional Qualification$_{local}$, Professional Qualification$_{overseas}$
GMAT Score	GMAT Score$_{<650}$, GMAT Score$_{\geqslant 650}$

Table 2. Choice relation table $\mathcal{T}_{ADMIT}$ for ADMIT

	Qualified Accountant$_{yes}$	Qualified Accountant$_{no}$	Professional Qualification$_{local}$	Professional Qualification$_{overseas}$	GMAT Score$_{<650}$	GMAT Score$_{\geqslant 650}$
Qualified Accountant$_{yes}$	⊏	⊄	𝔼	𝔼	𝔼	𝔼
Qualified Accountant$_{no}$	⊄	⊏	⊄	⊄	𝔼	𝔼
Professional Qualification$_{local}$	⊏	⊄	⊏	⊄	𝔼	𝔼
Professional Qualification$_{overseas}$	⊏	⊄	⊄	⊏	𝔼	𝔼
GMAT Score$_{<650}$	𝔼	𝔼	𝔼	𝔼	⊏	⊄
GMAT Score$_{\geqslant 650}$	𝔼	𝔼	𝔼	𝔼	⊄	⊏

(3) The choice relation between every pair of choices is determined according to ADMIT, as shown in the choice relation table $\mathcal{T}_{ADMIT}$ in Table 2. For example, we have (Professional Qualification$_{local}$) ⊏ (Qualified Accountant$_{yes}$), indicating that every complete test frame containing "Professional Qualification$_{local}$" must also contain "Qualified Accountant$_{yes}$". The rationale is that "Professional Qualification$_{local}$" assumes that the applicant must be a qualified accountant. An example of a partial embedding relation is (Professional Qualification$_{overseas}$) 𝔼 (GMAT Score$_{\geqslant 650}$). Any complete test frame containing "Professional Qualification$_{overseas}$" may or may not contain "GMAT Score$_{\geqslant 650}$". This is because a complete test frame containing "Professional Qualification$_{overseas}$" may contain "GMAT Score$_{<650}$" instead of "GMAT Score$_{\geqslant 650}$", or the complete test frame may not contain any choice from the category "GMAT Score" (when the applicant does not know the GMAT score when applying for the program). Finally, an example of the non-embedding relation is (Qualified Accountant$_{no}$) ⊄ (Professional Qualification$_{local}$). In other words, if the applicant is not a qualified accountant, whether the professional accounting qualification is obtained locally or from overseas is irrelevant.

In essence, the choice relations in $\mathcal{T}_{ADMIT}$ determine how choices are combined to form complete test frames.

(4) Suppose, for instance, the software tester judges that, according to experience in the application domain, "GMAT Score$_{<650}$" and "GMAT Score$_{\geqslant 650}$" are most likely to reveal faults in ADMIT. In this case, the tester will assign higher priorities to $r(\text{GMAT Score}_{<650})$ and $r(\text{GMAT Score}_{\geqslant 650})$ than other choices. As a result, "GMAT Score$_{<650}$" and "GMAT Score$_{\geqslant 650}$" will first be used to generate test frames. Suppose further that, after considering the testing resources available, the tester sets $\overline{M}$ to a very high value, indicating to the associated algorithms that all complete test frames are to be generated for testing. (See Section 3.4 for more details.)

Table 3. Complete test frames generated by CHOC'LATE for ADMIT

Complete Test Frames
$B_1^c = \{$Qualified Accountant$_{yes}$, Professional Qualification$_{local}\}$
$B_2^c = \{$Qualified Accountant$_{yes}$, Professional Qualification$_{local}$, GMAT Score$_{<650}\}$
$B_3^c = \{$Qualified Accountant$_{yes}$, Professional Qualification$_{local}$, GMAT Score$_{\geq 650}\}$
$B_4^c = \{$Qualified Accountant$_{yes}$, Professional Qualification$_{overseas}\}$
$B_5^c = \{$Qualified Accountant$_{yes}$, Professional Qualification$_{overseas}$, GMAT Score$_{<650}\}$
$B_6^c = \{$Qualified Accountant$_{yes}$, Professional Qualification$_{overseas}$, GMAT Score$_{\geq 650}\}$
$B_7^c = \{$Qualified Accountant$_{no}\}$
$B_8^c = \{$Qualified Accountant$_{no}$, GMAT Score$_{<650}\}$
$B_9^c = \{$Qualified Accountant$_{no}$, GMAT Score$_{\geq 650}\}$

(5) The associated algorithms generate a set of test frames SF_{ADMIT}(CHOC) for ADMIT. In particular, nine test frames are complete, as shown in Table 3. Obviously, the test frames B_2^c, B_3^c, B_5^c, B_6^c, B_8^c, and B_9^c are complete. The test frames B_1^c, B_4^c, and B_7^c are also complete because ADMIT allows an applicant to apply for the program before knowing the GMAT score, so that the score is not a necessary input to the system.

During the generation process, several incomplete test frames are also formed. An example is $\{$Qualified Accountant$_{yes}$, GMAT Score$_{<650}\}$. It is incomplete because it needs a choice from the category "Professional Qualification" to form a complete test frame. The tester needs to check SF_{ADMIT}(CHOC) and remove any incomplete test frames. After the removal process, the nine complete test frames in Table 3 remain in SF_{ADMIT}(CHOC). For each of these complete test frames, a test case is formed by randomly selecting and combining an element from each choice in that test frame. Consider, for instance, B_9^c. A test case $\{$Qualified Accountant = no, GMAT Score = 720$\}$ can be formed. ∎

2.2   CTM

CTM is similar to CHOC'LATE in its approach to test suite generation [6,10,12,22]. It consists of the following steps:

(1) Decompose the specification into individual functional units that can be tested separately. This step is identical to step (1) in CHOC'LATE.
(2) For each functional unit, identify *classifications* and their associated *classes*. Classifications and classes in CTM are identical to categories and choices, respectively, in CHOC'LATE. For ease of presentation, in the rest of this paper, classifications and classes will be stated as categories and choices.
(3) Construct a *classification tree* to capture the relation between any choice P_x and any category Q ($\neq P$).
(4) Use the associated algorithm to construct the *combination table*, through which valid combinations of choices are selected as complete test frames. A test case is then formed from each complete test frame as in CHOC'LATE.

Example 2 (Test Suite Generation by CTM)
Refer to the university admission system ADMIT in Example 1. Steps (1) and (2) of CTM are identical to their counterparts in CHOC'LATE. Let us illustrate steps (3) and (4) of

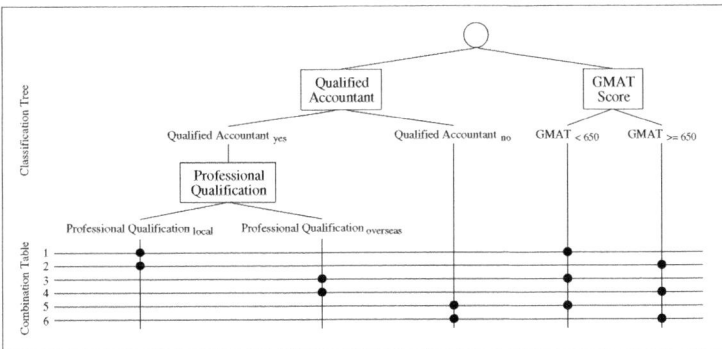

Fig. 1. Classification tree Υ_{ADMIT} and combination table for ADMIT

CTM for generating a set of test frames $SF_{\text{ADMIT}}(\text{CTM})$ and its corresponding test suite $TS_{\text{ADMIT}}(\text{CTM})$:

(3) We construct a classification tree Υ_{ADMIT} (as shown in the upper half of Fig. 1), capturing the relations between the relevant categories and choices. Categories in the classification tree are enclosed in boxes whereas choices are not.

A small circle at the top of a classification tree is the *general root node*, covering the entire input domain. The categories directly under the general root node, such as "Qualified Accountant" and "GMAT Score" in Fig. 1, are called *top-level categories*. In general, a category P may have several choices P_x directly under it. P is known as the *parent category* and P_x is known as a *child choice*. In Fig. 1, for example, "Qualified Accountant" is the parent category of "Qualified Accountant$_{\text{yes}}$" whereas "Qualified Accountant$_{\text{yes}}$" is a child choice of "Qualified Accountant". Similarly, a choice P_x may have one or more categories $Q (\neq P)$ directly under it. Then P_x is known as the *parent choice* and Q is known as a *child category*. In Fig 1, for example, "Qualified Accountant$_{\text{yes}}$" is the parent choice of "Professional Qualification" while "Professional Qualification" is the child category of "Qualified Accountant$_{\text{yes}}$".

(4) Use the associated algorithm to construct the combination table and to generate complete test frames (as shown, for example, in the lower half of Fig. 1). The process makes use of the following rules:

(a) Draw the grids of the combination table under a classification tree. The columns of the table correspond to the terminal nodes of the classification tree. The rows correspond to test frames.

(b) Generate a test frame in the combination table by selecting a combination of choices in a classification tree as follows: (i) select one and only one child choice for each top-level category, and (ii) for every child category of each selected choice, recursively select one and only one child choice.

For the given classification tree Υ_{ADMIT}, the above rules generate $SF_{\text{ADMIT}}(\text{CTM})$ containing six test frames. For instance, the test frame corresponds to row 1 of the combination table is {Qualified Accountant$_{\text{yes}}$, Professional Qualification$_{\text{local}}$,

GMAT Score$_{<650}$}. Since a classification tree may not fully capture the relations among the relevant categories and choices, resulting in the occurrence of incomplete test frames, we need to check the set of test frames generated and remove any incomplete ones. After checking, we find that all the six test frames in SF_{ADMIT} (CTM) are complete. For each of these test frames, a test case is formed by randomly selecting and combining an element from each choice in that test frame.   ∎

2.3   Applicability of CHOC'LATE and CTM

It is obvious that a testing method may not be applicable to all types of systems. CHOC'LATE and CTM are no exception. Both methods are not specifically developed for testing real-time systems or embedded systems. Having said that, it should be noted that CHOC'LATE and CTM are generic testing methods and, as such, they can be used to generate test suites when the following two conditions are met: (a) the software can be decomposed into functional units to be tested independently, and (b) categories, choices, and relations at the category-level or at the choice-level can be identified from the specification. For example, CHOC'LATE has been successfully applied to different application domains, including the inventory registration module and the purchase-order generation module of an inventory management system, an online telephone inquiry system, and the meal scheduling module of an airline meal ordering system [7]. As for CTM, its successful applications to an airfield lighting control system, an automatic mail sorting system, an integrated ship management system, and a parser as part of a software development environment have been reported [10].

3   Strengths and Weaknesses of CHOC'LATE and CTM

3.1   Relations among Categories and Choices

CHOC'LATE and CTM use different approaches to capture and represent relations among choices or categories. These relations then determine how choices are combined together to form complete test frames. CHOC'LATE captures the relation between every pair of *choices*. They are expressed in terms of three choice relations (full embedding, partial embedding, and nonembedding) and captured in a choice relation table. In contrast, CTM captures the relations at the *category* level, or more specifically, the relations between a choice P_x and a category Q ($\neq P$). Furthermore, these relations are expressed in a hierarchical tree structure known as a classification tree. Obviously, category-level constraints are coarser than choice-level constraints. On the other hand, since the number of category-level constraints is much less than that of choice-level constraints, the former type requires less effort to identify.

Consider, for example, the classification tree Υ_{ADMIT} in Fig. 1. According to the selection rules, because "Qualified Accountant$_{yes}$" is the parent choice of "Professional Qualification", whenever either "Professional Qualification$_{local}$" or "Professional Qualification$_{overseas}$" is selected to form part of any complete test frame, "Qualified Accountant$_{yes}$" must also be selected. This part of the tree structure is similar in effect to the definition of the choice relations (Professional Qualification$_{local}$ ⊏ Qualified

Accountant$_{yes}$) and (Professional Qualification$_{overseas}$ $\sqsubseteq$ Qualified Accountant$_{yes}$) in CHOC'LATE.

Because CHOC'LATE captures the relations at a more fine-grained level (namely, the choice level instead of the category level), CHOC'LATE is generally more comprehensive in generating complete test frames. Let us compare SF_{ADMIT}(CHOC) and SF_{ADMIT}(CTM). As explained in Example 1, SF_{ADMIT}(CHOC) contains all the nine complete test frames $B_1^c, B_2^c, \ldots, B_9^c$ that should be generated, as shown in Table 3. SF_{ADMIT}(CTM), however, only contains six complete test frames, namely $B_2^c, B_3^c, B_5^c, B_6^c, B_8^c$, and B_9^c, corresponding to rows 1, 2, ..., 6 in the combination table of Fig. 1 (see Example 2). In other words, CTM cannot generate the complete test frames B_1^c, B_4^c, and B_7^c. This problem affects the comprehensiveness of SF_{ADMIT}(CTM) and TS_{ADMIT}(CTM), and hence the effectiveness of testing.

A close examination of the structure of the classification tree Υ_{ADMIT} in Fig. 1 reveals the reason for the omission of B_1^c, B_4^c, and B_7^c. "GMAT Score" is a top-level category in Υ_{ADMIT}. According to the selection rules, a child choice of "GMAT Score" must be selected as part of any complete test frame. This requirement prevents B_1^c, B_4^c, and B_7^c from being generated, because all these three complete test frames do not contain any choice in "GMAT Score". [1]

In contrast, CHOC'LATE can generate B_1^c, B_4^c, and B_7^c by using the partial embedding relation. For example, by defining (Qualified Accountant$_{yes}$ $\sqsubseteq$ GMAT Score$_{<650}$), (Qualified Accountant$_{yes}$ $\sqsubseteq$ GMAT Score$_{\geqslant 650}$) and other relevant choice relations (see Table 2), any complete test frame B^c generated by CHOC'LATE containing "Qualified Accountant$_{yes}$" must be one of the following three types:

(a) B^c contains "GMAT Score$_{<650}$" but does not contain "GMAT Score$_{\geqslant 650}$",
(b) B^c contains "GMAT Score$_{\geqslant 650}$" but does not contain "GMAT Score$_{<650}$", and
(c) B^c does not contain both "GMAT Score$_{<650}$" and "GMAT Score$_{\geqslant 650}$".

Because of type (c), B_1^c and B_4^c (which are omitted from SF_{ADMIT}(CTM)) will exist in SF_{ADMIT}(CHOC). Similarly, we can define (Qualified Accountant$_{no}$ $\sqsubseteq$ GMAT Score$_{<650}$), (Qualified Accountant$_{no}$ $\sqsubseteq$ GMAT Score$_{\geqslant 650}$), and other relevant choice relations to guarantee the generation of B_7^c.

3.2   Inherent Limitation of Tree Structure

Given any pair of distinct categories P and Q, Chen et al. [6] define four possible types of hierarchical relations: (a) P is a *loose ancestor* of Q (denoted by $P \Leftrightarrow Q$), (b) P is a *strict ancestor* of Q (denoted by $P \Rightarrow Q$), (c) P is *incompatible with* Q (denoted by $P \sim Q$), and (d) P has *other relations with* Q (denoted by $P \otimes Q$). Note that, for the ancestor relation, type (a) is symmetric whereas type (b) is anti-symmetric. Readers may refer to [6] for details.

The hierarchical relations (b), (c), and (d) affect the relative positions of P and Q in a classification tree. Consider, for example, the categories "Qualified Accountant"

---

[1] One may argue that Υ_{ADMIT} is only one of the many possible tree structures with respect to the categories and choices in Table 1. We must point out, however, that no matter how a classification tree is drawn using these categories and choices, it is unable to generate all the nine complete test frames in Table 3.

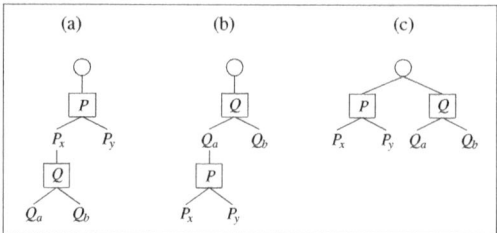

Fig. 2. Three possible classification trees

and "Professional Qualification" in the classification tree Υ_{ADMIT}. We have (Qualified Accountant $\Rightarrow$ Professional Qualification), causing "Professional Qualification" to appear under the choice "Qualified Accountant$_{yes}$" (but not "Qualified Accountant$_{no}$") of "Qualified Accountant".

On the other hand, for relation (a), it indicates a *symmetric* parent-child or ancestor-descendent hierarchical relation between P and Q, resulting in a loop in a classification tree. This relation violates an implicit assumption of classification trees, namely, that the parent-child or ancestor-descendent hierarchical relation must be *anti-symmetric* for any pair of categories; otherwise a classification tree cannot be constructed. Since CHOC'LATE does not use a tree structure to capture the relations among choices, the problem associated with the loose-ancestor relation is not applicable.

Example 3 (Loose-Ancestor Hierarchical Relation)
Suppose we have a pair of distinct categories P and Q, where P has two associated choices P_x and P_y, and Q has two associated choices Q_a and Q_b. Suppose further that, with respect to P and Q, only three complete test frames exist, namely, $B_1^c = \{P_x, Q_a\}$, $B_2^c = \{P_y\}$, and $B_3^c = \{Q_b\}$. In view of these complete test frames and according to the definitions of hierarchical relations [6], we have a loose ancestor relation $P \Leftrightarrow Q$. Thus, a classification tree cannot be constructed to *fully* capture the relations between P and Q such that B_1^c, B_2^c, and B_3^c can be generated.

If we ignore the ability of classification trees in generating all complete test frames, various tree structures can be constructed from P, Q, and their associated choices, including the three depicted in Fig. 2. [2] None of these classification trees (including the three in Fig. 2 and others not included in the figure) generates all the complete test frames B_1^c, B_2^c, and B_3^c. Consider, for instance, the tree in Fig. 2(a). It generates B_1^c and B_2^c but not B_3^c.

In CHOC'LATE, we can define the following choice relations between P and Q: (i) $P_x \sqsubseteq Q_a$ and $Q_a \sqsubseteq P_x$; (ii) $P_y \not\sqsubseteq m$ and $m \not\sqsubseteq P_y$, where choice $m = P_x$, Q_a, or Q_b; and (iii) $Q_b \not\sqsubseteq n$ and $n \not\sqsubseteq Q_b$, where choice $n = P_x$, P_y, or Q_a. These definitions will then cause the associated algorithms to generate B_1^c, B_2^c, and B_3^c, respectively.   ∎

---

[2] There are other feasible classification trees that are not shown in the figure, because a category and its associated choices may occur more than once in a classification tree [6].

3.3 Automatic Deduction and Consistency Checking of Relations

The comprehensiveness of the generated test suite depends on the correctness of choice relations and hierarchical relations in CHOC'LATE and CTM, respectively. However, it would be tedious and error prone to manually define all such relations. Chen et al. [7] have identified various properties of these relations in CHOC'LATE to form the basis for their automatic deductions and consistency checking. Two examples are:
(**Property 1**) Given any choices x, y, and z, if $x \sqsubset y$ and $x \mathrel{\boxed{E}} z$, then $y \mathrel{\boxed{E}} z$.
(**Property 2**) Given any choices x, y, and z, if $x \sqsubset z$ and $y \mathrel{\boxed{E}} z$, then $y \mathrel{\boxed{E}} x$ or $y \mathrel{\boxed{\not\sqsubset}} x$.

Property 1 provides a basis for automatic deduction of choice relations because its "then" part consists of a definite relation. Thus, once $x \sqsubset y$ and $x \mathrel{\boxed{E}} z$ are defined, $y \mathrel{\boxed{E}} z$ can be automatically deduced without manual intervention. As for Property 2, its "then" part contains two possible relations. Although the property cannot be used for automatic deduction, it nevertheless allows us to check the consistency of the relations among choices. For example, we know that when $x \sqsubset z$ and $y \mathrel{\boxed{E}} z$, we cannot have $y \sqsubset x$, or else it will contradict Property 2.

Similar properties and techniques have been identified in CTM [6]. Two examples are:
(**Property 3**) Given any categories P and Q, if $P \Rightarrow Q$, then $Q \otimes P$. (**Property 4**) Given any categories P and Q, if $P \otimes Q$, then $Q \Rightarrow P$ or $Q \otimes P$. Properties 3 and 4 can be used for automatic deduction and consistency checking of hierarchical relations, respectively.

The techniques of automatic deduction and consistency checking are more advanced and refined in CHOC'LATE than in CTM. In CHOC'LATE, there are five main propositions and three main corollaries, from which properties such as those mentioned above are derived. Some of these main propositions and corollaries are further refined into sub-propositions and sub-corollaries (see [7] for details). On the other hand, in CTM [6], only three propositions exist and they cannot be further refined.

3.4 Test Frame Generation

Often, many categories and choices can be defined from a real-life specification [3]. Consequently, CHOC'LATE and CTM will generate many complete test frames (and hence many test cases) to cover diverse valid combinations of the defined choices. For instance, it has been reported that real-world protocol software may have 448–2402 test cases per test suite [13]. Such a test suite can be prohibitively expensive to execute exhaustively owing to its large size.

To alleviate this problem, CHOC'LATE allows testers to control the total number of test frames generated by specifying (a) the *preferred* maximum number of test frames $\overline{M}$, (b) the relative priority level $r(x)$ of each individual choice x, and (c) the minimal priority level $\underline{m}$. For $\overline{M}$, the word "preferred" implies that the limit is not absolute, as it may be overwritten by $\underline{m}$. For the relative priority level of individual choices, they determine the *order* of choices used for test frame generation. The lower the value of $r(x)$, the higher will be the priority of x. $\underline{m}$ allows testers to ensure that those choices x with $r(x) \leqslant \underline{m}$ will always be selected for inclusion as part of a test frame, no matter whether the number of generated test frames exceeds $\overline{M}$ or not. In the situation where $\overline{M}$ should not be waived by $\underline{m}$, $\underline{m}$ should be set to zero, and $\overline{M}$ becomes the *absolute* maximum number of generated test frames.

Testers often face a dilemma that, on one hand, they prefer to set a maximum number $\overline{M}$ of generated test frames so as to control the testing effort, but on the other hand, the choices considered very important should always be used for test frame generation, even though this may cause the number of generated test frames to exceed $\overline{M}$. Allowing testers to set the values of $\overline{M}$, $\underline{m}$, and the relative priority level of choices will provide them with flexibility in dealing with such dilemma.

In contrast, CTM aims at generating valid combinations of choices as complete test frames without considering the testing resources involved. Grochtmann and Grimm [10] argue that maximality and minimality criteria can be incorporated into CTM, thus allowing testers to control the number of complete test frames to some extent. The *maximality* criterion naturally requires each valid combination of choices to form a complete test frame. The *minimality* criterion, on the other hand, requires each choice to be used in at least one complete test frame, so that the number of complete test frames can be reduced. Obviously, even with these two criteria, the ability to control the number of generated complete test frames in CTM is far more restricted than when compared with CHOC'LATE.

3.5   Documentation of the Software under Test

Both CHOC'LATE and CTM aim to generate a test suite for software testing. In addition, during the generation process, the choice relation table constructed in CHOC'LATE and the classification tree constructed in CTM can serve as useful documentation of the software under test [10].

Briand et al. [2] argue that "devising ... categories and choices is ... necessary to understand the rationale behind test cases and is a way for the tester to formalize her understanding of the functional specification". In CTM, a classification tree is constructed, capturing the relations among relevant categories and choices. Since it is in a graphic form, a classification tree is more concise and descriptive than a narrative specification [10]. Similarly, a two-dimensional choice relation table in CHOC'LATE captures the relation between every pair of choices. This table is better than a narrative specification for the purpose of documentation and reasoning.

When comparing a classification tree with a choice relation table, there are mixed opinions. On one hand, some people prefer a classification tree to a choice relation table for the purpose of *presentation*. They argue that the pictorial simplicity and vividness of a tree makes it more understandable [23]. On the other hand, others argue that a choice relation table is better than a classification tree because the former contains more fine-grained information to help readers understand the relations among individual choices (see Section 3.1 for details).

4   Selection Guidelines

Intuitively, every testing method has its own merits and drawbacks. CHOC'LATE and CTM are no exception. Neither of them is ideal for every testing situation. A software tester should be knowledgeable enough to decide whether CHOC'LATE or CTM is best applied to specific testing scenarios. The decision is not straightforward because both of them are input domain partitioning methods [11,16] and hence they are fairly similar. We provide below some guidelines to help a tester decide which of them should be used in a given testing scenario.

Given a specification, the tester should first consider the level of abstraction of the constraints and the relationships among constraints. If the constraints are specified at the choice level and the tester can afford the effort to identify their relationships, then CHOC'LATE is preferred because it will generate a more comprehensive set of complete test frames (see Section 3.1). On the other hand, if all or most of the constraints are only available at the category level, or if the tester can only afford to identify category-level relationships among constraints, or if the tester prefers an intuitive graphic presentation of the relations among constraints (see Section 3.5), then CTM is the option (see also Section 3.1).

In addition, the possible occurrence of the loose-ancestor hierarchical relation ($P \Leftrightarrow Q$) between two distinct categories P and Q is another factor to consider. If this relation exists, then CTM should not be chosen (see Section 3.2), unless the use of CHOC'LATE is prohibited by other factors such as the absence of choice-level constraints in the specification as explained above.

Next, we consider the process of generating complete test frames. Ideally, the process must be well executed so that no complete test frame will be missing. Otherwise, testing may not be comprehensive and some software failures may never be revealed. In the generation process, the correctness of the constraints (at the category or choice level) is of utmost importance because it will affect the comprehensiveness of the set of complete test frames generated. If the number of constraints to be manually defined is large (especially when the specification is large and complex), the chance of making mistakes is high. In this regard, the complexity of the choice relation table in CHOC'LATE is an additional consideration that needs to be taken into account when selecting between the two methods. In any case, both CHOC'LATE and CTM offer the features of automatic deduction and consistency checking of relations, with a view to improving the effectiveness and efficiency of constraint definitions. The two features provided by CHOC'LATE are more advanced and refined than those by CTM. This may serve to counterbalance the complexity of the choice relation table in CHOC'LATE (see Section 3.3).

The amount of testing resources available is also an important factor. As we have mentioned, it would be ideal to test the software with all the complete test frames. In reality, however, this may be infeasible because of the shortage of testing resources. If this happens, both CHOC'LATE and CTM allow the tester to select a subset of all complete test frames to be generated for testing. Among the two methods, CHOC'LATE is more refined in allowing the tester to control how this subset is generated. Therefore, if testing constraints are an issue, CHOC'LATE will be a better choice (see Section 3.4).

5   Related Work

Yu et al. [24] proposed some enhancements to CTM by annotating a classification tree with additional information (including selector expressions, occurrence tags, and weight tags) to reduce manual effort in the generation, selection, and prioritization of test cases. They also developed an automated tool (EXTRACT) that implements the proposed enhancements.

Amla and Ammann [1] analyzed the feasibility of applying the category-partition method (on which CHOC'LATE is based) to Z specifications and found that testing requirements can be defined from formal specifications more easily. Hierons, Singh and their co-workers [12,22] have also done similar work in the context of Z specifications. They introduce an approach [22] to generating test cases from Z specifications by combining CTM with disjunctive normal forms, and present another approach [12] to extracting predicates from Z specifications and building a classification tree from these predicates.

Obviously, the comprehensiveness of a test suite generated by CHOC'LATE and CTM depends on how well categories and choices are identified from the specification. In this regard, Chen, Poon, and their co-workers [4,19] have conducted several empirical studies to investigate the common mistakes made by experienced and inexperienced testers when the identification process is done in an ad hoc manner. Furthermore, they have recently developed a **D**ivid**E**-and-conquer methodology for identifying categorie**S**, choice**S**, and choic**E R**elations for **T**est case generation (**DESSERT**) for large and complex specifications that involve many different components [5].

6   Summary and Conclusion

In this paper, we have outlined the main concepts of two popular specification-based testing methods, namely, CHOC'LATE and CTM. We have used examples to illustrate how both methods generate a test suite from the specification, and contrasted their strengths and weaknesses with respect to five different aspects, namely, (a) relations among categories and choices, (b) inherent limitation of the tree structure, (c) automatic deduction and consistency checking of relations, (d) test frame generation, and (e) documentation of the software under test. Based on these strengths and weaknesses, we have provided guidelines to help the tester decide which method to use under different testing scenarios. Thus, the paper will help the software testing community better understand CHOC'LATE and CTM, and determine which of them is more appropriate in a specific testing scenario.

Acknowledgment. This research is supported in part by a Discovery Grant of the Australian Research Council (project no. ARC DP0771733) and the General Research Fund of the Research Grants Council of Hong Kong (project no. 717811).

References

1. Amla, N., Ammann, P.E.: Using Z Specifications in Category Partition Testing. In: Systems Integrity, Software Safety, and Process Security: Building the Right System Right: Proceedings of the 7th Annual IEEE Conference on Computer Assurance (COMPASS 1992), pp. 3–10. IEEE Computer Society, Los Alamitos (1992)
2. Briand, L.C., Labiche, Y., Bawar, Z., Spido, N.T.: Using Machine Learning to Refine Category-Partition Test Specifications and Test Suites. Information and Software Technology 51(11), 1551–1564 (2009)

3. Chan, E.Y.K., Chan, W.K., Poon, P.-L., Yu, Y.T.: An Empirical Evaluation of Several Test-a-Few Strategies for Testing Particular Conditions. Software: Practice and Experience (2011), doi:10.1002/spe.1098

4. Chen, T.Y., Poon, P.-L., Tang, S.-F., Tse, T.H.: On the Identification of Categories and Choices for Specification-Based Test Case Generation. Information and Software Technology 46(13), 887–898 (2004)

5. Chen, T.Y., Poon, P.-L., Tang, S.-F., Tse, T.H.: DESSERT: a DividE-and-conquer methodology for identifying categorieS, choiceS, and choicE Relations for Test case generation. IEEE Transactions on Software Engineering (2011), doi:10.1109/TSE.2011.69

6. Chen, T.Y., Poon, P.-L., Tse, T.H.: An Integrated Classification-Tree Methodology for Test Case Generation. International Journal of Software Engineering and Knowledge Engineering 10(6), 647–679 (2000)

7. Chen, T.Y., Poon, P.-L., Tse, T.H.: A Choice Relation Framework for Supporting Category-Partition Test Case Generation. IEEE Transactions on Software Engineering 29(7), 577–593 (2003)

8. Chusho, T.: Test Data Selection and Quality Estimation Based on the Concept of Essential Branches for Path Testing. IEEE Transactions on Software Engineering 13(5), 509–517 (1987)

9. Foreman, L.M., Zweben, S.H.: A Study of the Effectiveness of Control and Data Flow Testing Strategies. Journal of Systems and Software 21(3), 215–228 (1993)

10. Grochtmann, M., Grimm, K.: Classification Trees for Partition Testing. Software Testing, Verification and Reliability 3(2), 63–82 (1993)

11. Hierons, R.M., Harman, M., Fox, C., Ouarbya, L., Daoudi, M.: Conditioned Slicing Supports Partition Testing. Software Testing, Verification and Reliability 12(1), 23–28 (2002)

12. Hierons, R.M., Harman, M., Singh, H.: Automatically Generating Information from a Z Specification to Support the Classification Tree Method. In: Bert, D., Bowen, J.P., King, S., Waldén, M. (eds.) ZB 2003. LNCS, vol. 2651, pp. 388–407. Springer, Heidelberg (2003)

13. Jiang, B., Tse, T.H., Grieskamp, W., Kicillof, N., Cao, Y., Li, X., Chan, W.K.: Assuring the Model Evolution of Protocol Software Specifications by Regression Testing Process Improvement. Software: Practice and Experience 41(10), 1073–1103 (2011)

14. Kansomkeat, S., Thiket, P., Offutt, J.: Generating Test Cases from UML Activity Diagrams Using the Condition-Classification Tree Method. In: Proceedings of the 2nd International Conference on Software Technology and Engineering (ICSTE 2010), pp. V1-62–V1-66. IEEE Computer Society, Los Alamitos (2010)

15. Lemos, O.A.L., Vincenzi, A.M.R., Maldonado, J.C., Masiero, P.C.: Control and Data Flow Structural Testing Criteria for Aspect-Oriented Programs. Journal of Systems and Software 80(6), 862–882 (2007)

16. Myers, G.J.: The Art of Software Testing. Wiley, Hoboken (2004)

17. Ostrand, T.J., Balcer, M.J.: The Category-Partition Method for Specifying and Generating Functional Tests. Communications of the ACM 31(6), 676–686 (1988)

18. Poon, P.-L., Tang, S.-F., Tse, T.H., Chen, T.Y.: CHOC'LATE: a Framework for Specification-Based Testing. Communications of the ACM 53(4), 113–118 (2010)

19. Poon, P.-L., Tse, T.H., Tang, S.-F., Kuo, F.-C.: Contributions of Tester Experience and a Checklist Guideline to the Identification of Categories and Choices for Software Testing. Software Quality Journal 19(1), 141–163 (2011)

20. Richardson, D.J., O'Malley, O., Tittle, C.: Approaches to Specification-Based Testing. In: Proceedings of the ACM SIGSOFT 3rd Symposium on Software Testing, Analysis, and Verification (TAV 3), pp. 86–96. ACM, New York (1989)

21. Shepard, T., Lamb, M., Kelly, D.: More Testing should be Taught. Communications of the ACM 44(6), 103–108 (2001)
22. Singh, H., Conrad, M., Sadeghipour, S.: Test Case Design Based on Z and the Classification-Tree Method. In: Proceedings of the 1st IEEE International Conference on Formal Engineering Methods (ICFEM 1997), pp. 81–90. IEEE Computer Society, Los Alamitos (1997)
23. Subramanian, G.H., Nosek, J., Raghunathan, S.P., Kanitkar, S.S.: A Comparison of the Decision Table and Tree. Communications of the ACM 35(1), 89–94 (1992)
24. Yu, Y.T., Ng, S.P., Chan, E.Y.K.: Generating, Selecting and Prioritizing Test Cases from Specifications with Tool Support. In: Proceedings of the 3rd International Conference on Quality Software (QSIC 2003), pp. 83–90. IEEE Computer Society, Los Alamitos (2003)

Improving the Performance of Execution Time Control by Using a Hardware Time Management Unit

Kristoffer Nyborg Gregertsen and Amund Skavhaug

Department of Engineering Cybernetics, NTNU
N-7491 Trondheim, Norway
{gregerts,amund}@itk.ntnu.no

Abstract. This paper describes how a dedicated Time Management Unit (TMU) is used to reduce the overhead of execution time control. While the implementation described here is for Ada 2012 and a GNAT bare-board run-time environment, the principles should be applicable to other languages and run-time systems. The TMU has been implemented as a peripheral unit for the Atmel AVR®32 UC3 series of microcontrollers, and test results from simulation with the syntheziable RTL code of this system-on-chip are presented.

1   Introduction

Scheduling analysis of real-time systems relies on the worst-case execution time (WCET) of tasks being known. However, finding the WCET of an algorithm may be very hard, and performance enhancing techniques such as pipelines and caches makes it even harder [22]. This makes WCET analysis a costly and time consuming process. Also, the WCET will often be considerably longer than the average execution time, as it includes the unlikely event of many or all of the performance enhancing techniques failing. Therefore scheduling will often be pessimistic to provide an offline guarantee that all deadlines are met, which again leads to poor processor utilization.

Execution time control allows the total time a task has been executed on a processor to be measured, and a handler to be called when this execution time reaches a specified timeout value. Combined with a scheduling policy taking advantage of this feature, it allows online control of task execution time instead of relying exclusively on offline guarantees [21]. Execution time control also allows execution time servers for soft sporadic tasks [3], and algorithms where there is an increasing reward with increased service (IRIS) [13].

Many systems support execution time control, examples are real-time POSIX [19], real-time Java [16], and Ada since the 2005 revision of the language standard [11]. Common for most execution time control implementations is that they charge the running task the execution time of interrupt handlers. When the authors at NTNU implemented Ada 2005 execution time control for our AVR32 version of the GNAT bare-board run-time environment [7], separate execution

M. Brorsson and L.M. Pinho (Eds.): Ada-Europe 2012, LNCS 7308, pp. 177–192, 2012.
© Springer-Verlag Berlin Heidelberg 2012

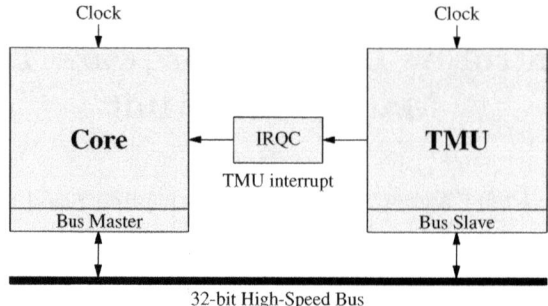

Fig. 1. Initial design with the CPU core and TMU connected to a high-speed bus

time measurement for each interrupt level was added [5, 9]. This improved accuracy of execution time measurement and allowed execution time control for interrupts. This solution was presented at IRTAW 14 [8]. Another solution presented by the developers of MaRTE measures the combined execution time of interrupt handling [15]. Following the recommendations of the workshop [14, 20], the draft for the Ada 2012 standard [12] includes both combined execution time measurement and separate for each interrupt. The new features have been implemented by the authors [10][1].

Performance testing has shown a significant overhead to context switches and interrupt handling, introduced by implementing execution time control [9, 10]. This motivated the authors to design a hardware Time Management Unit (TMU) to reduce the overhead [6]. The design has been implemented for Atmel AVR32 UC3 by a master student at NTNU in cooperation with Atmel Norway [18].

In the following there is a description of the TMU design and its UC3 implementation. Then follows a description of the Ada 2012 execution time control features, and our implementation of this without the TMU. After this it is shown how our implementation is modified for using the TMU and performance test results are given. Finally there is a discussion on the TMU design, the performance test results, and the portability of the solution.

2   The Time Management Unit (TMU)

The TMU was designed as a memory-mapped device accessible through a high-speed bus as shown in Figure 1. In addition to bus interface the TMU has a clock signal as input that need not be the same as the clock used by the core. The TMU generates an interrupt signal that will usually be routed to the core through an interrupt controller.

Internally the TMU has a 64-bit COUNT register that is incremented on every positive edge of the clock signal. After COUNT is incremented it is compared with the 64-bit COMPARE register. If COUNT ≥ COMPARE then the

---
[1] Code available at http://github.com/gregerts/GNATforAVR32

Table 1. User interface of the TMU

Offset	Register	Description
0x00	CTRL	Control register
0x04	MODE	Mode register
0x08	SR	Status register
0x0c	SCR	Status clear register
0x10	IER	Interrupt enable register
0x14	IDR	Interrupt disable register
0x18	IMR	Interrupt mask register
0x1c	COMPARE_HI	Compare register
0x20	COMPARE_LO	
0x24	COUNT_HI	Count register
0x28	COUNT_LO	
0x2c	SWAP_COMPARE_HI	Swap compare register
0x30	SWAP_COMPARE_LO	
0x34	SWAP_COUNT_HI	Swap count register
0x38	SWAP_COUNT_LO	

interrupt signal is asserted. In order to atomically swap a new set of COUNT / COMPARE values with the current, two swap registers are provided. The registers are swapped when the final word of the swap registers is written, and the previous values of COUNT and COMPARE can be read back. The swap registers allow for simple and efficient change of execution time clocks.

The COUNT and COMPARE register may also be accessed directly. When reading the high-word of the registers, the low-word is stored in an internal 32-bit buffer, and this buffered value is returned when the low-word is later read. Similarly, the high-word value is buffered when writing the high-word of COUNT and COMPARE. The whole register is updated when the low-word subsequently is written. Due to the buffering care must be taken not to interleave writing and reading of COUNT. If available it is recommended to use double-word load / store instructions so that registers are read and written atomically.

2.1   UC3 Implementation of TMU

The Atmel AVR32 [1] is a 32-bit RISC architecture optimized for code density and power efficiency. The AVR32 has four interrupt levels, and a number of exceptions. The UC3 is the second implementation of the architecture [2], intended for embedded control applications. It has a three-stage pipeline integrated with an internal SRAM allowing deterministic, single-cycle memory access.

When TMU was implemented for the UC3 some technical changes were needed [18]. The unit was moved from the high-speed bus to the peripheral bus to ease the implementation, and the clock signal driving the TMU was bound to the clock of the peripheral bus to allow a synchronous design. To make the TMU more like other UC3 peripherals and usable for a wider range of purposes, several registers were added as seen in Table 1. The control register allows enabling and disabling the TMU. It is disabled by default to save power. Even though the 64-bit COUNT register is not expected to overflow with the intended usage, an overflow interrupt was added to allow for other usages. Also interrupt control registers were added following the pattern of existing UC3 peripherals.

3   Ada 2012 Execution Time Control

The package Ada.Execution_Time defines the type CPU_Time and the function Clock for execution time measurement of tasks [12]. The execution time of a task is defined as the time spent by the system executing that task, including the time spent executing run-time or system services on its behalf [12]. For Ada 2005 it was implementation defined which task, if any, was charged the execution time used by interrupt handlers and run-time services on behalf of the system. Ada 2012 has the ability to account for the total or separate execution time of interrupts handlers. If supported the function Clock_For_Interrupts returns the total execution time of interrupt handlers since system start-up. The child package Interrupts is new for Ada 2012, and has a function Clock that returns the execution time spent handling the given Interrupt_Id since start-up if supported.

The child package Timers defines the tagged type Timer used for detecting execution time overruns for a single task. The type Timer_Handler identifies a protected procedure to be executed when the timer *expires*. Handlers are set to expire at an absolute or relative execution time using two overloading Set_Handler procedures, and may be cancelled using the procedure Cancel_Handler. To allow execution time control for interrupts in the same way as for tasks we have added a child package Interrupts . Timers. It defines the tagged type Interrupt_Timer that inherits Timer and its operations [10]. This package is not in Ada 2012, but should in the authors opinion be added to the next revision of the language.

4   Implementation without TMU

We have modified our earlier implementation of Ada 2012 execution time control [10] to use the TMU. To understand the changes and the overall design of the system a brief description of this implementation is needed.

4.1   Design

The real-time clock (RTC) and execution time clocks (ETCs) are quite similar in functionality: both clocks support high accuracy measurement of the monotonic passing of time since an epoch, and both support calling a protected handler when a given timeout time is reached. The main difference is that the RTC is always active, while an ETC is active only when its corresponding task or interrupt is executed. Our design takes advantage of this by having a single implementation of clocks and alarms in the internal package System.BB.Time.

In this package the type Time represents the passing of time since the epoch as a 64-bit modular integer, and Time_Span represents time differences as a 64-bit integer with range from -2^{63} to $2^{63} - 1$. The limited private types representing clocks and alarms are defined as shown in Listing 1, and there are access types Clock_Id and Alarm_Id for these. The package also defines public routines for clock and alarm operations, and procedures used by the run-time environment for changing the active execution time clock. Note that the alarm type is also used internally for task wake-up.

4.2   Hardware Timer

The 32-bit COUNT / COMPARE system registers of the AVR32 are used both for the RTC and execution time clocks in the implementation without TMU. The COUNT register is reset to zero at system start-up and is incremented by one every CPU clock cycle. The COMPARE interrupt is triggered when COUNT equals COMPARE, and cleared when COMPARE is written. The interrupt is disabled when COMPARE is zero, which is the reset value of the register.

The package CPU_Primitives provides three hardware timer operations for the COUNT / COMPARE registers. A snap-shot value of COUNT is returned by the function Get_Count. The procedure Adjust_Compare sets COMPARE according to the argument C, while making sure no interrupt is lost. If C is less than COUNT, an interrupt will be pending immediately after leaving the procedure. The procedure Reset_Count sets COUNT to zero and returns the previous COUNT value c_p in one atomic operation. The COMPARE register is not altered by the reset procedure and has to be updated with a call to Adjust_Compare if needed.

4.3   Clock Management

The package body has Clock_Descriptors for the RTC, interrupt clocks and the internal idle clock. Threads have a Clock_Descriptor stored in the Thread_Descriptor type. After initialization there are two active clocks: the RTC that is always active and the ETC that points to the clock of the running thread, that of the interrupt being handled or to the idle clock. The ETC is changed by the procedure Update_ETC as a result of a context switch, interrupt handling, or system idling.

The low-level interrupt handler calls Enter_Interrupt prior to calling the interrupt handler. This procedure activates the interrupt clock found in a look-up table as the new ETC. A stack is used to keep track of nested interrupts. After the interrupt has been handled the procedure Leave_Interrupt is called, and the interrupted clock is popped from the stack and reactivated.

The run-time environment has no idle thread. Instead the thread τ_a that finds the ready queue empty when leaving the kernel, enters an idle-loop waiting for any thread to be made runnable by an interrupt. Prior to entering the idle loop a call to Enter_Idle activates the idle clock as the ETC. If τ_a is made runnable it calls Leave_Idle to reactivate its clock. Also a context switch may change to a new running thread τ_b. When τ_a resumes execution the idle clock has to be activated by the context switch. Therefore the Thread_Descriptor has a field Active_Clock that points either to the task's own clock, or the idle clock if the task is executing the idle loop. Only one thread at a time will enter the idle loop.

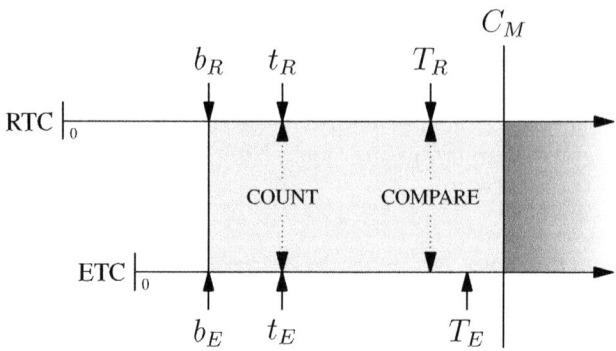

Fig. 2. Relation between the RTC and ETC, and the hardware timer registers. The base time of the two clocks are aligned in the figure.

4.4   Measuring Time

The use of the hardware timer is tick-less and does not require a periodic clock overflow interrupt. Instead COUNT is reset using Reset_Count when the ETC is changed by Update_ETC, and the Base_Time of the RTC and the old ETC is incremented with the previous COUNT value c_p. By doing this the same hardware timer may be used for both the RTC and the ETC as seen in Figure 2.

The elapsed time of a clock t since the epoch is retrieved by the function Elapsed_Time, and is computed from the base time b and the COUNT register value:

$$t = \begin{cases} b + \text{COUNT} & \text{if clock is active} \\ b & \text{else} \end{cases}$$

An interrupt may occur while within Elapsed_Time. This would reset COUNT and update the base time. To avoid an invalid result there is a check after reading COUNT to see if the base time has been updated, in which case the updated base time will be returned as the elapsed time.

4.5   Setting the Hardware Timer

The COMPARE register is adjusted after updating ETC and after the first alarm of an active clock is changed. This is done by calling the procedure Update_Compare. As seen in Figure 2, the value C given to Adjust_Compare is shortest remaining time until timeout T for the RTC and ETC. However, this value is never greater than the maximal COMPARE value C_M to avoid COUNT from overflowing. This safety region is marked with a darker shade in Figure 2. The interrupt will be pending within this region and COUNT is reset when it is handled, preventing overflow. The COMPARE interrupt handler will simply ignore this "false" interrupt. A large safety region of 2^{31} cycles is used to provide ample time for the interrupt to be handled.

4.6   Alarms

Each clock has a queue of pending alarms managed as a linked list and sorted in ascending order after the Timeout of the alarms. In the case of equal Timeout values alarms are queued in FIFO order. To avoid the special condition of an empty queue, there is a sentinel alarm with timeout at Time'Last that is always present at the end of the queue. The constant Time_Last seen by the user is set to Time'Last − 1 so that the sentinel is always last. This avoids an additional check when searching the queue. One sentinel alarm without handler is shared between all clocks to save memory. The procedures Set and Cancel both search the queue from the start for the place to insert or remove an alarm, and call Update_Compare if the first alarm in the queue of an active clock is changed.

4.7   Interrupt Handler

The COMPARE interrupt handler has the highest interrupt priority. The handler calls the procedure Alarm_Wrapper first for the RTC and then for the interrupted ETC on top of the stack. At this point the active ETC is that of the COMPARE interrupt itself, for which no alarms are allowed, so only the interrupt ETC on top of the stack or the RTC may be the cause of the interrupt. As the wrapper is called for both clocks there is no need to check which one caused the interrupt. The alarm wrapper removes all alarms with timeout less or equal to the base time of the clock from the head of alarm queue one at the time, clears the alarm and calls the handler with the data as argument.

5   Modifications for Using the TMU

The package specification of System.BB.Time was not altered when using the TMU. However, the routines interfacing with hardware and the COMPARE interrupt handler has to be updated. Also, an interrupt handler for the TMU has to be added, and an interface to the TMU in the package System.BB.Peripherals.

5.1   TMU Interface

A modular integer type TMU_Interval is defined to represent the 64-bit timer values of the TMU, and the memory-mapped interface is defined in the child package Registers. Public routines were added to read the COUNT register, set the COMPARE register and perform the swap operation. The TMU is configured and enabled as a part of the peripheral initialization.

5.2   Hardware Timer Usage

The updates needed to use two separate hardware timers are shown in Listing 2. The function Elapsed_Time is updated to use the TMU if the given clock is the ETC. No check for interruption is needed for this as the double-word read cannot be interrupted. If the clock is neither the RTC nor the ETC, it is not active and its elapsed time equals the Base_Time. The procedure Update_Compare updates the correct hardware timer if the given clock is active. The RTC is no longer updated by Update_ETC the TMU swap operation simplifies the procedure.

5.3   Interrupt Handlers

The COMPARE interrupt handler now only handles alarms for the RTC. As the RTC is no longer updated when changing the ETC, we reset COUNT and update the base time of the RTC first in this handler. The flag Defer_Updates is set while calling Alarm_Wrapper to avoid needless COMPARE updates. Notice the use of the flag in Update_Compare in Listing 2. The COMPARE register is updated after the user handlers are called.

The TMU interrupt handler only calls Alarm_Wrapper for the interrupted clock on top of the stack. This as before this interrupted clock is the only possible source of the interrupt. Updates to the TMU need not be deferred as the clock is not active.

5.4   Context Switch

The context switch routine now changes the active ETC directly as shown in Listing 3. First the Base_Time and First_Alarm . Timeout of the new running threads Active_Clock are loaded. Then a TMU swap operation is initiated using the multiple store instruction of the AVR32 architecture. Notice that the registers are stored in reverse order and therefore the high-word is stored before the low-word. After the swap operation the COUNT value of the previous ETC is read back and stored as its Base_Time. Finally, the ETC is updated to the new active clock.

6   Performance Testing

To evaluate the implementation of execution time control using the TMU, we execute performance tests and compare the results with those for the implementation using the COUNT / COMPARE registers [10]. We also compare to results without execution time control to find the absolute overhead caused by implementing this feature. The implementations are referred to as TMU-ETC, CC-ETC, and N-ETC respectively.

The testing of the TMU was done by simulation as it has not yet been included in a produced UC3 chip. However, since the syntheziable RTL code of the UC3 was used the results are the same as if obtained on hardware. The run-time environment and test programs are compiled and linked to an ELF file as normal, and no special code or libraries were needed to execute on the simulator. The test programs are the same with exception of the non-simulated tests sending data over the USART line, while the simulated store data in memory to be read directly using the simulator. Some updates to the run-time environment were needed as the simulated microcontroller is of version UC3L, while the earlier tests were for the UC3A [10]. These differences do not affect the test results.

Table 2. Performance test results in CPU cycles

Test	Implementation		
	TMU-ETC	CC-ETC	N-ETC
Reading the RTC	43	51	41
Reading the ETC	47	56	–
Context switch	529	602	471
Interrupt handler	294	324	204
Timing event	369	381	270
Interruption cost	244	295	–

6.1 Reading the RTC and ETC

The purpose of this test is to find the overhead of reading the RTC and the active execution time clock (ETC). This is important as this overhead affects most of the later test results. The test is done by a task reading the RTC twice, and then its own execution time clock twice before the results are stored in memory. After this the task is delayed for a short while so that COUNT is reset and there will be no interrupts while reading the clocks. The overhead is calculated as the difference between the two clock values read.

Due to the deterministic nature of the UC3 microcontroller and the simplicity of the test program, all samples for all implementations were of the exact same value for this test. As seen from Table 2, the time to read the RTC and the ETC is reduced by 7 and 9 clock cycles for TMU-ETC compared to CC-ETC, a reduction of 14% and 16% respectively. The overhead of reading the RTC for TMU-ETC is only 2 cycles or 5% more than for N-ETC.

6.2 Context Switch Overhead

The purpose of this test is to find the overhead to context switches by changing the execution time clock. We test without an alarm being set for the clock as the overhead is found to be the same regardless of alarm status. The test is done by task τ_a releasing a higher priority task τ_b that is blocked on a protected entry. The release time is read by the protected procedure opening the entry and is returned to τ_b. After being released τ_b reads the clock and stores the data in memory before it blocks again and the test is repeated. The time between the two clock readings thus include finishing the protected procedure, executing the entry by proxy on behalf of τ_b, leaving the protected object, the context switch to τ_b and retrieving the results of the entry call.

For the same reasons as the previous test, all samples were of the same value for this test. If we subtract the overhead of reading the RTC from the results in Table 2, it can be inferred that TMU-ETC has a context switch overhead caused by execution time control of 56 clock cycles compared to 121 for CC-ETC. This is an reduction of 65 cycles, or 54%.

6.3   Interrupt Handler Overhead

The purpose of this test is to find the interrupt handler overhead caused by implementing execution time control for interrupts. The test is done by using the 16-bit Timer / Counter (TC) peripheral unit of the UC3. The TC is set up to generate interrupts at regular intervals each time its counter is reset. The counter value is read by the interrupt handler and stored in memory. This provides a good measurement of the overhead from the interrupt line is asserted to interrupt handler is called. The sample values are multiplied with the clock division factor used by the TC to get the time in CPU cycles.

As before, all samples were of the same value for this test. As seen from Table 2, the overhead caused by execution time control is reduced from 120 clock cycles for CC-ETC to 90 clock cycles for TMU-ETC. This is a reduction of 30 clock cycles or 25%.

6.4   Timing Event Overhead

The system is required to document the overhead of handling timing event occurrences. While not related to the execution time control, this overhead is expected to be changed by our implementation using the TMU and had to be found. The test program has a single timing event that is programmed to occur with random intervals between 1 and 3 milliseconds. When the handler is called the difference between the timeout and the value of the RTC is stored in memory.

As before, all samples were of the same value for this test. By subtracting the overhead of reading the RTC from the results found in Table 2, it can be inferred the timing event overhead caused by execution time control is reduced from 101 clock cycles for CC-ETC to 97 clock cycles for TMU-ETC. This is a reduction of 4 clock cycles, or 4%.

6.5   Cost to Interrupted Task

The execution time cost to the task being interrupted is greater than zero, as the interrupt clock is activated by the low-level interrupt handler. The purpose of this test is to find this cost. The test is done by a task τ first setting its own execution time timer to expire in 20 ms, then reading its execution time clock, busy waiting 10 millisecond and then reading this clock again. The clock values are stored in memory and the test is repeated. Only the interrupt caused by the timer can occur between the two clock readings, and it can occur only once. To find the cost we compare the difference in execution time when interrupted to when the task is not interrupted. This test is not possible for N-ETC due to the lack of execution time measurement.

For this test there was a difference of one clock cycle between the maximal and minimal sample for CC-ETC. The maximal sample value for this implementation is shown in Table 2. If we subtract the overhead of reading the execution time clock from the results found in Table 2, it can be inferred that the cost to the interrupted task is 239 clock cycles for CC-ETC and 197 clock cycles for TMU-ETC. This is a reduction of 42 clock cycles or 21%.

Table 3. Performance improvements with TMU

Test	Improvement	
	CPU cycles	Reduction (%)
Reading the RTC	7	14
Reading the ETC	9	16
Context switch	65	54
Interrupt handler	30	25
Timing event	4	4
Interruption cost	42	21

7 Discussion

7.1 Performance Improvements

Testing showed that the TMU reduced the overhead and therefore improves the performance of the system. However, as seen from the overview in Table 3 some improvements were more significant than others. The overhead of handling timing events is hardly reduced at all. This is explained by the RTC now being reset before calling the handler in addition to the change of ETC. The implementation CC-ETC does both in one operation when the ETC is updated and is therefore almost as efficient as TMU-ETC. Also, while the relative overhead reduction for reading clocks is good, the absolute reduction is only a few clock cycles and does not affect the system performance much.

There is a noticeable improvement in interrupt handling latency. This is caused by the reduced execution time of Update_ETC using the TMU swap operation. Related to this is the improvement in cost to the interrupted task, that also has a noticeable improvement. Further improvements could be achieved if the swap operation was moved to the assembler part of the low-level interrupt handler. Yet, this has to be weighted against the added complexity and reduced maintainability by moving functionality from Ada to assembler.

The best improvement is for the context switch. This was expected as a complex procedure was replaced by the few assembly code lines seen in Listing 3. Combined with the general speed-up of changing clocks for the TMU, this more than halves the overhead introduced by execution time control compared to the earlier implementation. In systems with frequent context switches this should give a noticeable performance improvement.

7.2 Modifications of Run-Time Environment

As the package specification of System.BB.Time is unchanged the modifications for using the TMU are isolated to the package body, the context switch routine, the package System.BB.Peripherals and its child package Registers. The modifications within the package body of System.BB.Time are limited to the low-level parts interfacing with hardware clocks. The high-level parts concerned with alarms and managing clocks are unchanged.

The body of System.BB.Time has two logical code lines *less* when using the TMU. For the peripheral packages 50 logical code lines were added for interfacing with the TMU, whereof only 8 are statements. For the context switch only 8 additional instructions were needed, all simple load, store or move instructions. In essence the complexity of the run-time environment as a whole is unchanged when using the TMU.

7.3   TMU Design, Implementation and Portability

Our TMU is a simple, yet highly efficient, hardware mechanism for implementing execution time control that leaves the policy entirely for the software. This simplifies the hardware implementation and is also more flexible as the usage of the TMU is decided by software. In contrast, an earlier design [17] implemented for the LEON 2 architecture, changed clocks automatically before the processor started handling an interrupt [4]. This design also supported blocking the interrupt in hardware after the deferrable server pattern. While the benefit of this design is zero overhead to interrupt handling, it is costly to implement and also limits the choice of execution time control policy to one predefined in hardware.

When the TMU was implemented for UC3 some minor changes were needed for easing the implementation, and making the unit more usable for a wider range of applications [18]. The only noticeable change for our implementation of execution time control is that the TMU was moved from the high-speed bus to the peripheral bus. This eased the hardware implementation and reduced the cost in number of gates, but also increases the access latency for the registers. However, the UC3 allows the creation of a CPU local bus to the TMU [18]. If implemented this would provide single-cycle access to the TMU registers.

Since the TMU is designed as a simple memory-mapped device without any special system requirements, it should be portable to other architectures. In essence only the parts needed for interfacing with the memory-mapped bus need to be changed, and the TMU can be integrated with the system-on-chip by connecting the bus and interrupt line. In contrast the earlier TMU design modified the interrupt lines and is much harder to implement on existing architectures.

8   Conclusion

The careful design of our Time Management Unit (TMU) with 64-bit time measurement and the special swap operation, allowed us to develop a highly efficient implementation of Ada 2012 execution time control for the Atmel AVR32 UC3 microcontroller series. Only minor changes were needed to our earlier implementation in order to use the TMU. Performance testing with the UC3 has shown that the TMU gives a significant reduction of the overhead for context switches and interrupt handling, and also reduces the execution time cost for the interrupted task. This makes real-time applications taking advantage of execution time control more efficient and analyzable.

Acknowledgments. Thanks to Atmel Norway and Frode Sundal for facilitating the simulation work. Special thanks to Martin Olsson for the support during the simulation process.

References

1. Atmel Corporation: AVR32 - Architecture Document (November 2007), http://atmel.com/dyn/resources/prod_documents/doc32000.pdf
2. Atmel Corporation: AVR32UC3 - Technical Reference Manual (March 2010), http://atmel.com/dyn/resources/prod_documents/doc32002.pdf
3. Burns, A., Wellings, A.: Programming execution-time servers in Ada 2005. In: Proc. 27th IEEE International Real-Time Systems Symposium, RTSS 2006, pp. 47–56 (December 2006)
4. Forsman, B.: A Time Management Unit (TMU) for Real-Time Systems. Master's thesis. Norwegian University of Science and Technology, NTNU (2008)
5. Gregertsen, K.N.: Execution Time Management for AVR32 Ravenscar. Master's thesis. Norwegian University of Science and Technology, NTNU (2008)
6. Gregertsen, K.N., Skavhaug, A.: Functional specification for a Time Management Unit. Presented at SAFECOMP 2010 (2010)
7. Gregertsen, K.N., Skavhaug, A.: An efficient and deterministic multi-tasking run-time environment for Ada and the Ravenscar profile on the Atmel AVR32 UC3 microcontroller. In: Design, Automation & Test in Europe Conference & Exhibition, DATE 2009, pp. 1572–1575 (April 2009)
8. Gregertsen, K.N., Skavhaug, A.: Execution-time control for interrupt handling. Ada Lett. 30 (2010)
9. Gregertsen, K.N., Skavhaug, A.: Implementing the new Ada 2005 timing event and execution time control features on the AVR32 architecture. Journal of Systems Architecture 56, 509–522 (2010)
10. Gregertsen, K.N., Skavhaug, A.: Implementation and usage of the new Ada 2012 execution-time control features. Ada User Journal 32(4), 265–275 (2011)
11. ISO/IEC: Ada Reference Manual - ISO/IEC 8652:1995(E) with Technical Corrigendum 1 and Amendment 1, http://www.adaic.com/standards/05rm/html/RM-TOC.html
12. ISO/IEC: Ada Reference Manual - ISO/IEC 8652:201x(E) (Draft 15), http://www.ada-auth.org/standards/ada12.html
13. Krishna, C.M., Shin, K.G.: Real-Time Systems. McGraw-Hill International Edition (1997)
14. Michell, S., Real, J.: Conclusions of the 14th International Real-Time Ada Workshop. Ada Lett. 30 (2010)
15. Rivas, M.A., Harbour, M.G.: Execution time monitoring and interrupt handlers: position statement. Ada Lett. 30 (2010)
16. Santos, O.M., Wellings, A.: Cost enforcement in the real-time specification for Java. Real-Time Systems 37(2), 139–179 (2007)
17. Skinnemoen, H., Skavhaug, A.: Hardware support for on-line execution time limiting of tasks in a low-power environment. In: EUROMICRO/DSD Work in Progress Session. Institute of system science, Johannes Kepler University, Linz (2003)
18. Søvik, S.J.: Hardware implementation of a Time Management Unit. Master's thesis. NTNU (2010)

19. The Open Group: The Open Group base specifications issue 6, IEEE Std 1003.1, http://www.opengroup.org/onlinepubs/000095399/
20. Vardanega, T., Harbour, M.G., Pinho, L.M.: Session summary: language and distribution issues. Ada Lett. 30 (2010)
21. Wellings, A.J., Burns, A.: Real-Time Utilities for Ada 2005. In: Abdennahder, N., Kordon, F. (eds.) Ada-Europe 2007. LNCS, vol. 4498, pp. 1–14. Springer, Heidelberg (2007)
22. Wilhelm, R., et al.: The worst-case execution-time problem—overview of methods and survey of tools. Trans. on Embedded Computing Sys. 7(3), 1–53 (2008)

Listing 1. Definition of clocks and alarms

```
type Clock_Descriptor is
   record

      Base_Time : Time;
      -- Base time of clock

      First_Alarm  :  Alarm_Id;
      -- First  alarm  of  clock

      Capacity  :  Natural;
      -- Remaining alarm capacity

   end record;

type Alarm_Descriptor is
   record

      Timeout : Time;
      -- Timeout of alarm when set

      Clock  :  Clock_Id;
      -- Clock  of  this  alarm

      Handler  :  Alarm_Handler;
      -- Handler called  when alarm  expires

      Data  :  System.Address;
      -- Argument when calling handler

      Next  :  Alarm_Id;
      -- Next alarm  in  queue when set

   end record;
```

Listing 2. Updates to use TMU as hardware timer.

```
function Elapsed_Time (Clock : not null Clock_Id) return Time is
begin

    if  Clock = RTC'Access then
       return T : Time := Clock.Base_Time do
          T := T + Time (CPU.Get_Count);
          CPU.Barrier;
          if  T < Clock.Base_Time then
             T := Clock.Base_Time;
          end if;
       end return;
    elsif  Clock = ETC then
       return Time (Peripherals.Get_Count);
    else
       return Clock.Base_Time;
    end if;

end Elapsed_Time;

procedure Update_Compare (Clock : Clock_Id) is
   T : constant Time := Clock.First_Alarm.Timeout;
begin

    if  Clock = RTC'Access and then not Defer_Updates then
       declare
          R : constant Time := T − Time'Min (T, Clock.Base_Time);
       begin
          CPU.Adjust_Compare (CPU.Word (Time'Min (R, Max_Compare)));
       end;
    elsif  Clock = ETC then
       Peripherals.Set_Compare (Peripherals.TMU_Interval (T));
    end if;

end Update_Compare;

procedure Update_ETC (Clock : Clock_Id) is
   use Peripherals ;
begin
   pragma Assert (Clock /= null);

   Swap_Context (TMU_Interval (Clock.First_Alarm.Timeout),
                 TMU_Interval (Clock.Base_Time),
                 TMU_Interval (ETC.Base_Time));

   ETC := Clock;

end Update_ETC;
```

Listing 3. Context switch routine

```
/* Store address of running thread in r9 */
lda.w    r8, running_thread
ld.w     r9, r8

/* Add size of context */
sub r9, −CONTEXT_SIZE

/* Save CPU context of running thread */
stm −−r9, r0,r1,r2,r3,r4,r5,r6,r7,sp,lr
mfsr     r0, SYSREG_SR
st.w     −−r9, r0

/* Store address of first thread in r1 */
lda.w    r1, first_thread
ld.w     r9, r1

/* First thread is now also running thread */
st.w     r8, r9

/* Load Active_Clock of first_thread */
ld.w     r0, r9[THREAD_ACTIVE_CLOCK_OFFSET]

/* Load First_Alarm.Timeout and Base_Time */
ld.w     r1, r0[CLOCK_FIRST_ALARM_OFFSET]
ld.d     r4, r1[ALARM_TIMEOUT_OFFSET]
ld.d     r2, r0[CLOCK_BASE_TIME_OFFSET]

/* Do TMU swap operation */
mov r1, TMU_ADDRESS + TMU_SWAP_OFFSET
stm      r1, r2−r5
ld.d     r4, r1[8]

/* Load ETC address */
lda.w    r1, system__bb__time__etc

/* Load current ETC and store its Base_Time */
ld.w     r2, r1
st.d     r2[CLOCK_BASE_TIME_OFFSET], r4

/* Active_Clock of first_thread is now ETC */
st.w     r1, r0

/* Load CPU context of first thread */
ld.w     r0, r9++
mtsr     SYSREG_SR, r0
sub pc, −2
ldm r9++, r0,r1,r2,r3,r4,r5,r6,r7,sp,pc
```

Implementing and Verifying EDF Preemption-Level Resource Control

Mark Louis Fairbairn and Alan Burns

Department of Computer Science, University of York, UK

Abstract. To support Earliest Deadline First (EDF) dispatching of application tasks the Ada language has had to incorporate Baker's Stack Resource Protocol (SRP). This protocol has proved problematic both in terms of its language definition and implementation. This paper proposes a means of verifying the implementation of complex language features. It describes a prototype tool that allows a comparison to be made between the output of an executing program and a diverse simulator that directly implements EDF+SRP. The tool creates a collection of cases (scenarios); for each of which a program is automatically generated (and executed) and a separate simulation script produced. Tests on an existing run-time for Ada has shown that in certain circumstances an Ada program and its corresponding simulation diverge.

Keywords: real-time, EDF, resource control.

1 Introduction

Embedded systems that work in high-integrity applications are often subject to stringent timing requirements, which are usually expressed in terms of *deadlines*. They are also subject to severe resource constraints. Hence optimal (or at least near optimal) resource allocation is required together with *apriori* analysis that will determine that the implemented system will meet its timing requirements.

A key property of any real-time system is its scheduling policy. This will determine the means by which system resources are allocated to system activities. Two common algorithms are FP - Fixed Priority, and EDF - Earliest Deadline First. In the second, more dynamic algorithm, the activity that has the most pressing (i.e. earliest) deadline is the one that is executed first.

Whilst EDF has a number of theoretical advantages over FP, in particular it provides for greater utilization of the processor, FP is the scheme most usually provided in real-time operating systems. One of the reasons for this is ease of implementation; another comes from the way it deals with other resources. As well as determining how the processor is allocated, a scheduling policy must also deal with other (typically non-preemptable) shared resources. A naive approach can lead to *priority inversion* during which a high priority activity is prevented from making progress because a resource it needs is currently 'locked' by a lower priority activity. Some level of priority inversion is unavoidable due to the non-preemptive nature of the resource, but

M. Brorsson and L.M. Pinho (Eds.): Ada-Europe 2012, LNCS 7308, pp. 193–206, 2012.

if no further action is taken the high priority activity can be further delayed (this is termed *blocking*) by medium priority activities that preempt the low priority one. The result is extensive, and multiple, priority inversion. To reduce this blocking to an acceptable level some form of *priority inheritance* is needed. The most effective scheme is the Priority Ceiling Protocol (PCP) [1].

For single processor FP systems, the use of PCP has been shown to prevent dead-lock over the use of resources and to limit priority inversion to a single minimal duration. For this reason it is supported (in one form of another) in most real-time operating systems (RTOSs), standards (e.g. POSIX) and programming languages such as Ada and the Real-Time Specification for Java (RTSJ). With the PCP scheme, fixed priorities are assigned to each activity and each resource. For a resource, its priority (termed *ceiling priority*) is the maximum priority of all tasks that make use of the resource. Whilst this is a straightforward and efficient scheme for FP scheduling there is no similar simple equivalent for EDF scheduling.

In order to support EDF, Ada 2005 implements Baker's more general scheme for preemption level resource control [2]. This is a more complex algorithm and hence its implementation is not as straightforward. In this paper we describe a tool that has been produced to verify any Ada run-time system to ensure that it faithfully implements the required semantics. For the purposes of this work, Gnat, a reliable and dependable compiler, is used in conjunction with the runtime operating system, MarteOS, which defines itself as follows:

'The first objective of this implementation is to provide a reference platform for GNU/Linux, fully compliant with Ada 2005, available for industrial, research, and teaching environments' [3].

There is however, little verification as to the implementation of Ada 2005 within Mar-teOS, and with some recent corrections to the Ada 2005 specification [4], there needs to be added assurance that all the corrections have been applied correctly. As will be explained shortly, the version of MarteOS being employed was shown to produce output inconsistent with a direct simulation of Baker's scheme.

The objective of this paper is to describe a method by which confidence in the cor-rectness of the implementation of a complex language feature can be gained. The implementation of Baker's algorithm is the exemplar used to illustrate this method.

In this paper we first review Ada's implementation of Baker's algorithm. The verifi-cation tool is then described and evaluations undertaken. Conclusions are then drawn.

2   Analysis of Baker's Algorithm

The stack resource policy, as defined by Baker [2], deals with the currently executing task and relies on the system's ceiling and the preemption check being run for all waiting tasks upon every task arrival, departure and exit from a protected object (en-try to a protected object can be omitted as no waiting tasks will preempt the currently running task unless it decreases its active priority).

In the official Ada 2005 reference manual [5] another set of rules are defined that exhibit the same behavior as Baker's algorithm. These sets of rules are concerned with the position in which a task is placed within a priority ordered list of ready queues. When any tasks are added, removed or moved around the ready queues, the task at the head of the highest priority ready queue is always the task that should be chosen for execution.

The manual also states the criteria for a dispatching point (the instant in time when the rules for preemption are applied). These are when the deadline of a task changes; there are other tasks with earlier deadlines on this ready queue; or there are tasks on higher priority ready queues. At this dispatching point, the following rules are applied:

For a task T to which policy EDF Across Priorities applies, the base priority is not a source of priority inheritance; the active priority when first activated or while it is blocked is defined as the maximum of the following:

[A1] the lowest priority in the range specified as EDF Across Priorities that includes the base priority of T;

[A2] the priorities, if any, currently inherited by T;

[A3] the highest priority P, if any, less than the base priority of T such that one or more tasks are executing within a protected object with ceiling priority P and task T has an earlier deadline than all such tasks; and furthermore T has an earlier deadline than all other tasks on ready queues with priorities in the given EDF_Across_Priorities range that are strictly less than P.

When a task T is first activated or becomes unblocked, it is added to the ready queue corresponding to this active priority. Until it becomes blocked again, the active priority of T remains no less than this value; it will exceed this value only while it is inheriting a higher priority.

When the setting of the base priority of a ready task takes effect and the new priority is in a range specified as EDF Across Priorities, the task is added to the ready queue corresponding to its new active priority, as determined above. [5]

There was however, an issue within the original Ada 2005 specification of Baker's algorithm, with a correction submitted by Burns et al [6]. This was described in detail in a paper by Zerzelidis et al [4]. The error in question was in clause D.2.6(26/2) which originally stated:

'the highest priority P, if any, less than the base priority of T such that one or more tasks are executing within a protected object with ceiling priority P and task T has an earlier deadline than all such tasks'

This was corrected to [A3] above.

In short, the initial Ada rule stated that for a task to be placed upon a higher ready queue than another task, the task must have a deadline that is earlier than all preceding tasks on this queue.

This had to be amended due to an oversight that effectively omitted to include an additional requirement that must be considered when determining priority: the deadline must also be earlier than all lower priority ready queues. That is, 'all other tasks on ready queues with priorities strictly less than P' in [A3].

Thus, the amended rule states that for a task to be placed upon a higher ready queue than another task, the task must have a deadline that is earlier than all subsequent tasks on this queue and all lower priority queues, in addition to those accessing protected objects with a ceiling of this level.

Although this rectifies an error relating to the specific wording of Baker's algorithm within Ada, the issues that arise due to this omitted clause, relates to the comparative use of relative and absolute deadlines. This is an easy error to make as within Baker's algorithm, the preemption levels are assigned according to relative deadline and the assumption is made that if a task has a higher preemption level, then it must have an earlier deadline. In most cases, this assumption holds true and the system is consistent with Baker's algorithm. However, in unique cases, scenarios can be constructed where this does not hold [4].

In order to ensure that MarteOS does not suffer from this issue and that it is fully compliant with the specification, the work reported in this paper aims to test their claim. These tests, in the form of example programs, in conjunction with an in-depth understanding as to the various quirks that may occur within the protocol, aim to test all the issues that may arise when implementing Baker's protocol.

3   EDF Verification Tool

The tool developed to test any Ada run-time implementation, has the following features:

- An abstract representation of a task and its use of protected objects.
- A scenario generator that produces a multitask specification that explores a particular interaction of tasks and protected objects.
- A simulator that directly follows Baker's algorithm and determines when key interaction within the program should take place.
- A code generator that produces a valid Ada program that behaves according to the generated specification.
- An execution of the generated code on a bare board implementation (using MarteOS).
- A comparison of the outputs of the simulator and the actual program.

The remainder of this section described the properties and construction of the tool. Section 4 illustrated some example scenarios and shows that consistent behaviour was not always delivered. Note, as will shortly be explained, most of the above steps have been automated in the developed prototype tool. The final step however, the comparison, is currently undertaken by the user of the tool.

3.1   Abstract Specification

To make the tool simple to use, the following specification for a task was employed:

```
Task (TaskName, StartTime, Deadline, Period) { Code }
```

- The task name can be any sequence of alphanumeric characters, but must start with a letter.
- The Period can be omitted in the case of sporadic tasks.

The Code of a task must only contain the following:

- An integer, which is the amount of time to busy-wait.
- A string in the following format <ProtectedObjectName> {Code}, which enters the protected object before executing all the provided code.

This format can cover any sequence of events that may occur, for example a simple task that accesses a single protected object is presented on the left, and a task that accesses multiple nested protected objects is on the right:

```
Task (T1, 2, 8, 30) {          Task (T2, 2, 8, 30) {
    2                              2
    R1 {                           R1 {
        2                              2
    }                                  R2 {
}                                          2
                                       }
                                       R3 {
                                           1
                                       }
                                   }
                                   2
                               }
```

Both tasks presented are periodic, with a period of 30 time steps. Both are initially released at time 2 and have a deadline of 8 time units. After both tasks execute for 2 time units, enter R1 and execute for a further 2 time units, task T1 leaves the protected object and ends execution. Task T2 however accesses R2, from within R1 for 2 time units, followed by R3 from within R1 for one further time unit, before ending execution inside any protected resources. After 2 final time units task T2 finishes execution.

3.2   Scenario Creator

Given a maximum number of tasks the Scenario Creator (SC) manipulated four rules in order to generate a tree of potential scenarios (cases). The rules refer to task creation, task departure, task promotion (when entering a protected object, PO) and task demotion (leaving a PO). Combinations of these actions are explored to produce different scenarios. To prevent an exponential growth in the number of generated cases, a limit is placed on the depth of nested PO calls. To remove duplicates (similar scenarios that will exercise the language model in an identical way) the tool allows, via a pretty printer, the user to delete scenarios.

3.3   Simulator

In order to accurately model Baker's algorithm in the simulator, and to avoid any errors that may occur interpreting Baker's algorithm, it was decided to take a much slower, more accurate method than that defined by the Ada specification [5] and the scenario creator. This accurate method was to follow Baker's original rules exactly, these state that a task could be preempted by another task only when the deadline of the new task was earlier than the executing task and the preemption level of the new task was higher than the executing task.

As Baker's rules merely specify the conditions under which tasks may preempt the running task, as opposed to the ordering of tasks upon a list, the simulator is required to operate upon each time step throughout the system's execution. At each time step in the simulation, Baker's rules will be checked and a decision made as to whether or not the current task is to be preempted.

A simulation of each time step is not strictly necessary, as the preemption rules only need be applied when the currently running task completes, a new task arrives or a protected object is accessed or returned from. However, as the purpose of this simulation is to be as complete and robust as possible, it was deemed prudent to simulate each time step and omit any possible optimisations. These optimisations could be that event's occur only at dispatching points. However as the arrival of tasks needs to be checked constantly (to keep the complexity low), and as the amount of real-world time that the simulator takes is acceptable, then simulating every time step is acceptable.

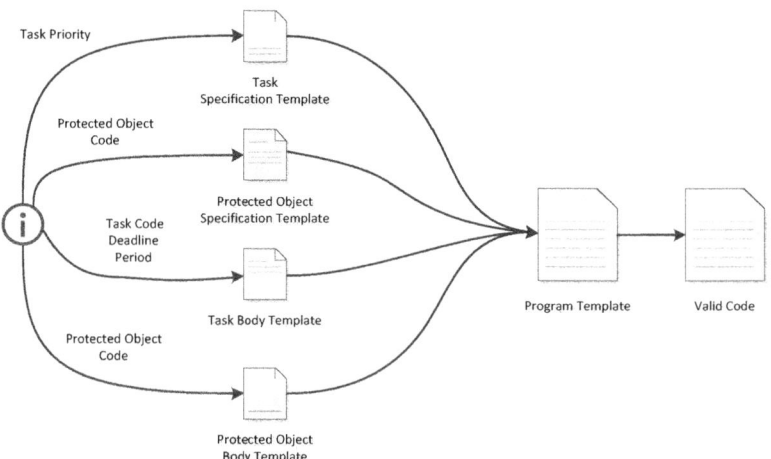

Fig. 1. Code generator workflow

3.4   Code Generator

To complete the analysis of the protocol, results must also be obtained from running the code upon MarteOS. In order to do this, the provided formal tests need translating into Ada code. The following diagram gives an overview of the process.

The initial task of the generator was to take the formal representation and import it into a useable programmatic form within python (see later discussion). This was done by the parser component. To do this in the simplest way, regular expressions were used to match each line into one of 4 categories, translating the input string to object form,

- Task Beginning – The start of a task's code. This start also contains the parameters StartTime, Deadline and Period
- Enter Protected Object – Signals that the current task is to enter the named protected object.
- Wait – States the amount of time that the tasks must busy wait at this point in its execution
- Exit – When a task leaves a protected object or a task definition.

When each line has been classified, it is then simply a matter of performing the correct actions to allow the rest of the parser to continue. The actions that are preformed are as follows:

- Create the basic object and store the collected parameters in the same object.
- Check if the named protected object exists in the protected object collection, and if it is absent then it must be created. In both cases a procedure within the protected object is created for this call. This means, that each time a protected object is entered, it will be entered through a unique procedure and thus there can be multiple execution paths through the protected object. The procedure call is appended to the callers code stack.
- A wait statement is simply inserted into the callers code stack; this wait call will be inlined by the Ada compiler to avoid problems of mutual exclusion over the wait procedure.
- Upon return simply remove the topmost item from the procedure stack should it have any members and the topmost item on the object stack is always removed.

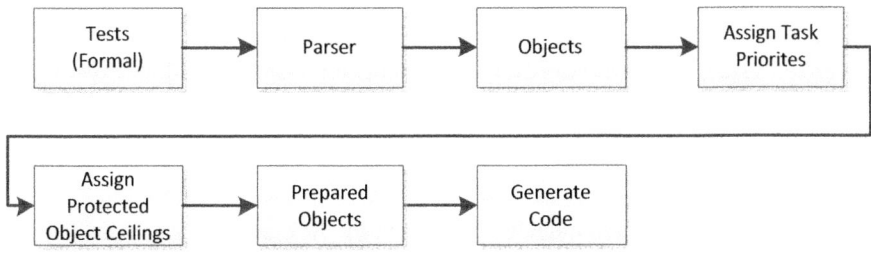

Fig. 2. Workflow from formal tests to the final generated code

Once the entire specification has been parsed into a set of objects, then they are passed onwards into separate sections to have priorities assigned to the tasks and the ceiling values assigned to the protected objects (see diagram above). Task priorities begin at 2 and are assigned so the lowest priority goes to the largest deadline and the highest priority to the smallest deadline, with the rest following in order. The ceiling values are simply the maximum of all the tasks that access the particular protected object.

3.5   Controller

This part of the project was created to bind the code generator and the simulator into a user friendly system that would not require the end user to have any programming knowledge to run the tests. This was initially realised as a method for re-running a large number of tests in sequence, as opposed to manually running each test. The tool iterates through all of the folders under the Tests directory, retrieve the formal specifications, simulate the code, generate the Ada code, compile, execute and retrieve the results. The simulation results, execution results and the code are saved into the directory for analysis by the user.

3.6   Implementation

In order to implement the simulator and the generator, Python was chosen as the programming language. The reasons for this choice were:

- Python allows for high level of programming.
- It provides a large number of string handling capabilities.
- It provides regular expression features that are sufficient for the purpose of parsing incoming strings.
- Outputting from Python to the user is simple, allowing the output to be displayed to the end user in a friendly manner.
- Another advantage of Python, is the inbuilt support for unit testing through the use of the 'unittest' module. This allows a set of unit tests to be defined that can be run manually or automatically through integration with suitable IDE's such as Komodo [7].
- The Python runtime can be freely downloaded for all popular operating systems.

The downside of python is the speed and the requirements of the python runtime in order to execute the code. However, as the program does not need to show any real-time characteristics, the time it takes (provided the user does not have to wait for an excessive amount of time) is deemed acceptable.

The implementation was achieved as a result of a careful, systematic, incremental process. Initially the Generator was created so that tests could be run and output produced. Secondly, the simulator was created to allow for faster verification of the results. These two components were then wrapped together using the controller to further automate the compiling and execution of the code. Finally, the scenario creator was constructed to generate a sequence of tests for use in the system.

3.7   Summary

A suite of tools have been produced that allow a given set of defined tests to be automatically simulated, code generated, and test executed. The simulator provides an accurate representation of Baker's algorithm by using the rules as specified in the original paper [2]. These simulation results are shown in a similar format to the generated codes output, thus aiding comparison between the expected output (as generated by the simulator) and the results obtained from MarteOS. The controller wrapping the generator and the simulator automates the full process; and uses the fact that the local execution is much faster.

To assist in the creation of the tests, another component called the scenario creator was developed, and using the same rules as specified in the Ada reference manual, it produces a complete set of scenarios for a given number of tasks and preemption levels. This set of Scenarios can then be applied by the user, to generate the formal specifications of the tests for use within the controller.

4   Evaluation

In this section the results of running the scenario generator with 3 tasks and two priority levels, to generate a large number of scenarios, is described. From this scenario listing a smaller sample of the tests were chosen for evaluation. This sample was selected by removing the scenarios that fell into the following criteria:

- The topmost task enters and leaves a protected object without any interaction from other tasks within the scenario.
- Any scenarios that are equivalent, due to the same set of tasks performing the same actions, with different task names.
- Any scenarios that are the same, with the only difference being the priority of the ready queue.

This then provided a smaller set of scenarios. Once all scenarios were translated, the controller as discussed was executed, systematically generating, compiling and executing the code, whilst saving the results of the execution into the same directory. During this process the code was also simulated and saved alongside the results.

4.1   Scenario Descriptions

A large number of scenarios were generated and evaluated – see full report [8]. Here we just describe four. For consistency with the original report they are numbered 1, 3, 6a and 6b.

Scenario 1
This scenario is a basic sequence of tasks that arrive in order, with each new task having a smaller deadline than any other in the system. The following table shows the scenario that was tested, along with the formal specification that was written to run this test, and the outputs of the system. A graphical representation of the execution sequence is also illustrated to help the reader visualize the ordering of the scenario.

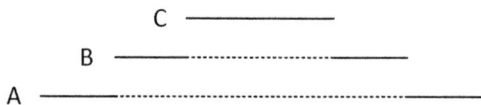

Fig. 3. Task release diagram for scenario 1

Table 1. Task release schedule for scenario 1 with sumlator and MarteOS results

Scenario	Formal Specification	Simulator Results	MarteOS Results

0:A
0:BA
0:CBA
0:BA
0:A
	`Task(TA,0,100) {`
	    `10`
	`}`
	`Task(TB,2,80) {`
	    `10`
	`}`
	`Task(TC,4,60) {`
	    `10`
	`}`
		0 in TA
		2 in TB
		4 in TC
		14 out TC
		22 out TB
		30 out TA
			0 in TA
			2 in TB
			4 in TC
			14 out TC
			22 out TB
			30 out TA

This test shows that in the absence of any protected objects, MarteOS correctly schedules the tasks in such a way that should the tasks arrive in order of deadline, the task with the earliest deadline is always the task currently executing within the system.

In order to conserve space, the full results tables for future tests that are deemed uninteresting will be omitted, for the full listings please consult the report [8].

Scenario 3
This scenario tests that a task, when raised to a higher priority ready queue, correctly blocks a task, along with preemption by a higher priority task after the protected object has been accessed.

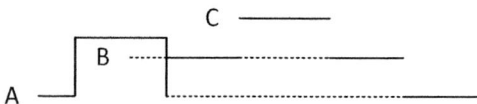

Fig. 4. Task release diagram for scenario 3

Within the following results table the output when the simulator accesses a protected object it is in the form

```
<Time, In/Out, TaskId, ProtectedObjectId>
```

MarteOS output is slightly different being

```
<Time, In/Out, TaskID, ProtectedObjectId, ProcedureId>
```

Where ProcedureId is part of the generated code as discussed in section 3.4. Along with the small difference of all MarteOS protected objects having Po prepended, makes simulator output of "3 out TA PoA" functionally the same as "3 out TA A P3" from MarteOS.

Table 2. Task release schedule for scenario 3 with sumlator and MarteOS results

Scenario	Formal Specification	Simulator Results	MarteOS Results

0:A
1:A
1:A 0:B
0:BA
0:CAB
0:BA
0:A
	`Task(TA,0,100){`
	`    1`
	`    A {`
	`        2`
	`    }`
	`    7`
	`}`
	`Task(TB,2,80) {`
	`    1`
	`    A {`
	`        2`
	`    }`
	`    7`
	`}`
	`Task(TC,4,60) {`
	`    10`
	`}`
		0 in TA
		1 in TA
		PoA
		3 out TA
		PoA
		3 in TB
		4 in TC
		14 out TC
		14 in TB
		PoA
		16 out TB
		PoA
		23 out TB
		30 out TA
			0 in TA
			1 in TA
			A P3
			3 out TA
			A P3
			3 in TB
			4 in TC
			14 out TC
			14 in TB
			A P10
			16 out TB
			A P10
			23 out TB
			30 out TA

As a description of the above results are as follows. At time 0 Task A begins execution. At time 1 Task A enter protected object A before leaving at time 3. At time 3 Task B begins executions (and as Task A has not finished execution it was preempted). At time 4 Task C preempts task B and finished execution at time 14.

Scenario 6a

This scenario is the first to test the protected object handling seen in scenario 3 above, in combination with the absolute/relative ordering change. Task A will initially block the execution of any other tasks, in which time tasks B and C will arrive, where B should execute before C, before both being allowed execution by task A departing the protected object.

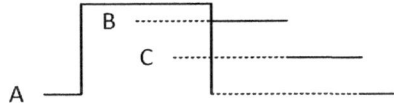

Fig. 5. Task release diagram for scenario 6a

Table 3. Task release schedule for scenario 6a with sumlator and MarteOS results

Scenario	Formal Specification	Simulator Results	MarteOS Results

0:A
1:A
1:A 0:B
1:A 0:BC
0:BCA
0:CA
0:A
	`Task(TA,0,100) {`
	`  2`
	`  A {`
	`    8`
	`  }`
	`  2`
	`}`
	`Task(TB,4,50) {`
	`  4`
	`  A {`
	`    2`
	`  }`
	`  2`
	`}`
	`Task(TC,6,80) {`
	`  10`
	`}`
		0 in TA
		2 in TA PoA
		10 out TA
		PoA
		10 in TB
		14 in TB
		PoA
		16 out TB
		PoA
		18 out TB
		18 in TC
		28 out TC
		30 out TA
			0 in TA
			2 in TA A
			P3
			10 out TA A
			P3
			10 in TB
			14 in TB A
			P10
			16 out TB A
			P10
			18 out TB
			18 in TC
			28 out TC
			30 out TA

Scenario 6b

In this related scenario there is a minor change to the task set. This diagram shows the differences between the two cases. Upon first glance, it is easy to overlook that in scenario 6b the length of task C (its relative deadline) is shorter than that of 6a. However the absolute deadlines of the tasks (the end of the line), are still in order. The results of this test were of significant importance as shown in the table.

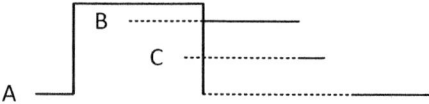

Fig. 6. Task release diagram for scenario 6b

Scenario 6a, where the absolute and relative deadline orderings are the same, successfully produces the expected results; however, 6b has an interesting error. In scenario 6b, when task A leaves the protected object A, task B preempts as expected, but as task B attempts to access the protected object A, task C preempts and executes to completion. Then Task B resumes and completes. This is incorrect, as in no circumstances should C complete before B.

Table 4. Task release schedule for scenario 6b with sumlator and MarteOS results

Scenario	Formal Specification	Simulator Results	MarteOS Results
0:A	`Task(TA,0,100) {`	0 in TA	0 in TA
1:A	1	1 in TA PoA	1 in TA A
1:A 0:B	A {	8 out TA PoA	P3
1:A 0:BC	7	8 in TB	8 out TA A
0:BCA	}	9 in TB PoA	P3
0:CA	2	16 out TB PoA	8 in TB
0:A	}	18 out TB	9 in TC
	`Task(TB,2,60) {`	18 in TC	19 out TC
	1	28 out TC	19 in TB A
	A {	30 out TA	P10
	7		26 out TB A
	}		P10
	2		28 out TB
	}		30 out TA
	`Task(TC,6,58) {`		
	10		
	}		

4.2   Summary

The above erroneous cases (and a number of other inconsistent scenarios) were checked by hand. It is our belief that the simulator is accurate and that some aspect of the run-time is therefore erroneous. This was been acknowledged by the team supporting MarteOS; a new version with the error corrected is expected and we will then rerun these tests.

5   Conclusions

The high-level aim of the work presented in this paper was to verify the implementation of the Earliest Deadline First scheduling scheme with Baker's algorithm in MarteOS. MarteOS aims to be fully compliant with the Ada 2005 specification, including the real-time annex. However, this work has identified, at the time of writing, that there are errors within the implementation.

The apparent glitch that appears when the active priority of a task changes under certain conditions. Theses have been shown in section 4 (and in greater detail in the full report [8]) to be when the following rules hold:

- The preemption levels of the tasks are such that the earlier absolute deadline tasks have a lower preemption level (as their relative deadlines are actually later).
- All the tasks with the reversed absolute deadlines (compared to the relative deadlines) are blocked from starting and the block is released from all tasks simultaneously.

- When one of the tasks accesses a protected object, the task with the earliest relative deadline will incorrectly preempt.

Notwithstanding these specific conclusions, the work reported here also highlighted the somewhat complex language model within Ada, and for the need to verification run-time systems via diverse implementations and scenario generation.

Acknowledgements. Although the work reported in this paper has shown there to be a problem with the current version of MarteOS we would like to thank the development team both for producing an Ada implementation in the first place, and for constructive and supportive interaction once a potential problem was identified.

References

1. Sha, L., Rajkumar, R., Lehoczky, J.P.: Priority inheritance protocols: An approach to real-time synchronization. IEEE Transactions on Computers 39(9), 1175–1185 (1990)
2. Baker, T.P.: A Stack-Based Resource Allocation Policy for Realtime Processes. In: IEEE Real-Time Systems Symposium, pp. 191–200 (1990)
3. Rivas, M.A.: (February 2010), http://marte.unican.es/
4. Zerzelidis, A., Burns, A., Wellings, A.J.: Correcting the EDF protocol in Ada 2005. In: 13th International Workshop on Real-time Ada, Vermont (2007)
5. Tucker Taft, S., Duff, R.A., Brukardt, R.L., Plödereder, E., Leroy, P.: Ada 2005 Reference Manual. LNCS, vol. 4348. Springer, Heidelberg (2006)
6. Ada Conformity Assessment Authority (April 2010),
   http://www.ada-auth.org/cgi-bin/cvsweb.cgi/ai05s/
   ai05-0055-1.txt?rev=1.1&raw=Y
7. ActiveState Software (April 2010), http://www.activestate.com/komodo/
8. Fairbairn, M.L.: An Assessment of Ada's new EDF Facilities, MEng Report. University of York, UK (2010),
   http://www-users.cs.york.ac.uk/~burns/FairbairnReport.pdf

Efficient Constraint Handling during Designing Reliable Automotive Real-Time Systems

Florian Pölzlbauer[1], Iain Bate[2], and Eugen Brenner[3]

[1] Virtual Vehicle, Graz, Austria
[2] University of York, Department of Computer Science, York, United Kingdom
[3] Graz University of Technology, Institute for Technical Informatics, Graz, Austria

Abstract. In modern embedded systems, e.g. avionics and automotive, it is not unusual for there to be between 40 and 100 processors with a great deal of the software having hard real-time requirements and constraints over how, when and where they execute. The requirements and constraints are essential to the overall systems dependability and safety (e.g. to ensure replicas execute on different hardware). This leads to a complex design space exploration (DSE) problem which cannot be practically solved manually especially if the schedule is to be maintained.

In this paper it is shown that dealing with the constraints using a conventional state of the art "System Configuration Algorithm" is less efficient, less effective and does not scale well. This issue can be improved by performing constraint pre-processing as well as constraint encoding. It is shown that our approach can handle typical industrial requirements that come from the automotive industry's AUTOSAR standard in an efficient way.

Keywords: design constraints, system configuration, task allocation, efficient design space exploration, real-time systems.

1 Introduction

In the past, automotive electronics were designed in a federated manner. Most functionality was implemented by special-purpose hardware and software. Therefore one control unit performed only one or at most a limited number of individual functions, and functions had their own dedicated hardware. As the functionality steadily increased, the number of control units has also increased. Nowadays cars contain up to 80 control units.

During the last several years, a paradigm shift has occurred in the automotive domain. The design of electronics has moved from a hardware-oriented to a software/function-oriented approach. This means that the functionality is mainly based on software that is executed on general-purpose hardware. In order to enable this trend a middleware (AUTOSAR [1]) was introduced, which separates the application software from the underlying hardware.

In order to develop such reliable and safety-relevant software-based systems, several engineering steps have to be performed. Besides developing the systems

M. Brorsson and L.M. Pinho (Eds.): Ada-Europe 2012, LNCS 7308, pp. 207–220, 2012.
© Springer-Verlag Berlin Heidelberg 2012

functionality, designing the software architecture and implementing software components, several configuration steps have to be performed. These are essential if systems are to meet their reliability requirements (e.g. in the form of timing requirements being met), availability requirements (e.g. where task replicas have to be placed on different processors), and safety requirements (e.g. where tasks have to be allocated and executed in a particular way).

- task allocation: local assignment of tasks to processors
- data routing: finding a route (via buses and gateways) for data transmission between tasks that reside on different processors
- frame packing: packing application messages into bus frames
- scheduling: planning of the temporal attributes of the system (e.g. priority assignment to tasks and frames)
- system performance evaluation: schedulability, resource utilization, etc.

Due to the increasing system complexity, high number of design constraints and safety as well as reliability demands, finding feasible system configurations is a challenging and error-prone task, if performed manually. In order to disburden engineers from these tasks, automized system configuration generation is needed. This will enable the engineers to spend more time on actually designing the systems functionality.

1.1   Related Works

In the literature, the task of finding a system configuration is often referred to as the task allocation problem (TAP). The TAP consists of two principal parts: allocating tasks to processors and messages to communication buses, and then assigning attributes such as the priority to tasks and messages. The TAP should be solved such that all essential requirements (or constraints) are met (e.g. task deadlines) and that the objectives are optimized (e.g. the minimum number of processors are used).

The TAP has been the subject of a great deal of research over the last couple of decades ranging from the early works that dealt with independent tasks to later work that handles more complex requirements, e.g. dependent tasks (or transactions) in [4, 6]. More recent work has considered other constraints, such as tasks having to reside on a particular processor [11].

In [16] the aspect of *extensibility* is tackled. Thereby system configurations are optimized to tolerate increasing worst-case execution times (WCET). This metric can be used to estimate how many tasks and messages could be included in future systems. In [9] even more attributes (e.g. periods) are subject to variation, and multi-dimensional robustness analysis is performed.

In [8] the issue of *system configuration upgrade* is tackled. Starting from a given initial system configuration, the search algorithm (based on simulated annealing (SA)) searches for an improved/optimized system configuration. Thereby minimal changes between the initial and the optimized system configuration are preferred.

Although the TAP has been addressed from different perspectives, some common issues can be identified: Firstly, almost all works focus on creating a new system configuration "from scratch". Although the configuration may be designed with respect to extensibility [9, 15, 16], the necessary design steps to actually perform a system configuration upgrade are not shown. Only [8] tackles this issue. Secondly, the works only deal with simple design constraints that are insufficient for the needs of many critical systems including those based on the AUTOSAR standard. However, when designing dependable, real-life, reliable, long-life software-based systems, more sophisticated design constraints need to be taken into account (for details see table 1).

1.2   Contribution and Outline

The contributions of this work are:

- provide an overview of industrial relevant design constraints
- provide methods that satisfy these constraints in an efficient way
- show how these methods can be incorporated into *system configuration optimization frameworks*
- present experimental results that evidence the efficiency of the approach

The work is structured as follows: In section 2 we present an overview of design constraints that typically are present in industrial system configuration problems. Then we present *when* each of these constraints can be satisfied (= constraint satisfaction time). Later we show *how* each of these constraints can be satisfied. In section 3 we present an *optimization framework* for finding near-optimal system configurations, which incorporates the methods for satisfying the design constraints. In section 4 we present experimental results that evidence the efficiency of the proposed methods. Finally we draw our conclusions and provide an outlook on future research directions.

The following symbols and abbreviations are used in this work.

Symbol	Description	Symbol	Description	Symbol	Description
t	task	B	set of bus systems	adm	admissible
c	task cluster	P	set of processors	ded	dedicated
m	message	dyn	dynamic	ex	excluded

2   Design Constraints

Design constraints may have a wide variety of sources. Most relevant are:

- safety considerations: If safety analysis of the entire system has been performed (e.g. hazard and risk analysis, in accordance with ISO 26262 [2]), safety requirements can be derived. These impose constraints on design decisions.

- compatibility to legacy systems: Automotive systems are usually designed in an evolutionary fashion. A previous version of the system is taken as a starting point and is extended with additional features, in order to satisfy current demands/requirements. Thus, legacy components may impose constraints on design decisions.
- engineer's experience: Engineers who have been designing similar systems typically have figured out "best practices". These may exclude certain design decisions, thus imposing additional constraints.

Within the automotive domain, the AUTOSAR standard [1] has positioned itself as a leading standard. Within the AUTOSAR standard, design constraints which might occur have been specified in the *AUTOSAR system template*. Therein, a variety of constraint-types can be found. However, these constraints are not only relevant for automotive systems, and could easily be applied to other domains (e.g. rail, aerospace, automation, ...). Table 1 provides a summary of the constraint-types. They can be categorized within 6 classes.

Table 1. Constraint-Types specified within AUTOSAR System Template

Constraint-class	Constraint-type	Literature
A: limited resources	A-1: processor CPU speed	yes
	A-2: processor memory	yes
	A-3: bus bandwidth	yes
B: real-time behaviour	B-1: task deadline	yes
	B-2: communication deadline	yes
	B-3: end-to-end deadline	yes
C: allocation (task to processor)	C-1: dedicated processors	yes
	C-2: excluded processors	yes
	C-3: fixed allocation	yes
D: dependencies (task to task)	D-1: grouping	no*
	D-2: separation	yes
E: data routing (data to bus)	E-1: processor-internal only	no*
	E-2: dedicated buses	no
	E-3: excluded buses	no
	E-4: same bus	no
	E-5: separated buses	no
F: frame packing (data to frame)	F-1: dedicated frame	no
	F-2: same frame	no
	F-3: separated frames	no

* not stated as a constraint, but used as means to reduce bus utilization

Some of these constraints are relevant for a wide range of software systems. E.g. all embedded software must content itself with limited resources. Thus these constraints are well studied in the literature. However, for reliable systems, additional constraints need to be taken into account. Most safety-related systems must guarantee real-time behaviour, especially if human life is at risk (e.g. drive-by-wire application in a car). Hence, safety analyses are performed in order to identify potential risks, and derive adequate safety goals how to address these risks. A strategy (safety concept) is derived, how to achieve these safety goals. The safety concept must be satisfied/implemented by the architecture. This imposes additional design constraints on the architecture. E.g. a typical safety concept is to use redundancy and replication [7]. If a triple modular redundant approach is used to improve availability and reliability then different physical processors and communication paths need to be enforced in order to avoid common mode failures or byzantine effects. Therefore replicated tasks must not reside on the same processor (task separation), certain processors are inadequate for handling certain tasks (excluded processors), and data must be transferred via separated buses, probably even within separated bus frames.

Concluding: In order to satisfy the safety goals and thus comply to safety standards [2] and legal regulations, a set of highly heterogeneous design constraints need to be handled. This imposes significant effort on engineers. Therefore methods for efficient constraint handling are needed.

It is interesting to note, that several constraint-types are not addressed in the literature. Especially constraints that focus on the configuration of the communication infrastructure have not been tackled. This can be explained, because most works on system configuration (e.g. task allocation) use simplified models for cross-processor communication. These models do not cover all relevant details of the communication infrastructure, and thus the use of detailed constraints seems obsolete. In real dependable systems though, these constraints are of high importance.

2.1   How to Satisfy Constraints in an Efficient Way

During designing safety-relevant distributed real-time systems, that are mainly empowered by the use of software architectures (like the AUTOSAR middleware), the question arises: How can the set of highly heterogeneous constraints be handled and satisfied in an efficient way? By analysing the constraints, we can identify two concepts to satisfy these constraints. Each concept can be applied to a sub-set of the constraints. By combining both concepts, all relevant constraints can be handled and satisfied.

1. pre-processing: Certain constraints can be resolved before the DSE. This way, the constraints are always satisfied during the DSE. Figuratively speaking: The constraints are removed from the design space, thus reducing the design space by removing infeasible regions.
2. encoding: Constraints that cannot be resolved have to be encoded into the search algorithm, e.g. into the objective-function. This way the search is guided towards configurations that satisfy the constraints.

Basically, each constraint-type could be addressed by "encoding". However, this option is not very efficient, since no guarantee of constraint satisfaction can be given. "Resolving" a constraint-type can give that guarantee. Thus the goal is to resolve as many constraints as possible.

Resolve Constraints before Design Space Exploration

Table 2 shows, which constraints can be resolved, which constraints cannot be resolved, and why that is the case. In order to resolve constraints before performing the DSE, the following rules have to be applied:

Table 2. Constraint Satisfaction Time: "before" or "during" Design Space Exploration

Type	before	during	Rationale
A-1		x	CPU utilization can only be checked after task allocation
A-2		x	memory utilization can only be checked after task allocation
A-3		x	bus utilization can only be checked after message routing and frame packing
B-1		x	can only be checked after scheduling
B-2		x	can only be checked after scheduling
B-3		x	can only be checked after scheduling
C-1	x		a set of admissible processors can be calculated
C-2	x		a set of admissible processors can be calculated
C-3	x		allocation algorithm does not modify the allocation
D-1	x		tasks can be grouped (forming a task cluster); task clusters are handled as "single elements" by task allocation
D-2		x	a set of excluded processors can be derived dynamically
E-1	x		sender- and receiver-tasks can be grouped
E-2	x		a set of admissible buses can be calculated
E-3	x		a set of admissible buses can be calculated
E-4	x		group sender-tasks; group receiver-tasks
E-5		x	message routing results from task allocation
F-1	x		only the dedicated frame will be used
F-2	x		demand E-4; perform frame packing in two phases
F-3	x		perform frame packing in two phases

F-1: Dedicated frame packing is typically used, because the same *frame catalog* is used within different cars. To satisfy this constraint, messages that have this constraint associated, will only be packed into the dedicated frame.

E-1: By grouping the sender- and the receiver-task (forming a task-cluster), we can make sure that the task allocation algorithm will allocate both tasks to the same processor. Thus, the communication between these tasks is always performed processor-internal.

D-1: Similar to E-1, this constraint can be resolved by grouping the associated tasks (forming a task-cluster).

E-2 & E-3: Based on these sets, a set of admissible buses can be calculated for each message.

$$B_{adm} = \begin{cases} B \setminus B_{ex} & \text{if} \quad B_{ded} = \{\} \\ B_{ded} \setminus B_{ex} & \text{otherwise} \end{cases} \tag{1}$$

This admissible message-routing implies a set of admissible processors X for the sender- and receiver-task of this message. Only processors connected to the

admissible buses of the message are potential candidates for hosting the sender-
and receiver-task.

$$P_{adm}^{(t \to m \to t)} = P \text{ connected to } B_{adm} \tag{2}$$

Since a task may send and receive several messages, only the intersected set X
is a potentially admissible processor for each task.

$$X = \bigcap P_{adm}^{(t \to m \to t)} \tag{3}$$

C-1 & C-2: Based on these sets, a set of admissible processors can be calculated
for each task. Thereby, the set of admissible buses (derived from E-2 & E-3) of
the sent/received messages has also to be taken into account.

$$P_{adm} = \begin{cases} (P \cap X) \setminus P_{ex} & \text{if} \qquad P_{ded} = \{\} \\ (P_{ded} \cap X) \setminus P_{ex} & \text{otherwise} \end{cases} \tag{4}$$

If tasks are grouped (forming a task cluster), the set of admissible processors for
a task cluster c is:

$$P_{adm}^{(c)} = \bigcap_{t \in c} P_{adm} \tag{5}$$

C-3: If an allocation is fixed, the task allocation algorithm will not modify that
allocation.
E-4: Two messages can only be routed via the same bus, if their sender-tasks
reside on the same processor and also their receiver-tasks reside on the same
processor. Thus, E-4 can be satisfied by two D-1 constraints.
F-2: Two messages can only be packed into the same frame, if both messages are
sent from the same processor and routed via the same bus. This can be stated by
E-4. In addition, frame packing is performed in two phases. In phase 1, messages
that must be packed into the same frame are packed into the same frame. In
phase 2, all remaining messages that have not been packed yet are packed into
frames (either into new frames or adding them into existing frames).
F-3: Frame packing is performed in two phases. In phase 1, messages that must
be packed into separated frames are each packed into a separate frame. In phase
2, all remaining messages that have not been packed yet are packed into frames
(either into new frames or adding them into existing frames).

Tackle Constraints during Design Space Exploration
Some of the constraints that cannot be resolved before performing the DSE, can
be addressed during the DSE, by applying the following rules:
D-2: The set of admissible processors can be updated dynamically (during the
DSE).

$$P_{adm.dyn} = P_{adm} \setminus P_{ex.dyn} \tag{6}$$

$$P_{ex.dyn} = P \text{ of tasks that the current task must be separated from} \tag{7}$$

Concluding: For a set of constraints (A-1, A-2, A-3, B-1, B-2, B-3, E-5) no rules how to satisfy them, could be derived. Consequently, these constraints must be tackled somehow else. An elegant way to do this, is to encode them into the search algorithm. Thereby they can either be represented as a *mandatory* or as *desired*. However, the following implications should be taken into account, when deciding between these options:

- mandatory: If a mandatory constraint is violated, the configuration is treated as being *infeasible*. Thus it will be rejected. Consequently, the configuration is not considered as the starting point for generating new configurations.
- desired: A configurations that does not satisfy a desired constraint is not rejected. Instead it is punished by a high *cost value*. However, the configuration can still be picked as the starting point for subsequent exploration steps.

The difference may sound minor, but actually has significant impact on the DSE. Using *desired constraints* enables the search to gradually traverse through infeasible regions. However, even configurations with "moderate" cost may be infeasible. Using *mandatory constraints* ensures that all constraints are satisfied for feasible configurations.

Table 3. Constraint Encoding: as "mandatory" or as "desired"

Type	mandatory	desired	Rationale
A-1	x		utilization $\leq$ 100% required for schedulability
A-2		x	utilization $\leq$ 100% not required for schedulability
A-3	x		utilization $\leq$ 100% required for schedulability
B-1		x	guide search through un-schedulable regions
B-2		x	guide search through un-schedulable regions
B-3		x	guide search through un-schedulable regions
D-2	xx	x	depending on source of constraint (e.g. safety analysis)
E-5	xx	x	depending on source of constraint (e.g. safety analysis)
F-3	xx	x	depending on source of constraint (e.g. safety analysis)

Note: All other constraint-types can be resolved, thus are always satisfied, and don't need to be encoded. Options marked as "xx" are preferred by the authors.

Table 3 provides a proposal, in which way each constraint-type could be encoded. The proposal tries to tackle the nature of the constraint-types as well as efficiency considerations, in order to find the most appropriate encoding for each constraint-type. If a constraint-type is encoded as "desired", the following representation is proposed/advised:

$$cost_i = \frac{\text{\# of elements that violate a constraint-type}}{\text{\# of elements that have a constraint-type associated}} \rightarrow \min \quad (8)$$

This way, each cost term is scaled between 0 and 1, which makes it easier to incorporate the cost term into the *cost function*. The individual cost terms (for constraint encoding) can then be grouped into a single cost term *constraint violation*, using a scaled weighted sum, inspired by [10].

$$cost_{\text{constraint violations}} = \frac{\sum w_i \cdot cost_i}{\sum w_i} \rightarrow \min \tag{9}$$

This cost term can then be included into the cost function, wherein the optimization objectives (e.g. minimize bus utilization) are encoded. Finding adequate weights for the individual cost terms is a challenging task. It is almost impossible to find weights that perform well for all problems. Therefore weights should be assigned to problem-classes. By applying a systematic experimental approach [12], weights can be found that perform well for these problem-classes.

2.2   Implications on Design Space Exploration

Within the pre-processing phase, constraints are resolved. Therefore two methods are used:

1. grouping of tasks, forming task clusters
2. calculating a set of admissible processors for each task

In addition, a set of rules how to tackle certain constraints during the DSE were presented. These information is exploited during the DSE. As a consequence the following principles will be used during the DSE:

- Task clusters are treated as single elements during task allocation. Therefore, if a task cluster is re-allocated, all tasks inside that task cluster will be re-allocated to the same processor.
- When picking a "new" processor for a task / task cluster, only processors from the set of admissible processors are used as candidates.
- Rules for satisfying constraints during the DSE are applied to the commensurate design steps (e.g. frame packing)

As a consequence, a large number of infeasible configurations is avoided, since constraints are not violated. Thus, the efficiency of the DSE increases.

3   System Configuration – Optimization Framework

In order to actually perform the system configuration DSE, we are using a metaheuristic search algorithm called *simulated annealing (SA)*, a well known algorithm in the domain of artificial intelligence. Its name and inspiration come from annealing in metallurgy, a technique involving heating and controlled cooling of a material. The main reason for using SA is that it is shown in [8] how SA can be tailored to address system configuration upgrade scenarios. To ensure that the temporal attributes of the system meet the requirements, traditional methods are used: WCET-analysis and WCRT-analysis. In order to apply SA to a specific problem (here: system configuration), some methods have to be implemented:

- neighbour: Which modification can be applied to a system configuration, in order to get a new system configuration? These represent the modification an engineer would perform manually.
- energy (cost): How "good" is a system configuration? This represents the metrics that are used to evaluate a system configuration.

The following optimization objectives are encoded into the cost function. Again a scaled weighted sum is used.

- number of needed processors → min
- bus utilization → min
- processor CPU utilization → max & balanced
- end-to-end delay → min
- constraint violations → min

In order to get a modified system configuration, the following neighbour steps are applied: 1) A task / task cluster (whose allocation is not fixed) is randomly picked. 2) A "new" processor is determined by randomly picking out of the set of admissible processors for that task / task cluster.

When solving the underlying forward-problem for each allocation iteration, the following assumptions are made and the following methodologies are used:

- Tasks are activated by the arrival of a message. Therefore, the task scheduling problem is equivalent to finding adequate priorities for tasks. This problem can be addressed by simple, yet efficient heuristics: rate monotonic (RM), deadline monotonic (DM) or "deadline minus jitter" monotonic (D-JM) priority assignment [3].
- The bus protocol is CAN [5]. Therefore, the bus arbitration scheduling problem is equivalent to finding adequate priorities for bus frames. Thus, RM, DM or D-JM can be applied as well.
- Data that is exchanged between processors via data buses is packed into bus frames using a heuristic inspired by [13], but additionally incorporating the methods for satisfying packing constraints.
- Schedulability of the system is checked using [14].

The simplifications and assumptions that are made within this work are only introduced for the sake of simplicity. The proposed methods for satisfying the design constraints are independent of these assumptions. Thus more sophisticated methodologies (e.g. for priority assignment) can be applied, if desired/needed.

4   Experimental Results

In section 2 we have presented a set of 19 constraint-types that may be present in a system configuration problem. Later, we presented a set of rules that can be used to resolve 11 constraint-types. In addition, we have presented rules that can be used to dynamically satisfy 1 constraint-type. Assuming that each constraint-type is used equally often, we can make sure that about 63% of the constraint-types are satisfied during the DSE. Thus a high number of constraint-violations can be avoided, making the DSE more efficient.

approach	#	%
resolve	11	57.89
dyn. satisfy	1	5.26
no guarantee	7	36.84

In order to show the impact of the design constraints on DSE efficiency, we have performed several experiments. On the one hand, we tried to solve the system configuration problem by state-of-the-art approaches. On the other hand, we applied a pre-processing phase, during which constraints are resolved.

Due to the high number of different constraint-types, it is infeasible to demonstrate all combinations of constraint-types here. Therefore, let us focus on a problem instance of medium scale size

- hardware: 6 processors, 1 external data bus
- software: 30 tasks, 45 communication-links between tasks

and having the following constraints

- limited resources for all hardware elements (A-1 .. A-3)
- deadlines for all tasks and messages (B-1, B-2)
- 2 tasks already allocated (C-3)
- 4 task-groupings (D-1)
- 1 internal communication-link (E-1)

In order to reduce the uncertainties that are introduced by the used meta-heuristic (SA) which uses random numbers, several solving-runs are performed. The results of all these runs are shown in table 4. The most interesting results are highlighted in bold.

Table 4. Impact of Resolving Constraints on DSE Performance and DSE Results (min./median/max. of 10 runs per scenario)

criteria	no pre-processing	with pre-processing
iterations	10000	10000
unique allocations	9546 / 9588.5 / 9595	9423 / 9430.5 / 9469
feasible allocations	**0 / 1 / 1**	**2026 / 2169 / 2231**
infeasible, due to constr. D-1 & E-1	**9541 / 9578.5 / 9589**	**0 / 0 / 0**
infeasible, due to CPU overload	0 / 1.5 / 8	4050 / 4177 / 4335
infeasible, due to memory overload	1 / 1.5 / 7	2653 / 2693 / 2759
infeasible, due to deadline violation	0 / 2.5 / 6	385 / 406.5 / 421
used processors	5 / 6 / 6 (of 6)	**4 / 4 / 4** (of 6)
bus utilization [%]	12.66 / 13.73 / 14.61	7.52 / 8.23 / 9.87
CPU utilization [%] (average)	47.69 / 47.69 / 57.23	71.54 / 71.54 / 71.54
Δ CPU utilization [%] (average)	7.69 / 10.77 / 20.25	3.85 / 5.19 / 8.08

The results impressively show the negative effect that the set of design constraints has on the DSE performance, if state-of-the-art solving approaches are used (see: *no pre-processing*). Almost no feasible configuration can be found. The main reason is that some constraints are violated. This is even more impressive if we consider that only a small number of constraints is used.

On the contrary, the results clearly evidence the positive effect of the pre-processing phase on the DSE performance (see: *with pre-processing*). If the pre-processing rules are applied, no more constraint violations stem from these constraint-types (here: C-3, D-1, E-1). As a consequence, more feasible configurations are generated and evaluated during the DSE. The median feasibility ratio is 0.217 (= feasible vs. all iterations). Overall, the DSE efficiency is significantly improved. In addition, the best obtained configuration is significantly improved, if pre-processing is applied: Fewer processors are needed, a lower bus utilization can be achieved, and processor utilization is more balanced.

However, it seems that pre-processing has a negative impact on resource utilization and real-time behaviour. Though, this is not the case, and can be explained: In these experiments we applied a hierarchical evaluation-schema. Constraints are checked in the following sequence: allocation, dependency, routing, packing, resource, timing. Thus, if allocation constraints are violated, other constraints (e.g. resource utilization or timing) are not checked/counted any more, since the configuration is already infeasible. This helps to speed up the entire evaluation process (since time-consuming schedulability-tests are performed only if all other constraints are satisfied). However, as a consequence resource overload and deadline violations are only counted if all the other constraints are satisfied. To get a more general comparison, the sum of all infeasible configurations can be taken as a metric.

Generality. In order to evaluate the generality of the proposed approach, several experiments have been performed. Therein, we varied both the size and structure of the problem instances, as well as the imposed design constraints. The problem sizes vary within the following ranges:

- 30..90 tasks / 45..135 messages
- 6..12 processors / system utilization: 0.331..0.493 per processor, if all processors would be used. Typically, a good configuration will not use all processors.

Besides limited resources and real-time behaviour, the following constraint-types are imposed on the systems:

1. scenario-type I: fault-tolerant system
    - excluded processors, for 15..25% of tasks (C-2)
    - task-separation, for 10..20% of tasks (D-2)
    - internal messages, for 5..10% of messages (E-1)
    - separated frames, for 10..15% of messages (F-3)
2. scenario-type II: system upgrade
    - fixed allocations, for 20..30% of tasks (C-3)
    - dedicated processors, for 10..20% of tasks (C-1)

- task-grouping, for 10..15% of tasks (D-1)
- dedicated frame, for 10..15% of messages (F-1)

10 examples of each category have been generated. For reason of space the full results cannot be presented. However the trends are similar to those in table 4. In summary: Without pre-processing almost no feasible configurations can be found, because of constraint violations. With pre-processing a significant larger number of feasible configurations can be found. The median feasibility ratio is 0.240, its min is 0.229, and its max is 0.547. So in general, the proposed method provides quite reproducible performance and results. This indicates the robustness of the method.

An even more general view can be derived from the results: All constraint-types can be categorized into 3 classes: (I) Those that can be resolved, (II) those that can be dynamically satisfied, and (III) those where no guarantee can be given. By applying the rules we have presented (I) and (II) will be satisfied. Thus only (III) are left. This means that any system configuration problem which contains the constraints presented in table 1 can be transformed into a problem where constraints of type (I) and (II) are no longer present. This transformation is performed by applying the presented resolving methods. Our experiments suggest that it is a robust method.

5   Conclusion

During the design of reliable software-based systems, a set of heterogeneous design constraints must be satisfied. These constraints stem from different sources. Most safety-relevant systems must guarantee real-time behaviour during operation, thus no deadline must be missed. Reliability is often enforced by applying replication. Consequently, replicated elements must be independent of each other. E.g. replicated tasks and messages must be assigned to separated resources. Manual configuration of such complex systems is time consuming and error-prone. Thus methods for automated system configuration are needed.

We have presented methods, how each of the relevant constraint-types can be addressed and satisfied. Several constraints can be resolved before the DSE, some can be dynamically satisfied, and for some no guarantee can be given. Experimental results evidence that by applying a pre-processing phase, during which constraints are resolved, significantly improves DSE performance. In addition, the quality of the best obtained configuration is improved.

In future research, the proposed methods will be incorporated into the DSE for *system configuration upgrade* (such as [8]) in order to make this DSE more efficient. Also, there are some indications that the presented approach can also be applied to (distributed) multi-core systems.

Acknowledgment. The authors would like to acknowledge the financial support of the "COMET K2 - Competence Centres for Excellent Technologies Programme" of the Austrian Federal Ministry for Transport, Innovation and Technology (BMVIT), the Austrian Federal Ministry of Economy, Family and Youth (BMWFJ), the Austrian Research Promotion Agency (FFG), the Province of Styria and the Styrian Business Promotion Agency (SFG). We also thank our supporting industrial (AVL List) and scientific (Graz University of Technology) project partners.

References

1. AUTOSAR (automotive open system architecture), http://www.autosar.org
2. ISO 26262: Road vehicles – functional safety
3. Audsley, N., Burns, A., Richardson, M.F., Wellings, A.J.: Hard real-time scheduling: The deadline-monotonic approach. In: IEEE Workshop on Real-Time Operating Systems and Software, pp. 133–137 (1991)
4. Chu, W.W., Holloway, L.J., Min-Tsung, L., Efe, K.: Task allocation in distributed data processing. Computer 13(11), 57–69 (1980)
5. Davis, R., Burns, A., Bril, R., Lukkien, J.: Controller area network (CAN) schedulability analysis: Refuted, revisited and revised. Real-Time Systems 35(3), 239–272 (2007)
6. Efe, K.: Heuristic models of task assignment scheduling in distributed systems. Computer 15(6), 50–56 (1982)
7. Emberson, P., Bate, I.: Extending a task allocation algorithm for graceful degradation of real-time distributed embedded systems. In: IEEE Real-Time Systems Symposium (RTSS), pp. 270–279 (2008)
8. Emberson, P., Bate, I.: Stressing search with scenarios for flexible solutions to real-time task allocation problems. IEEE Transactions on Software Engineering 36(5), 704–718 (2010)
9. Hamann, A., Racu, R., Ernst, R.: Multi-dimensional robustness optimization in heterogeneous distributed embedded systems. In: IEEE Real Time and Embedded Technology and Applications Symposium (RTAS), pp. 269–280 (2007)
10. Pölzlbauer, F., Brenner, E., Magele, C.: A transparent target function and evaluation strategy for complex multi-objective optimization problems. In: IEEE Real-Time Systems Symposium (RTSS) – Work-in-Progress, pp. 77–80 (2009)
11. Pop, P., Eles, P., Peng, Z., Pop, T.: Analysis and Optimization of Distributed Real-Time Embedded Systems. ACM Transactions on Design Automation of Electronic Systems 11(3), 593–625 (2006)
12. Poulding, S., Emberson, P., Bate, I., Clark, J.: An efficient experimental methodology for configuring search-based design algorithms. In: IEEE High Assurance Systems Engineering Symposium (HASE), pp. 53–62 (2007)
13. Sandström, K., Norström, C., Ahlmark, M.: Frame packing in real-time communication. In: International Conference on Real-Time Computing Systems and Applications (RTCSA), pp. 399–403 (2000)
14. Tindell, K., Clark, J.: Holistic schedulability analysis for distributed hard real-time systems. Microprocessing and Microprogramming – Parallel Processing in Embedded Real-Time Systems 40(2-3) (1994)
15. Zheng, W., Zhu, Q., Di Natale, M., Sangiovanni-Vincentelli, A.: Definition of task allocation and priority assignment in hard real-time distributed systems. In: IEEE International Real-Time Systems Symposium (RTSS), pp. 161–170 (2007)
16. Zhu, Q., Yang, Y., Scholte, E., Di Natale, M., Sangiovanni-Vincentelli, A.: Optimizing extensibility in hard real-time distributed systems. In: IEEE Real-Time and Embedded Technology and Applications Symposium (RTAS), pp. 275–284 (2009)

Author Index

GPSR Compliance

The European Union's (EU) General Product Safety Regulation (GPSR)
is a set of rules that requires consumer products to be safe and our
obligations to ensure this.

If you have any concerns about our products, you can contact us on
ProductSafety@springernature.com

In case Publisher is established outside the EU, the EU authorized
representative is:

Springer Nature Customer Service Center GmbH
Europaplatz 3
69115 Heidelberg, Germany

Batch number: 09490872

Printed by Printforce, the Netherlands